Dr. Chuck Johnson
79 E. Fayette St.
Hillsdale, MI 49242-1340
(517) 437-4645

THE
MARITAL-RELATIONSHIP
THERAPY
CASEBOOK

Theory and Application of the
Intersystem Model

THE
MARITAL-RELATIONSHIP
THERAPY
CASEBOOK

Theory and Application of the Intersystem Model

Edited by

GERALD R. WEEKS, Ph.D.
LARRY HOF, M.Div.

Marriage Council of Philadelphia
&
The University of Pennsylvania

BRUNNER/MAZEL *Publishers* • New York

Library of Congress Cataloging-in-Publication Data
The marital-relationship therapy casebook : theory and application of
   the intersystem model / edited by Gerald R. Weeks and Larry Hof.
      p.   cm.
   Includes bibliographical references and index.
   ISBN 0-87630-733-0
   1. Marital psychotherapy—Case studies.   I. Weeks, Gerald R.
II. Hof, Larry.   III. Title: Intersystem model.
RC488.5.M3583   1994
615.89'156—dc20

                                                                    94-4079
                                                                        CIP

Copyright © 1994 by Brunner/Mazel, Inc.

Published by
BRUNNER/MAZEL, INC.
19 Union Square West
New York, New York 10003

Manufactured in the United States of America
10 9 8 7 6 5 4 3 2 1

This book is dedicated to
MARTIN GOLDBERG, M.D.,
Director and Chief Executive Officer,
The Marriage Council of Philadelphia

Your professionalism, respect, and integrity...
Your friendship and your commitment to excellence...
Have facilitated the creation of a setting in which
we have been free to think, collaborate, and create...
A setting in which the therapeutic excellence described in this book
has become our norm.

Contents

Preface

The literature on couple/marital therapy is relatively scarce when compared to the literature on family therapy. During the last five years, the number of journal articles and workshop presentations at the Annual Conference of the American Association for Marriage and Family Therapy have increased. However, the number of books published on couple/marital therapy has not increased proportionally. Additionally, we are aware of only one volume being published that focuses on case studies. The dearth of recent, relevant literature has contributed to the need for a volume such as this—a casebook of clinically rich, in-depth cases that exemplify couple treatment.

The editors of this volume have over 40 years of experience between them in treating couples. Our practices, unlike those of most others in the field of psychotherapy, are devoted almost exclusively to couples and relationship issues and not to individuals or families. The contributors to this book are all supervisors and/or teachers at the Marriage Council of Philadelphia, which was founded in 1932 and is one of the oldest training and treatment centers in the U.S. Marital and couple therapy was developed at Marriage Council by Emily Mudd, who wrote the first books ever published on this new approach. The staff at Marriage Council is immersed in couples work. We teach, supervise, and maintain clinical practices with a large number of couples. Most of the contributors to this volume have 10 to 20 years of experience in doing couple therapy and supervising other clinicians.

As a result of our considerable experience in training clinicians in a post-degree institute, where most students have backgrounds in individual therapy, we have come to realize just how unique couple therapy is when compared to other therapeutic modalities. Many of the skills learned in other fields are helpful, but those skills alone do not make for an effective couple therapist. The clinician must master a new set of skills, and, more importantly, adopt a theoretical stance toward the couple that does not pathologize one partner at the expense of the other. The therapist must primarily be aware of treating the relationship and not the individuals. The focus is on the interlocking nature of each partner's personality, interactional style, intergenerational history, and, sometimes, pathology in the relationship.

Textbooks on marital and couple therapy tend to describe one approach, or a variety of approaches, to couple therapy. They focus on methods, techniques, and strategies. With the exception of our most recent book on couple/marital therapy (Weeks & Treat, 1992), none of these books devote chapters to the process of working with the couple. This fact has created the need for a text that not only demonstrates how to conceptualize and treat couples, but also shows the process of doing couples work. The cases in this book were chosen not because they were spectacular successes, but rather because they were conceptually and clinically rich cases that illustrated the process of doing couple therapy.

The present volume is actually the third in a series focusing exclusively on marital and couple therapy. The series began with a theoretically oriented text entitled, *Treating Couples: The Intersystem Model of the Marriage Council of Philadelphia* (Weeks, 1989). In that volume, the theoretical orientation of Marriage Council was described, and various members of our staff contributed chapters dealing with issues such as extramarital affairs, divorce and children, and marital violence. The second volume, *Couples in Treatment: Techniques and Approaches for Effective Practice* (Weeks & Treat, 1992), focused on the approaches, methods, and techniques of the couple/marital therapist. That book was intended for the beginning level couple therapist and the clinician engaged in training those just starting in this field. The book was essentially atheoretical, practical, and pragmatic and, unlike other books in this area, which focus on pathology, it also focused on promoting health in couples through the use of a variety of techniques.

The purpose of this third volume is to demonstrate the theory and techniques described in the first two books. This book differs from other casebooks in our field in that those books have included a wide range of treatment modalities, whereas this book demonstrates the application of the Intersystem Model across a wide range of cases. In order to accomplish this goal, we asked that each contributor from the Marriage Council staff use a standard format, the Case Formulation Form used by all of our clinical interns and staff members in presenting cases. The Case Formulation Form was described in detail in *Couples in Treatment* (Weeks & Treat, 1992). The Intersystem Model is described in the first chapter of this book. It is a multilevel, comprehensive, integrative, and contextual approach. The success of our model stems from our belief that it is absolutely essential to fit the therapy to the client-system, not the client-system to the therapy.

Because each contributor used the Case Formulation format provided by the editors, each chapter contains a formulation section which examines the problem from the individual, interactional, and intergenerational perspectives. The next section of the chapter examines treatment from these three perspectives. This redundancy is an integral part of the model which helps the clinician provide the systematic and programmatic treatment. Rather than have a theoretical analysis at the beginning or end of each chapter, the editors and authors have blended the concepts from Chapter 1 into their cases as they unfold. The case is finally reviewed in the Conclusion of the chapter. The concepts in this volume are new to most clinicians and require detailed explanation, exemplification, and repetition. Chapter 1 also contains appendices which help the reader further organize and understand the concepts.

The book contains two chapters which focus on Inhibited Sexual Desire (ISD). This is a common couple problem. The reader will see how the same problem may have very different roots and require different treatment. This idea is certainly in opposition to traditional sex therapy approaches where the problem is treated with one standard approach.

The cases in this book are clinically rich, exemplify how the model works, and required lengthy treatment. In an era of managed care which stresses short term treatment, we hope to show that some problems cannot be fully resolved in 10 or fewer sessions. The cases in this book were successfully treated in a responsible manner. These cases are essentially an argument against brief therapy.

A NOTE ON ETHICS

During the period of time the book was being prepared, the American Psychological Association (1992) revised its 1981 *Ethical Principles of Psychologists*. This comprehensive revision was published in the 1992 issue of the *American Psychologist*. Standard 5.08 pertains to confidentiality of material in lectures and publications. For the first time, the Standard requires that case material be disguised so that not even the patient can recognize herself or himself. Obviously, this has meant that the authors had two choices. First, authors could thoroughly disguise material by changing names, gender, ages, places of residence, number and gender of children, intervention content, etc. Some authors chose this option. Other authors chose to change names and information that might identify the client to others, but not enough to satisfy the requirement that the client be able to identify self. These authors obtained permission to use the chapter from the clients, after they had read and approved the chapter. The clients then filled out an appropriate release form.

The editors wanted to fulfill the ethical standards regarding consent. In order to fulfill this standard, we consulted an attorney and had the following form drafted. We are including this form, along with an explanatory note from the attorney who created it, so the reader can see what clients signed in giving their permission, and as a guide for others who are now confronted with the implementation of the new ethical standards.

Steven V. Turner, Esquire, notes:

> This draft agreement provides the broad outlines of a release between a therapist and his or her clients when that therapist writes for publication concerning therapy sessions and the therapist's observations and conclusions concerning those therapy sessions. This agreement also contemplates that audiotaping and/or videotaping of therapy

AGREEMENT

Agreement made this   day of   , 199_, by and between [*Therapist's professional corporation*] a Pennsylvania professional corporation, and [*Therapist's name*] (individually and jointly herinafter referred to as "Therapist") on the one hand, and [*Clients' full names*], clients of Therapist (hereinafter referred to as "Client") on the other hand.

1. Client has entered into and had continuing therapy sessions under the guidance of and/or with Therapist.

2. After discussion, Client and Therapist have agreed that Therapist may write a case study chapter for a book to be published by Brunner/Mazel based upon therapy sessions and/or audiotaping and/or videotaping of therapy sessions by and between Therapist and Client.

3. After discussion, Client and Therapist agree and believe that the case study chapter and the utilization of any or all tapes and other similar items could prove beneficial and/or useful for purposes of professional education, supervision, training, treatment, or research and could, therefore, be useful in the advancement of mental health programs.

4. In consideration of the premises and of the mutual covenants contained herein, the parties hereto, intending to be legally bound hereby, agree as follows:

    a. Client has reviewed the proposed case study chapter that was forwarded to Client on or about   , 199_ by Therapist.

    b. Client has had the opportunity to make any changes to the case study chapter that client wishes to. Client agrees that the case study chapter is acceptable to Client and Client permits the case study chapter to be submitted to and published by the publisher.

    c. Client agrees and acknowledges that Therapist is and shall be the sole owner of all rights in and to the aforementioned videotapes, audiotapes, case study chapter, or other similar products for all purposes and that Client shall receive no financial compensation for the use of the case study chapter or related materials in any book, other publication or for any other purpose.

    d. Client covenants and agrees that Client will never sue Therapist or Therapist's estate, successors or assigns nor attach the assets thereof for any purpose relating to the case study chapter, consents, authorizations, and acknowledgements encompassed by this agreement, and this covenant may be pleaded as a defense to any such action or proceeding instituted by Client relative thereto.

5. The parties hereto have duly executed this agreement the day and year first above written.

_____   _____
Therapist's Professional Corporation   Client

_____   _____
Therapist   Client

sessions has occurred. If audiotaping and/or videotaping is contemplated, please check with an attorney in your state to determine any applicable state laws concerning wiretapping and electronic surveillance. Some therapists may unknowingly be audiotaping and/or videotaping without a separate agreement between themselves and their clients and could potentially expose themselves to disagreement and liability concerning the audiotaping and/or videotaping.

Before utilizing this type of agreement, you should consult with your attorney to conform the agreement to current nuances and requirements of your state laws.

(Steven V. Turner is a member attorney of the law firm of Cozen and O'Connor in Philadelphia, Pennsylvania. Cozen and O'Connor is national law firm with seven regional offices around the country.)

Acknowledgments

The authors would like to thank Bill Murray, Jr. for his technical assistance in generating this text. Bill spent many hours organizing material and editing and formatting text. We would also like to thank Margaret S. Roth, M.S., for her editorial assistance. She served as a proofreader, and also helped to clarify ideas, so they could be more easily understood.

Contributors

Stephanie Brooks, M.S.W., L.S.W., Adjunct Supervisory Faculty, Marriage Council; Clinical Associate in Psychiatry, University of Pennsylvania, School of Medicine.

Michael J. D'Antonio, Ph.D., Clinical Director, Paoli and Concordville Offices, Marriage Council; Clinical Associate in Psychiatry, University of Pennsylvania, School of Medicine.

Larry Hof, M.Div., Chief Operating Officer, Marriage Council; Clinical Assistant Professor of Pastoral Counseling in Psychiatry, University of Pennsylvania, School of Medicine.

Bea Hollander-Goldfein, Ph.D., Staff Member, Marriage Council; Clinical Associate in Psychiatry, University of Pennsylvania, School of Medicine.

Joellyn L. Ross, Ph. D., Staff Member, Marriage Council; Clinical Associate in Psychiatry, University of Pennsylvania, School of Medicine; Private Practice.

Kate Sexton-Small, M.S.S., Adjunct Supervisory Faculty, Marriage Council; Clinical Associate in Psychiatry, University of Pennsylvania, School of Medicine; Private Practice.

William Silver, D.S.W., Adjunct Supervisory Faculty, Marriage Council; Clinical Associate in Psychiatry, University of Pennsylvania, School of Medicine; Private Practice.

Diane Logan Thompson, Ph.D., Staff Member, Marriage Council; Clinical Associate in Psychiatry, University of Pennsylvania, School of Medicine.

Nathan Turner, Ed.D., Adjunct Supervisory Faculty, Marriage Council; Clinical Associate in Psychiatry, University of Pennsylvania, School of Medicine; Private Practice.

Gerald R. Weeks, Ph.D., Director of Training, Marriage Council; Clinical Associate Professor of Psychology in Psychiatry, University of Pennsylvania, School of Medicine.

April Westfall, Ph.D., Director of Clinical Services, Marriage Council; Clinical Assistant Professor of Family Study in Psychiatry, University of Pennsylvania, School of Medicine.

THE MARITAL-RELATIONSHIP THERAPY CASEBOOK

Theory and Application of the Intersystem Model

Part I

THE INTERSYSTEM MODEL AND THE THEORY IN PRACTICE

The first section of this book consists of two chapters. Chapter 1 describes the theory on which the book is based. The remainder of the book consists of case material which illustrates the application of the theory. The reader will find the theory chapter is densely packed with new concepts. Much of the material will be new and the reader may need to read this chapter twice to comprehend the concepts. This chapter also contains a Glossary and an Outline at the end, in order to assist the reader in assimilating the concepts.

The concepts in this chapter have universal applicability in couple therapy. The main thrust of the chapter is to promote integration among different theories of couple and family therapy. Thus, readers will not be asked to sacrifice any of their theoretical background. Rather, they will be given a theory that allows the clinician to continue building a richer theoretical perspective. This model is comprehensive enough to permit the clinician to integrate the individual, interactional, and intergenerational aspects of the client-system in both assessment and treatment. The reader who is looking for simple answers and approaches, with a singular focus, will not find it in this approach. The Intersystem Model is challenging, intellectually and clinically, but the clinician who utilizes it will be able to think about the client-system at multiple levels, while directing treatment at one issue at a time.

Chapter 2 describes the assessment and treatment of a couple over a number of years, for a variety of diverse yet core issues, and at a variety of levels. Unlike the chapters in Part II, this case presentation includes significant material from the clients themselves, which illustrate the applicability of the theory of the Intersystem Model. It demonstrates the need for an integrated and dialectical approach to the assessment and treatment of the couple's individual, interactional, and intergenerational issues. With this particular case, the flowing back and forth between surface and depth; between past and present; between him and her; between affect, cognition, and behavior; and between the individual, the interactional, and the intergenerational, created a rich therapeutic milieu that permitted significant growth and change for the couple.

CHAPTER 1

The Intersystem Model: An Integrative Approach to Treatment

Gerald R. Weeks

The purpose of this chapter is to describe the therapeutic model on which this book is based. Dialectic metatheory is the philosophical basis for this model. While psychology and systems of family therapy have traditionally borrowed heavily from the natural sciences, such as physics, this chapter begins with the assumption that the natural sciences have been a poor model. The natural sciences view phenomena in linear (cause-effect) terms and strive to break complex phenomena down into fundamental units (a molecular approach). In marital therapy, a theory is needed that allows us to view the couple as an interlocking system and as intrinsically connected to many other social systems. The best metatheory to meet this goal is dialectics. This chapter will describe how to use this philosophical theory in a psychological and pragmatic way.

The Intersystem Model is a comprehensive, integrative, and contextual approach to treatment. Whenever a couple (or for that matter any other client-system)is being treated we believe it is essential to simultaneously consider three systems: the individual, the interactional, and the intergenerational, all within the context of the society and its history. Later in this chapter, these three systems will be considered in terms of how they fit together in the treatment.

HISTORICAL PERSPECTIVE

The development of the systems theories and therapies has represented a major paradigmatic shift in psychotherapy. These new therapies all represented a shift away from the individual and intrapsychic theories developed and employed by Freud and the psychoanalytic/dynamic therapists. The systems theories all share the concept of the individual-as-part-of-the-system and they focus on interpersonal variables.

The past 30 years has been the "systems era" in the history of psychotherapy. In this short period of time, eight major schools of family therapy have developed, which Kaslow (1981) grouped under the following headings: (a) psychodynamic/analytic; (b) Bowenian; (c) relational or contexual; (d) experiential; (e) structural; (f) communications-interactional; (g) strategic-systemic; and (h) behavioral. These schools of thought all share some basic assumptions about the nature of dysfunction and treatment, but they are clearly different in content. Unfortunately, some of these school were originally presented as if they were to be used exclusively, without "cross-fertilization" from others (see Gurman & Kniskern, 1981).

However, the practice of marital/family therapy has been much different than the theory. In practice, the clinician is rarely a theoretical purist and many practitioners have moved toward a position known as technical eclecticism, i.e, taking what works from many different approaches and using it in their treatment. In an effort to bring theory into line with what clinicians were already doing, a few theorists started to develop integrative approaches to treatment. This effort started in the mid-70's and resulted in a number of papers and books.

Kaslow (1981) advocated a dialectic approach to family therapy in which practitioners could draw "selectively and eclectically" from various theories. Duhl and Duhl (1981) developed an "integrative family therapy" which looked at various levels of the system, such as developmental level, individual process, and transactional patterns. Their discussion focused primarily on how the therapist thinks and intervenes. Berman, Lief, and Williams (1981), staff members of the Marriage Council, published a chapter on marital interaction and how several theories could be integrated therapeutically. They discussed combining contract theory, object-relations theory, multigenerational theory, systems theory, and behavioral analysis within a developmental and therapeutic framework. In addition, other efforts have been made. These include: Hatcher (1978) on blending gestalt and family therapy; Abroms (1981) on combining medical psychiatry and family therapy; Stanton (1981) on integrating the structural and strategic; Lebow (1984) on the need for integration; Duncan and Parks (1988) on the integration of strategic and behavioral; and, Pinsof (1983) on an integrative problem-centered approach.

The problem with all of these approaches and others not cited above is that they fail to meet the criteria for being truly integrative as described by Van Kaam (1969), and described in the next section. The integrative movement in family therapy has actually been a movement toward technical eclecticism.

Theorists have been attempting to find a way to "integrate" two or more theories and have not been attending to the need to consider *both* the "foundational construct" and the "integrational construct" noted by Van Kaam. For the most part, the best efforts have been directed toward constructs that are integrational, such as a theory of interaction to unify theories (Berman et al., 1981), but without clearly developed foundational constructs. The weakest attempts have been simple efforts to rationalize what is done in clinical practice. For a brief review of the efforts made toward integration the reader should consult Case and Robinson's (1990) article.

DEVELOPMENT OF THE INTERSYSTEM MODEL

The best word to describe the Intersystem Model is that it is integrative. Integration refers to the act of making a whole out of parts. The word is derived from the Latin *integratus*, which means to make whole or renew. The principles for developing an integrated or comprehensive psychology were developed in a seminal book entitled *Existential Foundations of Psychology* (van Kaam, 1969). The author pointed out that psychology consisted of many "differential" theories of behavior. Each theory focused on behavior from a different perspective. As theories proliferated there eventually arose a need for some unification. The history of psychotherapy and marital therapy has followed this same course of development, as we shall shortly show.

Two constructs are needed for the creation of a comprehensive theory—the foundational and the integrational. The foundational construct provides the frame of reference for the integration of the phenomena from various differential theories. This construct requires a close examination of the philosophical assumptions on which the theories are built. Interestingly, family therapists have become interested in this endeavor in the last few years and a number of articles have been published on epistemology (see Weeks, 1986).

The integrational construct is that which is used to unify disparate phenomena. For example, organisms learn to respond to their environment in a number of specific ways. The constructs of operant and classical conditioning help to explain these patterns of responding in a way that allows us to make sense of different instances of learning.

In developing the Intersystem Model, dialectic metatheory served as the foundational construct and three integrational constructs were used: (1) paradox as a universal aspect of therapy; (2) the spontaneous compliance paradoxes, i.e., affirmation and negation paradoxes; and, (3) a model of social interaction based on research in social psychology.

THE FOUNDATIONAL CONSTRUCT OF THE INTERSYSTEM MODEL: DIALECTIC METATHEORY

As noted, the *foundational construct* refers to the philosophical assumptions underlying a particular theory. It is not the theory itself, but rather the underlying concepts. It is, literally, the foundation on which a theory is built; thus, it is called *metatheory*.

Every theory of personality and psychotherapy is guided by an implicit or explicit theory. In most instances the theory is implicit, and, hence, not easily examined or questioned. The Intersystem Model is based on *dialectic metatheory*. A metatheory is a theory of theory. It is the philosophical underpinning on which a specific theory is built.

Dialectic metatheory is not new in psychology, but it is rarely used in formulating theories of family therapy (Rychlak, 1968). Weeks (1977) was the first to publish a paper that explicitly described a dialectical approach to intervention. In 1984 Bopp and Weeks published a paper that examined dialectic metatheory in family therapy. This analysis showed that some of the basic concepts of family therapy such as "system," "relationship," "reframing," "double-bind," "paradox," and "change" are defined in terms of dialectic metatheory.

The term "Intersystems Approach" (now, Intersystem Model) was actually coined in a paper that was part of a special edition of the *American Journal of Family Therapy* on philosophical and pragmatic issues in the field (Weeks, 1986). The Intersystems Approach was then described as a synthesis between two approaches—the individual and the systems. In traditional dialectical thinking, the individual pole was the thesis, the systems pole the antithesis, and the Intersystem Model the synthesis. This particular description is not intended to suggest that dialectics is as simple as thesis, antithesis, and synthesis. Dialectic metatheory is a complex philosophical system unto itself. In this chapter, we will be considering the dialectical theories of two psychologists, Riegel and Bassaches.

Riegel was one of the most influential dialectical psychologists in the 70's. He was a developmental psychologist and the editor of the journal, *Human Development,* where many of the papers on dialectics were published. Riegel (1976) had developed a theory of human development that stressed the need to consider four concurrent temporal dimensions: (1) *inner-biological*; (2) *individual-psychological;* (3) *cultural-sociological;* and (4) *outer-physical.* Different theories of family therapy stress these dimensions differently. From Riegel's perspective, a comprehensive theory would need to give attention to each of these four aspects of functioning.

The Intersystem Model has emerged as an attempt to consider all dimensions of the couple/family. The Intersystem therapist is much like the conductor of an orchestra. Unlike the pianist who is playing alone and wishing to create harmony within one section or system, the conductor wishes to create harmony across different sections or systems. In order to relate Riegel's (1976) concept of dialectics to couple therapy, we have chosen concepts already familiar to the clinician. Thus, we stress the assessment and treatment of the couple from the perspectives of the individual, interactional, and intergenerational. The figure below shows how "inner-" and "outer-dialectics" are related.

Although Figure 1 does not show it, we also include considerations that are cultural-sociological, such as race, ethnicity, economics, and the outer-physical such as living conditions and natural disasters. These aspects of the couple should be reflected in the Case Formulation (Weeks & Treat,1992) developed by the therapist.

Bassaches' (1980) work on dialectics is much more psychologically sophisticated than Riegel's, and offers us much more focus and many more specifics. His definition was encompassing in that it lent itself to motion and change, and applied to both ontology (a branch of philosophy concerned with the study of being) and epistemology (a branch of philosophy concerned with knowledge). He defined dialectic as: "developmental transformation (i.e., developmental movement through forms) which occurs via constitutive and interactive relationship" (p. 46). Bassaches was primarily interested in cognitive opera-

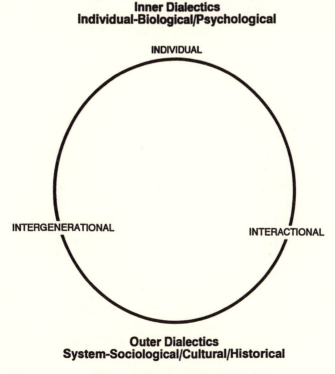

Inner Dialectics
Individual-Biological/Psychological

INDIVIDUAL

INTERGENERATIONAL

INTERACTIONAL

Outer Dialectics
System-Sociological/Cultural/Historical

Figure 1. Inner-outer Dialectics

tions. He formulated a new stage of cognitive development called dialectical thinking, which allow us to comprehend the "dynamic relations among systems" (p. 401). The ability to think dialectically is an absolute must for a systems therapist. Without this ability the therapist would not be able to conceive of a system, see the dynamic relationships within the system, or comprehend the contradictions that exist within systems and help to bring about change.

Bassaches (1980) argued that dialectical thinking involves 24 specific ways of conceptualizing that can be organized into four major categories. These four categories are *motion, form, relationship*, and *meta-formal integration*. The dialectical assumption is that *motion* or change, not inertia, is the fundamental tendency. No external force is required for change to occur. Reality is not a linear series of discrete and unrelated parts. It is motion, change, and interrelated activity, which is fundamental.

His concept of *form* emphasizes context. A dialectical description of phenomenon encompasses the structural, functional, and equilibrational qualities. Behavior is seen as a complex phenomenon with all qualities being interrelated. There may be periods of homeostasis, but qualitative changes inevitably follow. When describing couples, one does not change unidirectional phenomena. This view would be considered linear. A couple therapist emphasizes the circular nature of interactions—how one partner influences the other and is in turn influenced. This is one important aspect of "form."

The dialectical concept of form is pervasive in family therapy. For example, when describing the symptom, the couple therapist may utilize all three of the specific ways of conceptualizing within the category of form. These specific ways of dialectical thinking include: 1) *contextualization*; 2) *equilibration*; and 3) *contextual relativism*.

Contextualization refers to seeing phenomena with a context. In couple therapy, this involves seeing the problem within the context of the couple, a systems perspective, not as an individual problem.

Equilibration refers to how the system balances itself in order to exist. In family therapy, this concept is called homeostasis. Couples may use symptoms in order to avoid those issues that threaten their existence as a couple. For example, a couple may fight over sex rather than admit that they are, as individuals, too afraid to deal with their sexuality, and, in turn, too afraid to predicate their marriage on having a healthy sexual relationship.

Contextual relativism refers to how the symptom can be understood only in the context in which it occurred. For example, crying may be viewed as appropriate in one situation, but seen as a statement that the other partner did something wrong in another context. In other words, the meaning of a behavior may vary depending on the context in which it occurs.

Bassaches' third category is *relationship*. Relationships are defined as both interactive and constitutive. The *interactive* points to the fact that the relationship is defined by the members. The members are also defined by the relationship. For example, the husband and wife define how they are to be married while at the same time the role of being married defines the behavior of each participant. The definition is reciprocal. The *constitutive* part of the definition pertains to how family members or the spouse imbue each other with particular qualities. A wife, for example, might state that her husband is non-emotional and he might accept this definition. On the other hand, the *interactive* part of the definition pertains to how the relationship is defined by each partner. For example, if each partner defines the relationship as one in which fights are not allowed, then the couple may say they are always loving and, to prove it, say they have never had a fight.

Bassaches' fourth and last concept, *meta-formal integration*, is the most difficult to grasp. This concept defines how change occurs. A dialectician sees change as both qualitative and quantitative, internal and external, and producing both equilibrium and disequilibrium. The meta-formal category of dialectical thinking also allows for contradictions to occur within systems. A behavior may simultaneously mean A and not-A. For example, anger may be defined both as a sign of aggression and a sign of love, or changing one's behavior may be seen both as a sign of taking responsibility for oneself and simply trying to please the other person. The concept of metacommunication is an example of how contradictions are expressed in the couple. A communication may mean one thing at one level and the opposite at another level.

This concept of meta-formal thinking also allows us to conceptualize transformations. Systems change as a result of many factors, sometimes internal factors and sometimes external factors. The changes may be first-order, such as rules within the system, or second-order, such as the rules of the system itself. For example, parents may create new rules to govern the behavior of their children (first-order) or they may decide the children should be self-responsible, so they decide that it is no longer appropriate to have any rules (second-order). In the case of second-order change, it is the system itself that changes, rather than the elements of the system. The ability to "see" all these facets of the system depends on the extent to which the clinician has achieved the ability to use the dialectical schemata of meta-formal thinking.

This dialectical metatheory provides the basis for the three integrational concepts of the Intersystem Model. These include the following: 1) paradox as a universal aspect of therapy; 2) the spontaneous compliance paradoxes, i.e., affirmation and negation paradoxes; and 3) a model of social interaction. These concepts and their connection to dialectics will be described in the pages that follow.

THE INTEGRATIONAL CONSTRUCTS

Paradox as a Universal Aspect of Therapy

The first integrational concept to be discussed will be that of paradox. Psychotherapy and couple therapy have hundreds of interventions that have proven to be effective. How can it be that so many different kinds of interventions are effective in producing change? Is there a common thread? Is there an underlying explanatory principle? In this section, these questions will be explored and the concept of paradox will be proposed as that which integrates the various kinds of interventions in terms of the process of therapy.

The concept of paradox also requires that we be able to conceptualize dialectically. Weeks (1977), Weeks and L'Abate (1982), and Bopp and Weeks (1984) grounded paradox in the dialectical understanding of human nature. Two examples can be easily understood in light of the previous section, although many others could be offered. (The reader may wish to consult our earlier work for a more detailed understanding.) A symptom is a behavior. A behavior is not a symptom until it is labeled as such. The same behavior may simultaneously be a symptom and not a symptom (A and not-A). This kind of logic is embraced only by those who think dialectically. For example, in a couple, one partner's lack of sexual desire may become a symptom only when the other desires sex.

In this section, paradox is discussed in terms of both the therapeutic relationship and the intervention itself. In order to understand the therapeutic relationship as a paradox, the reader must be able to comprehend the contradictions inherent in relationships. The ability to comprehend contradictions is one of the aspects of meta-formal dialectical thinking. In addition, using a paradox as an intervention as usually conceived (the negation paradox) requires a dialectical perspective. An example would be that of prescribing the symptom. Suppose a couple have been fighting incessantly and the therapist prescribes that they fight even more under certain carefully prescribed conditions. To the couple, such an intervention appears to be in contradiction to what they came to therapy seeking. If the therapist does not understand the nature of this contradiction, s/he would never make such an intervention. Grasping the fact that producing more disequilibrium under controlled conditions may produce change is a uniquely dialectical concept.

In previous publications, this author has argued that paradox is the common element in all psychotherapies, including the family therapies (Weeks, 1977, 1985, 1986, 1989, 1990; Weeks & L'Abate, 1982; Weeks & Wright, 1979). In their book on paradox, Weeks and L'Abate (1982) compared and analyzed the Adlerian, Behavioral, Gestalt, Logotherapeutic, Provocative, and several other approaches to therapy in order to demonstrate that paradox was a part of each one's theory of change. Seltzer (1986) built on this work in a lengthy analysis of paradox in both Eastern and Western approaches to therapy. He showed us just how prevalent paradox is in the different schools by considering the labels used to describe paradox within just a few. He stated:

> From the psychoanalytic perspective, which includes the work of paradigmatic psychotherapists, we have inherited the descriptors "antisuggestion," "going with the resistance," "joining the resistance," "reflecting" (or mirroring") the resistance," "siding with the resistance," "paradigmatic exaggeration," "supporting the defenses," "reductio ad adsurdum," "reenacting an aspect of the psychosis," "mirroring the patient's distortions," "participating in the patients's fantasies," "outcrazying the patient," and "the use of patient as consultant." From the vantage point of behavior therapy, we may appreciate paradoxical elements in such procedures as "blowup," "implosion," "flooding," "instructed helplessness," "massed practice," "paradoxical intention," "stimulus satiation," and "symptom scheduling." In gestalt therapy, an approach where the term paradox is rarely employed, the attempt to foster change paradoxically may be recognized in the therapist's cruel-to-be-kind suggestions to "stay with the (negative) experience," or to "exaggerate the feeling" (sensation, experience, speech, movement, etc.) (p. 20).

Both Weeks and L'Abate (1982) and Seltzer (1986) realized that what was needed was a metatheory of paradox in order to account for its universality in psychotherapy. Such attempts had been tried before in the literature. In an effort to find the single common denominator of therapeutic change, Omer (1981) proposed the concept of symptom decontextualization. This idea consisted of the therapist modifying both the form and context of the symptom. By definition, modification of the form involved a request to continue the symptom under different conditions (e.g., scheduling, exaggeration). Modifying the context referred to allowing the expression of that which one had been trying to stop. Weeks and L'Abate (1982) referred to this concept as changing the direction of control. The patient can take charge of the symptom by enacting it consciously and voluntarily, which sets up a paradox. Doing that which one has been trying not to do, but doing it under one's own control, changes the meaning of the symptom. It is no longer that one cannot control it, because by doing it, it is brought under control. The patient's attitude toward the symptom is thus fundamentally altered.

Deissler (1985) also recognized this phenomenon in therapy, but called it "recontextualization." This term is highly descriptive of what systems therapists do. In his theory, the symptom is changed by alteration of the "recursive context" (i.e., the number of people involved in the problem and/or the temporal and spatial contexts) such that when the patient is able to change the context of the symptom, the meaning inevitably changes. Once again, this is the idea that the patient is able to demonstrate some control over the heretofore uncontrollable, some volition over the nonvolitional, and some mindfulness over the spontaneous (mindless or automatic) behavior.

Seltzer (1986) argued that all therapies are inherently paradoxical. He discussed this thesis from several perspectives. First, the therapeutic relationship requires that the therapist be in control of the process. The therapist takes control by helping the client eliminate the problem, but not by simply eliminating the problem. The therapist provides the techniques and the relational context in which the patient learns to manage and/or change his/her symptoms. Therapy is built on the paradox of taking control by giving it back to the client. Under this condition, the patient learns to develop self-control.

Second, the client must learn to see the symptom positively through the help of the therapist. In all systems of therapy, the symptom is never directly attacked. The symptom is seen as serving some need of the client or as providing some needed information. The therapist's attitude toward the symptom is one of acceptance. Weeks and L' Abate (1982) stated that symptoms should be redefined positively because they may represent allies, communications, existential statements, or vehicles of change. Not surprisingly, symptoms are routinely defined in positive ways in the strategic school of therapy.

Third, the therapeutic relationship is another paradox. The client usually enters therapy expecting to be changed and fearing that the therapist may disapprove of his/her symptomatic behavior. The therapist, on the other hand, responds to the person in attentive, empathetic, friendly, and supportive ways. The attitude is one of acceptance, even when the client is being actively resistant, since this phenomenon is viewed as part of the therapeutic process and as having utility.

The therapeutic relationship is "odd" in several other ways. The therapist has an attitude of detached concern, of uninvolved involvement, and takes control by giving it away. Change is not attributed to something the therapist does to clients. It is attributed to the something that occurred via their interaction, with the therapist encouraging clients to attribute change to themselves.

Fourth, Seltzer (1986) stated that the process involves helping the client work through, rather than around, the symptom. In every system of therapy the symptom is the point of departure. Change results from working with the symptom—not from fleeing from it.

By definition, a symptom is a behavior that the client defines as uncontrollable, involuntary, and/or spontaneous. Every system of therapy has methods to teach clients how to make their so-called symptomatic behavior controllable, voluntary, and volitional. Every system also has a set of rules that encourage the therapist to deny, disqualify, and externalize any responsibility for the occurrence of change. This set of contradictory conditions creates the context in which the attribution for change must reside in the client. This thinking now brings us to the second integrational construct—the spontaneous compliance paradoxes (i.e., the affirmation and negation paradoxes).

The Spontaneous Compliance Paradoxes

Therapy is seen as a paradox, and the ultimate goal of therapy is to bring about change. According to Strong and Claiborn (1982), there are two ways to effect this change. Change may be forced or it may be spontaneous. When people are forced to change, they attribute the change to someone or something else. They experience themselves as doing something different, but not as being different. Generally, when the source of the change is removed, they begin to behave as they did prior to the change. This type of change is called forced compliance. Anyone who has ever tried to force another person to change is familiar with the futility of this approach.

The second type of change is spontaneous. When people change spontaneously, they attribute change to themselves. They experience themselves as being different, rather than as just doing something in a different way. When they are actually different, their new behavior persists. Removing the source of the change (the change agent) does not result in a loss of change. This type of change is called *spontaneous compliance*.

The term spontaneous compliance appears to be a contradiction. However, therapeutic change is best defined as the therapist's ability to create a context for spontaneous compliance. The task of the therapist is to create the conditions for this type of change by taking control without appearing to take control. Hence, therapy is a paradox. Farming and therapy are much alike. The farmer cannot force his crop to grow. He plants the seeds at the proper time of the year, fertilizes, cultivates, and protects the crop from harmful insects and diseases; with some cooperation from nature, the crop grows. In our day-to-day interactions with people, we do not try to force them to comply with our wishes, but rather, like the farmer, we create the context for compliance by requesting or inviting others to join with us in doing things in certain ways.

In therapy, Strong and Claiborn (1982) describe the "affirmation" and "negation" paradoxes as the two ways to facilitate spontaneous compliance. The *affirmation paradox* is made up of three elements. First, the therapist defines the desired behavioral change and suggests that this change become a part of the definition of the therapeutic relationship. Second, the therapist communicates that the change is a result of some process internal to the client and is not a change forced by the therapist. Third, the therapist identifies an agent of change that is beyond the client's volitional control. For example, the therapist might suggest that the change desired is one which the client knows is really in his/her best interest and that it was the client's unconscious mental processes that helped to bring about the change.

The *negation paradox* is what has been called the "the paradox" in psycho-therapy (Weeks & L'Abate, 1982). In simple terms, the client is encouraged to not change that which the client defines as in need of change. A variety of techniques are available to effect change in this way. For example, a client might present with depression. The client views depression as something bad and fights against it. The more the client fights it the more depressed he becomes. The therapist might prescribe the depression and give it a positive connotation. This would have the effect of changing the meaning of the depression and of putting the client in charge of having it. Learning to control depression then leads to an elimination of the problem as it has been defined by the client.

A Model of Social Interaction

The third integrational construct is that of interaction. In dealing with a couple system, we need a theory of interaction that helps us make sense of their interactions and also allows us to draw from particular theories. The theory of interaction is meta- to the specific theories from which interventions are derived, which means that this theory serves as the framework used to bring together ideas from disparate theories. This theory of interaction is also grounded in our foundational construct of dialectics. While paradox is more closely related to the concepts of motion and meta-formal thinking, the theory of interaction is more closely associated with the concepts of form and relationship, which were described in the section on the foundational construct.

The theory of interaction is based on social psychology and was formulated by Strong and Claiborn (1982). Their theory is based on three assumptions, namely, people are open systems, they desire social interactions, and they behave in order to seek control. Control is defined as an attempt to get others to do what we wish spontaneously. It is an effort to get others to want what we want, such that when two people are working together, each party is giving something to the other that the other wants.

This model of social interaction has two components—an *intrapsychic* and an *interactional*. The *intrapsychic component* is comprised of three elements. *Interpretation* is the first element and refers to the fact that the behavior of another is not some objective reality. The other person's behavior is interpreted within a psychological framework and this framework serves as a mental template. Pinsof (1992) refers to this concept as interactive constructivism, in that a person' psychological history or experiences plays a major role in how social events are interpreted.

Definition is the second element of interpretation. Every relationship is defined in some way, and relationships are always in search of definition. Each partner in a relationship wishes to define the other in a particular way and to be defined in a particular way. Both desire a particular definition of the relationship, for example, as a loving, caring, relationship.

Prediction is the third element of interpretation. In this case, prediction refers to being able to predict that which will stimulate the desired feedback from another. For example, a partner may predict that his spouse will take care of him when he is feeling hurt or sick. If this behavior does not occur it leaves the spouse bewildered. The spouse begins to wonder what has happened and, in some cases, whether he or she knew the partner at all. In our experience, when partners believe they have lost the ability to make predictions, they experience confusion and begin to say they do not know who their partners are anymore.

The *interactional component* of the model also has three elements. *Congruence* is the first element, and exists when the feedback from the partner matches each partner's desired definition. In other words, the definition each partner wants for the relationship is shared by the other. For example, each may desire fidelity. When they both act according to this definition, their relationship is congruent. If one, or both, violates this definition, then they are incongruent, and a state of tension results from the discrepancy. When too much discrepancy exists in a relationship it will probably terminate or lead to dissatisfaction.

Interdependence is the second interactional element. Partners rely on each other to fulfill certain needs. The more these needs are fulfilled in actuality or in potentiality, and the greater the desire that the partner, and only the partner, fulfill these needs, the greater the level of interdependence. The degree of interdependence helps us predict which couples are likely to stay together and which partner is most likely to change. The partner who is most dependent is most likely to be accommodating to the one who is threatening to leave. This variable also gives the therapist some sense of how much leverage may be applied. Some couples have such a low level of interdependence that intervening too quickly and with too much force may dissolve the relationship. Other couples have such a high a level of interdependence that they can withstand the most aggressive therapist's attempts to force change.

The final interactional element is that of *impression management and attribution.* Impression management refers to how we present ourselves to others. A partner who presents himself to his wife in a loving way will probably be seen as loving. The partner who is seen positively will elicit a desire to be loving, helpful, etc. Attribution is the more clinically useful concept. This concept refers to the meaning we attribute to the behavior of others. We may define behavior in such terms as "good," "bad," "insensitive," and "uncaring." In a close relationship, attributions have two important uses. The first is whether the (other partner's) behavior and/or motives are viewed positively or negatively. For example, a partner may give advice to his spouse. This may be seen as helpful, controlling, or bossy.

The second use for attribution refers to the linear or circular attributional strategy. The linear attributional strategy is one in which behavior is conceptualized in cause-effect terms, i.e., a behavior causes an effect. For example, one partner externalizes responsibility onto the other by blaming or vilifying. It is the idea of "You *caused* me to..." It should be noted that the term linearity has several meanings. These include proportionality, unilinearity, and temporality (Cottone & Greenwald, 1992). In this chapter, the term is used in terms of its most common meaning which is that of unidirectionality of behavior—going from cause to effect.

In the circular attributional strategy, behavior is viewed as both cause and effect. Partners can see themselves linked together in circular patterns, hence, each takes responsibility for problems in the relationship. The circular strategy is consistent with systems thinking. A couple may conceptualize their problem in circular terms. For example, a husband may constantly withdraw from his partner because his partner relentlessly approaches him when he withdraws. Their behavior is reciprocally tied together. Each one's behavior provokes the other in such a fashion that further polarization occurs.

STRATEGIES FOR SPONTANEOUS COMPLIANCE

This chapter began with a discussion of dialectic metatheory as the foundational construct for the Intersystem Model—that is, the assumption that it is essential to think dialectically and to use some of the basic concepts from dialectics, such as inner-dialectics, outer-dialectics, motion, form, relationship, and meta-formal integration. Then, three integrational constructs were described: 1) paradox as a universal aspect of therapy; 2) the spontaneous compliance paradoxes (i.e., affirmation and negation paradoxes); and, 3) a model or theory of social interaction. The integrational constructs allow us to draw from different theories of psychotherapy in a systematic way. The foundational construct provides the context. The context of treatment is one in which the therapist does not force compliance, but creates the conditions for spontaneous compliance. Therapists have two very broad ranges of strategies available to them to accomplish this goal. These strategies are reframing and prescriptions.

Reframing

This strategy is one of the most common in all psychotherapy. Reframing was originally defined as a technique that allowed the therapist to change the perceptual and/or emotional meaning attributed to a situation (Watzlawick, Weakland & Fisch [1974]). The purpose of reframing is to alter the attributional process occurring in a client-system. In a couple, there are two basic unfortunate attributional strategies. One is for a partner to attribute negative meaning to the other's behavior or motives, when such behavior or intent does not exist, or when there are other ways of viewing the same behavior. The second attributional strategy is what was referred to earlier as a linear strategy. Strong and Claiborn (1982) identified the following four common variations of the linear attributional strategies:

1. *Justification.* When a person assigns negative or harmful effects of his behavior onto external causes (e.g., "I cannot help the way I acted because I had a bad day.");
2. *Rationalization.* When a person denies that his or her behavior was intended to be harmful (e.g., "You don't understand that I wanted to help you.");
3. *Debilitation.* When a person assigns hurtful behavior to internal causes, beyond one's control (e.g., "You know I can't stop myself when you do that.");
4. *Vilification.* When a person ascribes negative intent to another (e.g., "When you told me you didn't like my new slacks, you were treating me like a child.").

The first use of reframing is to alter these *linear and negative attributional processes* in the couple, to change them to *circular and positive attributional processes.* In previous writings, many examples of reframing have been provided (Weeks & L'Abate,1979,1982; Weeks & Wright, 1979; Weeks & Williams, 1984). For that reason, we will only briefly describe these two uses in this chapter. However, it is important to state first that while reframing is similar to the traditional concept of interpretation, there is an important difference. Interpretations are generally made with the idea in mind that they represent some truth or reality. Perhaps the therapist believes the interpretation is true because of a particular approach to therapy. A reframing statement does not imply truth from an objective point of view. The statement is true only if it works, i.e., helps to bring about the desired change. Such a view would be consistent with William James' (1907) pragmatic theory of truth. The client-system judges whether the reframe has truth for them. The reframing statement cannot be too incongruent with the client's view of reality or it will be rejected. In constructing the reframe, the therapist goes through a process of highlighting certain facts in a certain way in order to lead the client to see the truth inherent in the reframe (Jones,1986).

Most of the reframes in this first category are designed to move the client from seeing a behavior negatively to seeing it positively. Occasionally, the direction will be changed because that which is negative may be therapeutically useful. For example, Weeks and Williams (1984) used a techniques known as developmental reframing in treating adolescents. In some of these cases the adolescents' behavior was defined as childish and childlike. Adolescents do not like to be told they are children. Because it was their defiance that had gotten them in trouble in the first place, we used the same dynamic to help them get out of trouble. By rebelling against our negative label, they could not continue the problematic behavior. In couple relationships, an affair is often redefined as an opportunity for change, growth, and recommitment.

The second use of reframing is to *shift the responsibility for the problem or the symptom from the individual-intrapsychic level to the interpersonal-systems level.* As long as the symptom is defined in terms of one person, the symptom bearer, the other members of the system escape the need for change. The reframe is an attempt to circularly define the problem in such a way that all members of the system accept some responsibility for the problem. This particular use of reframing was used almost exclusively by the Palazzoli group (1978) and is called positive connotation.

In our system, reframing has multiple effects. It changes the definition of the relationship, changes the meaning of the behavior by altering or disrupting the interpretative framework, and disrupts members' ability to predict each other's continued problematic behavior. It also puts the members on the same level, so that one cannot take advantage of the other, thereby creating greater congruence and interdependence by showing how each depends on the other to fulfill appropriate psychological needs. Finally, when one attributes positive intentions to unrewarding behavior, each partner is implicitly invited to try something different in order to achieve a mutually sought after goal.

Although reframing is an essential part of therapy, it alone is rarely enough to effect change. Of course, there are exceptions. In some of the references cited above, the reader will find instances where reframing was enough to free the client-system to bring about change on their own. Normally, therapy proceeds with a combination of continuing reframes and prescriptions.

Prescriptions

A prescription is a set of instructions or injunctions the client is requested to follow. Unlike reframing, a prescription possesses some demand for change. The prescription may be given in the session or it may be given at the end of a session for homework. The prescription may be directed toward the client's affective, behavioral, or cognitive functioning. The choice of this term was made because it has been used in the literature frequently (see L'Abate, 1986; Weeks & L'Abate, 1982) and it is synonymous with the term "directive" (Haley, 1976). Nichols (1984) also noted how commonly this term was used. He noted that experientialists use directives to promote affect, behaviorists to teach new ways to teach parents, structural family therapists to give homework, Bowenians to improve relationships with parents, and strategic therapists to outwit resistance and facilitate change. In our use, the prescription is the call to action. It is not something the therapist does to the client. The prescription grows out of the goals the client has established.

Establishing goals means the therapist has gone through a systematic process of assessing the functioning of the client-system and arriving at mutually agreed upon goals. To reach this point requires that a collaborative set be formed. The therapist and the client-system decide to collaborate with each other. The therapist does not do something *to* the client, the therapist does something *with* the client.

The prescriptions to be used fall within the two categories described earlier. They may be *affirmation or negation paradoxes*. However, in either case it should be noted that therapy is fundamentally paradoxical. The prescription chosen should be consistent with Seltzer's (1986) principles of taking control by giving it away; maintaining a positive view of the symptom and the person; not attempting to force change; allowing the client to have the symptom; helping the client attribute change to self rather than to outside forces; and placing the client in charge of the symptom so it is seen as controllable, voluntary, and/or volitional.

The choice between affirmation and negation paradoxes may be guided by a number of considerations. Empirical research has shown that certain problems respond well to certain methods of intervention. L'Abate and McHenry (1983) have reviewed much of the empirical literature on marital therapy to show which methods work in which cases. Ascher, Bowers, and Schotte (1985) and Kim, Poling, and Ascher (1991) have published comprehensive reviews of when paradox is the method of choice for problems. Unfortunately, the reviews on paradox have focused primarily on non-relational problems. Only two publications have focused directly on when to use and when not to use paradox in dealing with systems. Fisher, Anderson, and Jones (1981) and Weeks and L'Abate (1982) presented some clinically useful guidelines.

Fisher et al. (1981) linked family characteristics to three paradoxical techniques. They stated that reframing could be used when the family was moderately resistant, nonoppositional, had an ability to reflect and was not action-oriented, could handle frustration and uncertainty, had little or no acting-out behavior, possessed no pressing external problems, had a rigid family structure, and may have experienced repeated but not severe crises. Escalation should be used when the family has a vague style, excessive verbal manipulation,is oppositional,shows power struggles,has marked resistance, needs to move slowly, has a potential for acting-out, is excessively rigid, shows no compromise, and where the adults are competitive with the therapists. Finally, redirection (i.e., changing some aspect of the symptoms occurrence) should be used with families when the child is the presenting problem with specific symptoms, the symptoms are repetitive, and the family is basically compliant.

Weeks and L'Abate (1982) described five family patterns where paradox would be the method of choice. These patterns are defined by excessive fighting and bickering, unwillingness to cooperate with each other and to complete assignments, continuing the same patterns in spite of all types of interventions, divide and conquer strategies, and verbal and non-verbal disqualification. These five patterns can be distilled to two basic characteristics. When the client-system is resistant and the symptom is chronic, then a negation paradox is probably needed. Otherwise, an affirmation paradox is the intervention of choice.

The degree of resistance in a client-system can also be conceptualized from a social-psychological perspective. J.W. Brehm (1966,1972) and S. Brehm (1976) developed a theory of psychological reactance. According to them, reactance is the need to maintain one's sense of freedom. Loss of freedom may be self- or other- imposed. The degree of reactance is based on three variables: 1) the significance of the free behavior to the client; 2) the number of freedoms threatened; 3) the perceived magnitude of the threat. If the client views the symptom as the free behavior because it is that which others, including the therapist, want to take away, then we may utilize these three variables to assess resistance. This concept of resistance is similar to that of oppositionality in L'Abate's (1976) theory of differentiation of self and Millon's (1969) use of negativism in psychopathology.

Rohrbaugh, Tennen, Press, and White (1981) further refined the use of paradox when they divided paradoxical interventions into two major classes. They delineated compliance- and defiance-based interventions. The compliance-based intervention should be used when the client-system is likely to comply with whatever request is made. In general, these clients demonstrate symptoms over which they believe they have no control, but they are not resistant to change. Defiance-based interventions are those in which the therapist expects the client to not follow the intervention. In order to prove the therapist wrong, etc., the client must give up the symptom. This type of intervention should be used when the resistance is high and the client has control over the manifestation of the symptom.

THE INTERSYSTEM MODEL AS A METAFRAMEWORK

The evolution and combination of dialectic metatheory with foundational and integrational constructs drawn from social psychology has led to the development of this integrative perspective, which we call the Intersystem Model. Pinsof (1992) and Breunlin, Schwartz, and Karrer (1982) use the term metaframework to refer to the development of this kind of approach. A metaframework allows us to transcend any particular model of family/couple therapy by linking family processes to all facets of human development. An approach such as this does not culminate in specifying which approaches, techniques, or methods should be used in treating particular problems. That kind of specifying is based on the conception of therapy as outcome, i.e.,the idea of treatment X for problem Y, a medically driven model.

This integrative approach is based on the concept of therapy as process. Pinsof (1992) noted that similar disorders can have different etiologies and be maintained in very different ways. What works for one client-system may not work for another. This is not to say that we should not be thoroughly grounded in the empirical literature on outcome research. But, if this is all we know, we run the risk of doing therapy out of a "cookbook." The process component of therapy is what informs us about *how* to use *what* has been learned from outcome research.

The Interactional Context of Therapy

An essential part of the therapeutic process is to create a context for change to occur. As we have stated, change is best accomplished when it occurs spontaneously. Strong and Claiborn (1982) describe three principles that are useful in creating *spontaneous change or compliance.*

The first principle is called *choice.* The client needs to sense choice in his or her decisions. The therapist should never tell the client what to do nor use terms that may be polarizing or pejorative. This concept is especially important with couples. Most couples in treatment describe each other in language that is commanding, polarizing, pejorative, and judgmental. One partner usually assumes the moral high ground by claiming to know "the facts." The couple therapist strives to eliminate this kind of language by asking questions and modeling the use of language that stresses perceptions, opinions, beliefs, and appearances. The therapist focuses on what will work, be useful, and fit for the couple, rather than on someone's "right" or "perfect" solution that then leaves no choice. The therapist needs to listen to both partners carefully and respectfully in order to construct an intervention with which they will want to comply. If a partner believes s/he has no choice in the situation, the intervention will probably fail.

Personalism is the second principle used to facilitate spontaneous compliance. This concept refers to the idea that the compliance stems less from the client's personal desire for change and more from the requirements of the problem. Once again, the therapist collaborates with the couple in designing a program, system, or treatment plan they both believe is needed to solve their problem. Paradoxically, each partner must be willing to give up some control in the situation in order to gain control. For example, a couple in conflict might work on developing a set of communication and fair fighting rules. In the process, each partner might believe s/he is losing some advantage, but the idea of being able to be heard and understood thus permits the possibility of compromise. Once the rules are completed, they govern each partner's behavior—not the behavior of the other partner.

Awareness of this concept also means the therapist must monitor his or her language and attitude toward the couple. The therapist does not impose his/her standards, ideas, values, or treatment onto the couple. The language used by the therapist must reflect this attitude. Rather than say, "You should...," the therapist might say, "Let's think about what the two of you need to do...."

The *implicitness vs. the explicitness* of the intervention is the third principle for producing greater compliance and self-attribution of change. Implicit interventions grow organically from the therapeutic interactions and are "seamless." These interventions seem so obvious when they occur as to be either unnoticed or monumental. In modern psychotherapy, one school has emphasized these interventions. The Ericksonian school uses stories and metaphors during waking trances to bypass the clients conscious defenses (Rosen, 1982; Lankton & Lankton, 1991). The couple therapist is constantly making choices about what is noticed or emphasized in the session. Making points of difference explicit is not always the best idea. Focusing on similarities and on common goals and needs helps to reveal that which had been implicit in the relationship and which binds the couple together. The reader may wish to consult Weeks & L'Abate (1982) for a more complete description of indirect forms of therapeutic communication, including paradoxes, indirect and cryptic messages, metaphor, and trance-inducing messages.

Keeping the concepts of spontaneous compliance, personalism, and implicitness vs. explicitness in mind is pertinent whether the therapist chooses affirmation or negation paradoxes. They are part of the process of therapy. When these ideas work to create a spirit of cooperation, the therapist may choose to use affirmation paradoxes or compliance-based paradoxes. When these principles fail to produce the desired spirit of cooperation, then defiance-based paradoxes are in order.

Interpersonal/Interactional Integrative Principles

In Strong and Claiborn's (1982) model, there are six integrative principles, three interpersonal/interactional, and three intrapsychic. *The three interpersonal/interactional principles are congruence, interdependence, and attribution.* These principles are useful in conceptualizing the therapeutic relationship and the relationship of the partners. In this section, we will focus on these interpersonal/interactional principles. (The three intrapsychic principles are discussed in a separate section to follow.)

The first principle is that of *congruence.* In order to form any relationship, the partners must be in a state of relative congruence. Congruence could be used to refer to similarity or to sharing similar expectations, needs, etc. In marital and family therapy, the concept of congruence has been discussed in terms of the concept of joining (see Sauber, L'Abate, & Weeks, 1985). The basic idea has been that the therapist must join with the clients in ways that are not too dissimilar from them. Otherwise, the therapist is likely to be rejected. Congruence may be further thought of as the therapist being sensitive to the clients' expectations, needs, and explanatory model of change.

The first task of the therapist is to learn what the clients expect of, or from, therapy. Some clients expect the therapist to be active and directive while others expect the therapist to listen quietly. Some expect the therapist will ask questions about the past, others think talking about the past is a waste of time. Once the therapist has learned what the expectations are, s/he can begin to weave the therapy around these expectations and gradually change them through education and the process of therapy.

The prescriptions the therapist uses must also be consistent with the principle of *congruence.* It is obvious to say that prescriptions should be congruent with the couple. Part of what this means is that they should be acceptable within the framework of the clients' expectations. One way to view prescriptions is along a space-time continuum (L'Abate, 1976). Space refers to the depth of the intervention, ranging from surface-conscious to deep-unconscious material. Time refers to the past-historical or present-future perspective.

Prescriptions may be drawn from different schools of therapy with different spatial and temporal foci. In general, prescriptions from the Analytical/Bowenian schools emphasize the past and the intrapsychic; prescriptions from the Contextual and Experiential schools emphasize both the past and present, and the intrapsychic and interpersonal; prescriptions from the Strategic, Structural, Communications, and Behavioral school emphasize the present and the interpersonal (Kaslow, 1981).

The second concern in being congruent focuses on whether or not the clients' needs are being meet. The therapist cannot do everything the partners expect. The therapist is expected to bring some expert knowledge; otherwise, why see a therapist? Once the therapist and couple have moved into a congruent relationship, it is much easier for the therapist to move them to another position with regard to what they expect and what they need. Couples often do not know what they need. If the therapist presents this information according to the guidelines mentioned at the beginning of this section, and does so with confidence, the couple is likely to accept the information.

The needs of the couple are reflected in the treatment plan of the case formulation. The therapist carries out a comprehensive assessment of the couple based on the *Intersystem Assessment: Case Evaluation Form* (pp. 26-27).

The case formulation is multileveled and focuses on individual factors, interactional factors, and intergenerational factors. It is further fleshed out with much more information, including "outer- and inner-dialectics." The treatment plan should reflect both the therapist's expert knowledge, as well as what would be congruent with the couple.

The third consideration regarding congruence deals with the partners' implicit theory of change. It is important to ask not only what they want to change, but how they believe this change will occur. Some couples can actually articulate what approach will help them to change. Others, perhaps most, will have difficulty with this question. However, they render this information indirectly in the way in which they frame their problems. If a couple begins treatment by stating they have a communication problem, they are implicitly saying the solution is in better communication. If the couple says they are from dysfunctional families (a phrase common these days), then they imply a perceived need for family-of-origin work.

The second principle is *interdependence*. This principle should evolve naturally from the first (i.e., congruence) in the therapeutic relationship. The clients develop a sense of trust, confidence, and belief that by working together, needs can be fulfilled. The therapist does not want to foster dependence. Interdependence comes through the collaboration with the therapist, who disclaims responsibility for change, as was described earlier in this chapter.

The third principle is that of *attribution and impression management.* The therapist is in a position to help the partners question attributions they have made of each other in the past. For example, it is frequently helpful to have the couple split intents from effects. Just because something has been experienced as hurtful in the past does not necessarily mean it was intended in a hurtful way.

Most importantly, the therapist strives to evoke positive attributions and to change unidirectional attributions to bidirectional attributions so that each partner can see their part in the problem.

Thus far, the three interactional concepts have been applied to the therapeutic relationship. These concepts also apply to understanding the relationship between the partners. The therapist and the couple need to understand how they are in a congruent relationship and how they are different; the couple need to understand their interdependence on each other in terms of what is healthy and what is unhealthy; and, finally, the couple need to understand the relative nature of attributions and how changing their perceptions can have beneficial effects in their relationship.

The Intrapsychic Context of Therapy

The intrapsychic principles pertain to what we call the individual component of the Intersystem Model. These concepts deal with the internal events in each partner. Three integrative principles are used to help the therapist understand each partner, and how the two individuals form a relationship. They are (1) *definition*, (2) *interpretation*, and (3) *prediction*.

The first component is *definition* (Strong & Clairborn, 1982). The reader will recall that this concept refers to how each partner defines the relationship and how the relationship defines each partner. In traditional theory, it has to do with marital or relational expectations. Whatever the language, it is essential to learn as much as possible about these two facets of their definition. In a previous volume, Weeks and Treat (1992) described the use of Sternberg's (1986) triangular theory of love as an essential part of understanding this definition. In this theory, love consists of three parts—commitment, passion, and intimacy. The relationship may have definitional problems in one or all of these areas. For example, one partner may be defining the relationship as committed while another believes it is over or wants to leave. The fundamental task of the therapist is to raise the question of definition and help the couple negotiate toward a congruent definition of the relationship.

The second intrapsychic component is *interpretation*. Partners are constantly interpreting the meaning of each other's behavior. Sometimes the meaning given an event is not the meaning intended. When this happens, the couple will experience problems. Much of what the couple therapist does is to help interpret experience in the way in which it was intended. Communications work consists primarily of teaching the couple how to share in the same meanings of behavior.

When one partner distorts the meaning of a behavior, the therapist may choose a cognitive approach to deal with the distortion or s/he might choose to do family-of-origin work in order to determine the source of the distortion.

INTERSYSTEM ASSESSMENT: CASE FORMULATION FORM

FAMILY NAME:_____   Date of 1st interview:_____

Partner's name:_____   Age:_____ Occupation:_____

Partner's name:_____   Age:_____ Occupation:_____

Children & other family in home: _____   _____

_____   _____   _____

Ethnic group:_____   Years married/in relationship:_____

Referred by:_____   Reason for referral:_____

1. Initial Impressions and Reactions.

2. Presenting Problem(s)—Give a concrete description including the who, where, what, how. What is each member's view of the problem? How is the problem maintained in the system?

3. History of the Problem—Abbreviated form of No. 2, above.

4. Solutions Attempted—(including previous therapy).

5. Changes Sought by Client(s).

6. Recent Significant Changes—Stressors and Life Cycle Changes (new job, move, death, divorce, child leaving home, etc.). (Include here notations regarding individual/relationship/family life-cycle issues.)

Individual/Interactional/Intergenerational Assessment

7. Individual System(s)—Intrapsychic components, i.e., cognitive distortions and irrational thinking, defense mechanisms (denial, projection), definitions, predictions, interpretations. Also include DSM-III diagnosis on Axis I, II, and III.

8. Interactional System—e.g., emotional contracts, styles of communication, patterns of dyadic interaction, linear attributional strategies (debilitation, justification, vilification, rationalization, problem-solving and conflict-resolution skills).

9. Intergenerational System—e.g., anniversary reactions, scripts, boundaries, cutoffs, triangles, closeness-distance issues.

Treatment Plan

10. Hypothesis Regarding the Client(s).

11. Treatment Plan & Strategies—(Individual, Interactional, Intergenerational).

Problems:	Change Strategies:
1.	1.
2.	2.
3.	3.

12. Prognosis & Expected Length of Therapy—(provisional).

13. What are your strengths and weaknesses in dealing with this client system?

A concept that reflects the tendency to see the other in particular ways is projective identification (Feldman, 1982,1985), in which the partner projects onto the other those aspects of self that are unacceptable and identifies with them negatively in the other. For example, in one case a husband complained that his wife was always angry. The fact was that the husband was chronically angry, but could not admit this in himself, because in his family anger was taboo. When projective identifications exist, the therapist helps to make these explicit and encourages ownership of the projected wishes, desires, thoughts, behaviors, or feelings.

Prediction is the third intrapsychic concept. People search for safe and secure environments, including social environments. In close relationships we generally believe we know other people well enough to trust them, which really means well enough to predict their behavior. Trust and predictions are practically synonymous. By helping the couple redefine their relationship in a congruent way, and helping them to eliminate distortions in their interpretative process, the therapist is, in fact, creating predictability. For example, let us suppose a husband has had an affair. He would have the affair after work and tell his wife he was staying late. She would now predict that when he is "working late" he might be having an affair again. She must be able to trust her predictions about his behavior. If she cannot believe he is, in fact, working late, and he cannot accept the fact that he must be more accountable, then they will be trapped in the situation where the wife cannot trust him.

Integrating the Individual, Interactional, and Intergenerational Approaches

The couple/marital therapist is always confronted with the question, "Upon which component of the client-system should I focus?" Historically, marital therapists have tended to think in terms of focusing exclusively or primarily on the individual/intrapsychic part of a couple (which essentially means doing individual therapy with each partner), or working from a systemic perspective by focusing on the couple in the here-and-now (the interactional), or focusing on the family histories of the partners (intergenerational).

Conceptually and clinically, it may be easier and less anxiety provoking to think of these approaches as being mutually exclusive. However, one purpose of this chapter has been to break down these conceptual and clinical barriers in order to suggest that the best way to fit the therapy to the client, rather than the client to the therapy, is to have a comprehensive model that recognizes the complexity and wholeness of individuals and couples, and permits and encourages the therapist to function in an integrated manner.

This chapter began with a discussion of dialectic metatheory as the foundational construct for the Intersystem Model. The reader will recall how Riegel

(1976) stressed the need to consider the inner-biological, inner-psychological, cultural-sociological, and outer-physical. Bassaches (1980) also stressed the need to comprehend the dynamic relationship among systems. The dialectical concepts of *form* and *relationship* were particularly relevant. *Form* refers to viewing phenomena within context and *relationship* to viewing the interactive and constitutive aspects of relationships. Dialectic metatheory requires us to examine all aspects of a system. Because marital and family therapy has, at least, focused on these three aspects, our task is to think of them integratively rather than exclusively. A couple is composed of two separate individuals, each with his or her own dynamics (individual), who form a system that transcends the individual selves (interactional), and who possess family histories which impact on both of the above (intergenerational).

The *foundational construct* of *dialectic metatheory* provides us with a view of phenomena that stresses the need to see things contextually, historically, relatively, reciprocally, biologically, psychologically, etc. In short, the foundational construct demands that we transcend the existing theories to form a more encompassing theory.

One of the *integrational constructs* was a model of social interaction. This model of interaction had six principles. The first three were individual/intrapsychic and the second three were interactional/interpersonal. These six principles, as well as the other concepts in this chapter, help to guide the clinician in integrating the individual, interactional, and intergenerational approaches.

The first task in doing therapy with a couple is to view them as a system (a dialectical perspective). The assessment is done from the perspective that they constitute a system that is also composed of individuals. Treatment begins the process of helping the individuals to see themselves as a couple—they must begin to see their behavior as interlocking or circular. This task is accomplished by the neutrality of the therapist, the kinds of questions asked (circular questions, e.g., "and what you do when your partner does x"), and through the use of reframing. Achieving this task is the sine qua non of couple therapy and is a dialectical perspective.

The second task is to understand and treat the couple in terms of how they understand themselves and their problems. Oftentimes, multiperspectives are needed in order to fully resolve the problems. The six principles of the model of interaction inform us regarding which perspective(s) to utilize.

For example, suppose partners consistently misinterpret each other's behavior. The concept of *interpretation* from the model of interaction would become the focused perspective. The problem would then be explored in terms of the three approaches. At the individual level, the misinterpretation may have to do with cognitive distortions, individual psychopathology, or overuse of defense mechanisms. At the interactional level, the misinterpretation may stem from poor communication skills, unresolved conflict/anger, or confusion over intentions vs. effects. At the intergenerational level, it might have to do with the fact that, in the past, certain behaviors were consistently and rigidly defined in one way or that the individual has a need to project certain traits from family-of-origin members onto the partner. (The Intersystem therapist also realizes the interactional nature of all these perspectives—that the individual, interactional, and the intergenerational all impact upon, and are impacted, by each other.)

This example illustrates how using the six principles in our assessment and treatment can lead us to one or more of the three approaches and their interlocking circularity. The process begins by assessing where difficulties exist in these six areas and then moving to explore and treat.

CONCLUSION

Until recently, theories of marital and family therapy have generally been developed with an emphasis on promoting theoretical consistency within their own system rather than on integrating ideas from other approaches or systems of therapy. In the Intersystem Model the emphasis is on the systematic integration of the differential therapies, which comes through an appreciation and understanding of the dialectical process.

Dialectic metatheory served as the foundation for this Intersystem Model. The use of this metatheory directed our attention toward all aspects of the couple system—inner-dialectics and outer-dialectics; the intrapsychic, inter-personal, and intergenerational; affect, cognition, and behavior. In order to use this metatheory in a way which is conceptually compatible with our present thinking, this approach attempts to be comprehensive, contextual, historical, and multileveled. Conceptually, it points us toward integrating approaches that have, in the past, been seen as mutually exclusive—the individual,the interactional, and the intergenerational aspects of the couple system. This kind of theoretical and technical integration was accomplished through the use of three constructs: 1) paradox as a universal aspect of therapy; 2) the spontane-ous compliance paradoxes (i.e., affirmation and negation paradoxes); and 3) a model of social interaction. The model of social interaction applied to the couple's interaction as well as to the interaction between the couple and the therapist.

First, it was argued that paradox is the universal aspect of all psychotherapy, and that all of the techniques of change could be reduced to the affirmation or negation paradoxes. Consequently, the basic task in psychotherapy (marital therapy) is for the therapist to create the conditions for spontaneous compliance. Once the need for this task is understood, the therapist assesses and treats the couple, integrating a variety of concepts and techniques. The couple's relationship is examined using the constructs of definition, interpretation, prediction, congruency, interdependence, and attributions. The interventions flow from these constructs. Therapy is not conceptualized in terms of outcome, but in terms of process, and the therapist uses these concepts in creating a therapeutic process. The therapeutic process, in turn, points toward specific issues and ways of dealing with those issues.

The success of this approach depends on the therapist being able to think abstractly or, as Riegel (1976) has shown, to have reached the stage of dialectical thinking. This level of thinking is holistic and relativistic, and it is antithetical to thinking that is fragmented and compartmentalized, i.e., the kind of thinking that has pervaded the field of marital and family therapy. Dialectical processes are never-ending; there is never a product, always a process. This approach will evolve as new constructs are developed, old ones are better articulated, and as we move back and forth between differential and comprehensive theories.

The differential theorist plods along in step with the tenets of traditional scientific methodology. The theory is empirically tested one step at a time. In order for the therapist to work with this kind of theory empirically , human behavior is investigated in units—not as a whole. Unfortunately, the family and couples theorists who developed theories have become victims of their own success when it comes to practice. Developing and researching a theory in its pure form is a scientifically acceptable undertaking. Using the theory as the only theory in clinical practice is another matter. In practice, human behavior is not presented in units that fit nicely into theories. Many of the early proponents of family therapy theories have acted as if their theory were wholly sufficient for understanding and treating the client-system. They have also led others in the field to accept their view. It is our contention that the clinician must be a dialectician. Otherwise, the therapist will always be trying to fit the client to the theory and not the theory to the client-system.

AFTERWORD

Because this chapter is filled with so much information which is unfamiliar to the couple therapist, and because of the number of categories and subcategories of concepts, we have included this short addendum. First, a glossary of the key concepts is provided. Second, a topic outline of the chapter is provided, in order to help the reader clearly comprehend the organization of the concepts that comprise the Intersystem Model. We hope the reader will be able to use these tools in conceptualizing their own cases.

Key Concepts of the Intersystem Model

Foundational Construct–The underlying assumptions that constitute the philosophical basis for a theory. This construct is known as the metatheory. It serves as the frame of reference for the integration of differential theories of behavior.

Integrational Construct–The set of principles that is used to integrate disparate phenomena. These constructs have a unifying function and are commonly recognized in the field of study.

Dialectic Metatheory–One of the two most common metatheories in human behavior. In the Intersystem Model, two approaches to dialectics are used. Riegel's (1976) theory, which stresses the inner-biological, individual-psychological, cultural-sociological, and outer-physical, and Bassaches' (1980) work on dialectical thinking, which is categorized in terms of motion, form, relationship, and meta-formal thinking.

Paradox–A complex concept that is used in two ways in the Intersystem Model, both as Integrational Constructs: first, to describe the paradoxical or contradictory nature of the therapeutic relationship, and second, to describe two types of spontaneous compliance (affirmation and negation) both of which are paradoxical.

Theory of Interaction–the third integrational construct.

There are six integrative principles of the theory of interaction, representing concepts from social psychology. They are:

Interpretation - Refers to how events are interpreted. Interpretations are seen as relativistic and based on each partners own particular psychological predisposition to see events in a certain way.

Definition - Refers to how the partners define the relationship and how the relationship defines the partners.

Prediction - Refers to each partner's tendency to make predictions about the other's behavior. When predictions are accurate the partner has a sense of safety, security, and trust.

Congruence - Refers to the degrees to which the partners agree on such matters as definition, expectations, etc.

Interdependence - Refers to the degree to which the partners can fulfill each others needs in actuality or potentiality.

Attribution - Refers to the fact that meaning is attributed to behavior subjectively. Couples use both linear and circular attributional strategies. Linear strategies are based on cause-effect thinking and are counterproductive. Circular strategies allow each partner to assume some responsibility for the problem(s) and are encouraged by the therapist (e.g., reframing).

Reframing - Changing the meaning attributed to a behavior through a systematic process of recontextualizing the problem from another perspective; one of the two strategies for spontaneous compliance.

Prescriptions - Refers to the use of either affirmation or negation paradoxes; one of the two strategies for spontaneous complicance.

THE INTERSYSTEM MODEL:
AN INTEGRATIVE APPROACH TO TREATMENT

I. Introduction
II. Historical Perspective
III. Development of the Intersystem Model
    A. Integrative vs. differential theories
    B. Foundational construct
    C. Integrational construct
IV. The Foundational Construct of the Intersystem Model: Dialectic Metatheory
    A. Dialectic metatheory
    B. Riegel's theory of dialectics
        1. Inner-biological
        2. Individual-psychological
        3. Cultural-sociological
        4. Outer-physical
    C. Bassaches' theory of dialectics
        1. Motion
        2. Form
        3. Relationship
        4. Meta-formal integration
V. The Integrational Constructs
    A. Paradox as a universal aspect of therapy
    B. The spontaneous compliance paradoxes

      1. Affirmation paradox
      2. Negation paradox
   C. Theory of interaction
      1. Intrapsychic components of the interactional model
         a. Interpretation
         b. Definition
         c. Prediction
      2. Interactional components of the interactional model
         a. Congruence
         b. Interdependence
         c. Impression management and attribution (linear vs. circular)

VI. Strategies for Spontaneous Compliance
   A. Reframing
      1. Linear vs. circular attributional strategies
         a. Reframing negatives as positives and vice versa
      2. Reframing from the individual level to the systems level
   B. Prescriptions
      1. Affirmation and negation paradoxes

VII. The Intersystem Model as a Metaframework
   A. The interactional context of therapy
      1. Spontaneous change or compliance
         a. Choice
         b. Personalism
         c. Implicitness vs. explicitness
      2. Interpersonal/interactional integrative principles
         a. Congruence
         b. Interdependence
         c. Attribution and impression management
   B. The intrapsychic context of therapy
      1. Intrapsychic integrative principles
         a. Definition
         b. Interpretation
         c. Prediction

VIII. Integrating the individual, interactional, and intergenerational approaches.
IX. Conclusion

CHAPTER 2

The Tale of the Two Seekers

Larry Hof
with Mary and David Seeker

The following case study is a joint effort of the author and two clients. Near the end of their therapeutic process, the clients commented that they had been wondering if the therapist had ever thought of "writing them up" in one of his books. They expressed the belief that the telling of their "story" might enable them to "put endings" to some of the chapters of their lives, and also might be of help to others. Their last name, Seeker, is a metaphor for their process in treatment. The first names are those of historical figures whom they admired, and with whom they identified. Metaphors, images, stories, and dreams played a significant part in each of their lives, and were an integral aspect of the treatment process. For those reasons, they are also an important part of this case study.

The Tale of the Two Seekers is written in three parts: Phase I: The Seekers Join Forces For The Quest; Phase II: The Quest; Phase III: Coming of Age in The Promised Land. An introductory metaphor begins the Tale, and is woven throughout the case presentation in a limited way. A descriptive section in each phase is followed by a discussion of Assessment and Treatment. The "therapist" also appears in the guise of "Wizard," "Nurturing Parent," and "Guide," for reasons that will become obvious.

THE TALE BEGINS . . .

Theirs is a story of two people seeking together a more satisfying present and a future with a hoped-for family. Yet, it is also a story with many echoes from the past, some soft and consoling, but others insidious and pernicious.

David's Germanic ancestors often found themselves amidst the forests. Within the wind-driven shadows and sounds of the glen, they saw and heard signs of the presence of the gods, and found comfort therein. As a child, he had come to love the solitude of being amongst the trees, for there he was safe from the warlocks and the witches, those who sought to destroy him with the brands and the secret sins. In a new age, the weary, fire-scarred, tempered and toughened veteran sought safety from the never-ending battle, sought sanctuary, within the community of followers of a new God.

Mary had a regal heritage. Almost two thousand years of recorded family history. A long-haired, intelligent, Asian beauty, yet too dark of skin for the rigid caste culture from which she sprang. Her people had followed the new God for nineteen centuries, yet ethnic demons, untold intergenerational secrets, and family curses had combined to drive her to seek the perfection that would enable her to secure her holy grail, the parental acceptance and love that would give her peace. Paradoxically, she sought to defy them and yet to gain their approval by becoming the best of priests, and she too sought sanctuary with the followers of this God.

In the sacred place, the place of training, the seminary, they met, they talked, they worked, and they even played together. They found security and safety, and the beginning of what they both desperately desired—love. Yet, when they sought to deepen it in a commitment to marriage, they found that they lacked the skills to achieve their ends, and they each had a vague sense that something malevolent lurked nearby or within. With anticipation and apprehension, they sought the aid and counsel of a supposed holy man and wizard, one they believed knew the rituals and held the secrets of effective relationships. The guided journey of the Two Seekers had begun.

PHASE I: THE SEEKERS JOIN FORCES FOR THE QUEST

The Myth: "Someday my Prince/Princess will come!"
The Reality: "You're mean"; "You're shrill"; "You're just like your..."

The Seekers sat in the waiting room, each dressed in black clerical garb and collar. (Were they pastors or were they dressed for mourning? Perhaps both.) They greeted the Wizard with genuine, but slightly anxious smiles, good eye contact, and firm handshakes. Seated in the office, they "fit" into the chairs, rather than merely sitting upon them. There was a strength and determination about each of them. Yet, the Wizard could hear a river of anxiety rushing within and beneath her shrill torrent of words, and a deep rage, sadness, and pain beneath his composed and calm exterior, rational discourse, and forced smile.

Mary was a 26-year-old, dark-skinned female from a traditionally oriented Asian family. A Protestant pastor, she was bright, determined, "with places to go and people to see," at the beginning of a potentially very successful career. Her drive towards success and perfection would serve her well, if she did not succumb to a self-induced, but career supported, "burn-out." The overt anxiety in her voice was electric-like, and the Wizard wished he could turn the volume and the pitch down, and halve the speed at which the "tape" was running.

David was a 32-year-old, Caucasian male from an American family with Germanic heritage. He too conveyed a sense of intelligence and determination, also at the beginning of a potentially successful career as a parish pastor. His performance orientation and compulsive personality would serve him well. However, beneath his calm exterior, beneath his apparently armored strength, behind the fog created by his chain-smoking, the Wizard could sense the anxiety and fragility of a hurting child, a fragility with which he himself had been very familiar.

They had met during their seminary training and had found that they shared many and varied intimacies, and could risk beginning vulnerability with each other. Their relationship was egalitarian in many respects, yet, at times, he conveyed the sense of all-knowing, more worldly-wise, benevolent parent, and she the sense of need-to-be-guided child. They were learning to be empathic, and they obviously shared deep commitment and caring with each other. Their shared religious faith was solid and genuine, providing a strong bond and source of hope. After a four-year relationship, they became engaged, and sought premarital counseling, sensing they lacked some of the skills needed for effective marital living, namely communication and role-renegotiation skills.

At times, she said, he could be patronizing and verbally mean to her. At times, he said, she could be shrew-like, accusatory and distancing. She said that what he did caused her to do what she did; he said the reverse was true. The Wizard suggested that they both might be right, and they laughed, and thought he was truly wise. (They had heard from others that he had powerful potions, spells and incantations, and that he, too, was a priest of the same God.) From the Wizard's perspective, their failure to deny the reality of this truth, their failure to reject the idea of personal responsibility, and their willingness to even temporarily lay aside the vilification and blaming of the other led him to believe that, in fact, they were genuine Seekers of their truth.

When each of the Seekers discussed the family of origin, it was apparent that they had much knowledge regarding the facts, but just the beginning of a fully conscious awareness of the impact of the family upon their development. Mary was the third child of her materialistically oriented, success-driven, caste-aware family, in which she was constantly degraded by her mother, who was perceived to be a selfish, self-centered individual, doted on by a passive father/

husband. As was the tradition in families from their Asian country, children were expected to be extremely loyal to the family unit, especially to the parents.

David was the eldest child of a family that had become accustomed to, and had accommodated to, the decades-long alcohol addiction of his father. The parentified role and triangulation with his mother were something with which this Seeker had become comfortable. He spoke as if the family was very close and connected in a "healthy" way, as compared to that of his partner.

Assessment during Phase I

The therapeutic assessment of this couple was done from the perspective of what has become known as the Intersystem Model (Weeks, 1989), using the assessment structure suggested by Hof and Treat (1989).

Within the first few sessions, it was apparent to the therapist that this was a genuinely committed couple, with many individual and couple strengths, with a limited agenda for short-term, premarital counseling. At the same time, the therapist could see and sense clear individual issues that needed to be addressed, including the following: (1) her anxiety; (2) her hidden low self-esteem and pursuit of acceptance and love, which provided the fuel for her relentless drive for perfection; (3) his apparent nicotine addiction; (4) his compulsive personality and rigidity, which gave him a needed sense of control of the present, which served him well, but also suggested something repressed that needed to be overcontrolled lest it be exposed; (5) the inability of each to sufficiently nurture themselves, together and individually, except through the vicarious caring for others—partner or parishioners.

A multiaxial diagnosis for each of them, according to DSM-III-R (American Psychiatric Association, 1987) criteria yielded the following for Mary:

Axis I - 300.0, Anxiety Disorder Not Otherwise Specified (Insufficient symptoms for classification as a specific Anxiety Disorder, and not classifiable as an Adjustment Disorder with Anxious Mood);
V62.81 – Other Interpersonal Problem (Difficulties with romantic partner);
Axis II–V71.09–No diagnosis on Axis II;
Axis III–None;
Axis IV–Severity of Psychosocial Stressors: 3 (Moderate);
Axis V–Global Assessment of Functioning: Current–70 (Some mild symptoms, but generally functioning pretty well, with some meaningful interpersonal relationships); Past Year–70.

A multiaxial diagnosis for David yielded the following:

Axis I–305.10–Nicotine dependence;
  309.28–Adjustment Disorder with Mixed Emotional Features;
  V62.81–Other Interpersonal Problem (Difficulties with romantic partner);
Axis II–Obsessive Compulsive Personality Traits;
Axis III–None;
Axis IV–Severity of Psychosocial Stressors: 3 (Moderate);
Axis V–Global Assessment of Functioning: Current–70 (Some mild symptoms, but generally functioning pretty well, with some meaningful interpersonal relationships); Past Year–70.

Developmentally speaking, from an individual perspective, neither of them had yet fully entered the so-called "Age 30's Transition" (Gould, 1978), in which there is genuine individuation from roles and the reclaiming of laid aside or suppressed pieces of the self. Rather, each was still in the final aspects of the stage of "Provisional Adulthood" (Gould, 1978), in which each person is learning how to "play the game of life" according to other people's rules. Much of what was occurring for Mary and David Seeker was "role behavior," rather than behavior based upon conscious, value-based integrative choice. However, as therapy progressed, they both moved into their "Age 30's Transition."

For this couple, it was also meaningful to view each of them from the perspective of their development in terms of Fowler's (1981) stages of faith. Evidence of a maturing, age-appropriate faith was present in each of them. Having moved through virtually all of the aspects of the stages of Undifferentiated Faith, Intuitive-Projective Faith, Mythical-Literal Faith, and much of the Synthetic-Conventional Faith stage, they stood in the doorway of the Individuative-Reflective Faith, in which there is a "reflective construction of ideology [and the] formation of a vocational dream" (p. 290). Their capacity for "critical reflection on identity (self) and outlook (ideology)" (p. 182), along with an inner drive and restlessness to move on and experience new life stories, even if this requires challenging past beliefs and neatly pieced-together theologies, gave clear evidence that most of the previous stage's tasks were completed, or well on their way to completion. In the nascent stage, the Individuative-Reflective, a reclaiming and reworking of one's past becomes necessary, along with opening oneself to the "deeper self" (pp. 197–98). There is a permeability that is "alive to paradox and the truth in apparent contradictions" (p. 198), and the individual strives for unity and wholeness, and is vulnerable to the processes necessary to attain those goals.

When they were viewed from the perspective of the relationship life cycle (Monte, 1989), they clearly fit within and between the following three stages, which for them overlapped to varying degrees: (1) Starting Up, in which the focal issues of differentiation, identity, intimacy and trust are central; (2) Settling In, in which the focus is on issues of identity, inclusion/exclusion, and power and control; and (3) Decision Time, with its focal issue of commitment.

With regards to the family life cycle, each was moving from the stage of being between families as the unattached young adult to the stage of the joining of families through marriage and the emergence of the newly married couple. Thus, issues of acceptance of parent/offspring separation and commitment to a new system were normative for this couple, but complicated by the intergenerational issues noted below (Carter & McGoldrick, 1980, 1989).

From an interactional perspective, it was evident that they desired to communicate effectively and in a caring way, and they did quite well at the rational level. However, they lacked certain specific skills in communications, (especially regarding affective awareness and expression), conflict utilization, and decision-making. In addition, they had no real sense of the need to continuously renegotiate marital roles, and little understanding of the concept of a flexible marital contract. Since they were embarking upon a dual-career marriage, failure to address those issues could lead to a rapid deterioration of the marital relationship; at intake, these were the most pressing issues and those about which they were most aware.

From the intergenerational perspective, it was clear that one function served by the formation of a marital dyad was the creation of a third entity in the relationship—Mary, David, The Couple—to help them protect each other from their respective families of origin. She needed to differentiate from her family, yet lived in fear of losing the unconditional love she never had but desperately sought. Interactionally, he would offer her the supportive strength and support to do it, and, hopefully, provide the genuine love desired. Of course, there was a *quid pro quo*, written in invisible ink on the reverse side of one of the "pages" of their marital contract: "If I do that for you, you will never betray, hurt, or abandon me."

David was less clear regarding his need to differentiate from his family. After all, it was clearly "more healthy" than hers, and even offered her something she lacked, a family that seemed to value her highly as long as the couple remained loyal and did not abandon any of the family "traditions," for example, weekly dinners together, laughing at or ignoring father's alcoholism, and David remaining a parentified child and surrogate husband for his mother. The impact of being an adult child of an alcoholic family (ACOA) was unknown to him at this point in treatment. Interactionally, Mary was willing to participate actively in the family, and in the charade. Of course, here too, there was a *quid pro quo*: "If I do that for you, you will always unconditionally love and accept me." Neither was able to fulfill these unrealistic goals of their initial marital contract.

The therapist, as well as Mary and David, was quite sensitive to the fact that theirs was a multicultural relationship, and although Mary was quite assimi-lated into American society, she had a strong commitment to her Asian heritage and was aware of many cultural clashes (cf. Berg & Jaya, 1993; McGoldrick, Pearce & Giordano, 1982). For example, her culture put the family first and the individual second, and this conflicted with her strong, Americanized, feminist inclination towards at least an equal balance between the two. Also, within the family, ultimate allegiance was to the parents, and children were expected to care for them, in their old age, even if such care was detrimental to the welfare of the children or their families. This conflicted with her strong, faith-centered sense of justice and fairness. However, David and Mary appeared quite comfortable with the cultural differences, showed genuine respect and appreciation for each other's heritage and traditions, and demon-strated clear ability and willingness to discuss and negotiate differences in this area.

Treatment during Phase I

In the descriptive section of Phase I, the therapist was referred to as the Wizard, to reflect his belief that this couple entered therapy at the stage of the process often referred to as Magical Thinking (Rado, 1956, 1962, 1969). In this stage, The Seekers were placing their hope more in the therapist and his skill than in themselves. He was expected to provide "wonderment and awe," because they perceived themselves to not have the skills they needed to resolve their issues (a reality), nor the ability to extract themselves from the negative reciprocal spirals of interaction that led them to seek treatment (a fallacy). They "simply" needed the first in order to accomplish the second.

The fact that the therapist was also a clergyman was important to them in their search, because their faith was a core aspect of their personal being and interpersonal relating. At a time when issues related to gender, ethnicity, and race appear regularly in the literature, it is surprising how seldom the issue of spirituality or sensitivity to religious/faith orientation is addressed (cf. *Religious values in psychotherapy*, 1991). With this couple, the therapist's sensitivity to, knowledge of, and respect for their religious/faith heritage and beliefs contributed to rapport building and the creation of a therapeutic alliance. He was able to affirm the positive use of their faith in their personal lives and in their relationship: (1) the utilization of their spiritual or transcen-dent beliefs, values, and resources to give them encouragement in times of trouble, and a sense of meaning beyond themselves, both of which are central aspects in the development of hope (Hof, 1993); (2) their creation of a "surrogate" family in their "household of faith," with a nurturing parental deity, "siblings" within the priesthood, "children" to nurture and receive nurture from within their congregations, all of which served a reparative function with regards to their family-of-origin issues, enabling them to experience and practice aspects of healthy family-like functioning, from which they could generalize to their own marriage and future family (cf. Friedman, 1985).

In addition, the therapist was able to challenge their misuse or abuse of their religious values and principles (see Lovinger, 1984). For example, each of them had a rather relentless pursuit of perfection, which meant to be without a blemish, and without anger and selfish thoughts or desires. Difficult to accomplish, to say the least! Their belief was based, in part, upon a verse in the New Testament book of Matthew (5:48), which directly states that one must be "perfect" as their "heavenly father" is perfect. When confronted, through some bibliotherapy (Sanford, 1974), with the full meaning of the Greek word for "perfection" upon which the English translation is based, they were forced to deal with the fact that it refers to "wholeness" rather than to "purity." This helped them to redefine and reinterpret their expectations regarding themselves, and to be more tolerant, accepting, and forgiving of themselves and each other. This also paved the way for the addressing of other relevant self/other definitions and cognitive distortions (Beck, 1976; Burns, 1986, Chapter 3; Datillo & Padesky, 1990; Seligman, 1991).

Interestingly, the overly critical aspects noted above were applied only to themselves and each other, but not to others outside of that small circle. Thus, the ability and willingness of the clients and the therapist to permit some convergence regarding religious issues and values created a therapeutic congruence that permitted and fostered significant change within the client system. This, in turn, contributed to an increasing congruence with their external world.

The therapist, aware of the limited agenda, but also cognizant of the developmental and other issues noted above, chose to utilize a premarital approach that could be effectively constructed to limit and constrain their change, but could also become more open-ended if they desired to pursue a broader agenda. Their high level of commitment to and love for each other contributed to the decision to use a prescriptive approach at this point in treatment and led to its success. Plainly and simply, their hope regarding the relationship possibilities was quite high at the outset of treatment (Hof, 1993), they wanted and expected the experience to be helpful, and, therefore, it was (cf. Frank & Frank, 1991).

Psychoeducational or premarital/marital enrichment techniques were utilized because there were clear interactional skill deficits (i.e., communications, conflict utilization, decision-making). The correction of those deficits could have conceivably provided them with the tools needed to delve further into the individual or intergenerational issues on their own, or even obviated the need for such exploration at this point in their marital life cycle (cf. Bandura

& Walters, 1963).

The listing of individual and marital strengths (Hof & Miller, 1981), the assessing of the variety and quality of intimacies they shared (Hof & Miller, 1981), and training in communication skills and assertiveness (Stuart, 1980), were all utilized to enhance the perception and reality of their relationship strengths. A limited focus on affective awareness and expression [using the technique and principles of the "World of Feelings" (Hof & Miller, 1981; Weeks & Treat, 1992)] enabled them to communicate their vulnerabilities to each other more effectively, enhance their empathy for each other, and begin to manage anger in a more constructive manner. Sager's (1976; Sager & Hunt, 1979) contract theory was utilized to begin the process of developing a specific, flexible, marital contract, and to provide the basis for practicing conflict resolution skills (Stuart, 1980; Weeks & Treat, 1992), and role renegotiation skills (Hof & Miller, 1981).

Because Sager's approach initially focuses on expectations of marriage, the development of a written contract also provided a gentle entree to the exploration of family-of-origin issues, where the therapist believed the most important work needed to be done. The word "gentle" is important to remember, because there was the sense of a great deal of pain and anger related to those issues that the couple was appropriately reluctant to deal with just prior to their marriage.

Sager's approach and the psychoeducational/enrichment approach were also employed because both Mary and David used abstract conceptualization and active experimentation as two primary learning styles (Kolb, 1979). The skill-building techniques and the marital contracting process gave them the opportunity to actively experiment with new approaches to their problems. Sager's marital typologies and contract theory also enabled them to utilize their abilities in the area of abstract conceptualization, effectively creating concepts that helped them integrate their observations or life experiences.

During the first six weeks of therapy, David and Mary were extremely responsive and cooperative, both during the sessions and with the weekly "homework" assignments. Although they initially utilized vilification and blaming, they were quick to grasp the concepts of personal responsibility and circular causality. Said Mary, "So, what you mean is that what I do is part of what causes him to do what he does, which is then part of what causes me to do what I do. Is that right?" And, David replied for the therapist, "That makes it a never-ending circle!"

Mary was especially enthusiastic, although extremely anxious. In her own words:

I called Larry Hof to set up four to six weeks of premarital therapy with my soon-to-be husband, David. After the first session, Larry asked us to read the book, *Intimate Partners*. The very word, "Intimate," made me anxious. I read the book and immediately identified with the couple who wanted a parental spouse. I was shocked, since I consider myself a feminist. I went through those first six sessions very anxious, and I had no idea why my mind was racing and my heart was pumping so fast, until Larry spoke the absolutely magical words, "Mary, you continue to appear to be extremely anxious, and I believe that if you would consider taking some anti-anxiety medication for a brief period of time, you might be able to enter these sessions in a manner that would enable you to benefit from them more and have a more healthy marriage." My sources of anxiety were the lack of love from my parents, because I was dark-skinned, (a major source of embarrassment for the whole family), because I did not receive admission into medical school and make my parents' dreams come true, because I was marrying a white man outside of my culture (the first woman in my family to marry outside the culture in over 1500 years), and because I could never make my parents love and accept me. Larry said the word, "anxiety," and it was as if I had never heard this word before, because I cried for an hour after the word was spoken. Soon after we were married, the anxiety remained very high, and I reluctantly agreed to use the medication prescribed by my physician. In just a few weeks, I knew what it was to live with less anxiety!

As is evident from the above, therapy did not end with those six premarital sessions. After their wedding, a joyous celebration of their "coupleness" and faith, shared with their many close friends and their families, they returned to continue the work they had begun. Mary accepted a referral for medication for her anxiety, and accepted the challenge to use progressive relaxation techniques and a planned aerobic exercise program to manage the anxiety more effectively. The medication gave her a much needed, never before experienced frame of reference—to be without excessive anxiety. With her typical determination, it was only a matter of months before she was managing most of the anxiety without medication. She was so pleased that she was determined to attack the other sources of anxiety noted above.

In this initial phase of treatment, David was involved, but maintained somewhat of a cautious distance, permitting Mary to lead the way and responding to her lead with the aura of a somewhat benevolent parent. When she would confront him regarding this, he would acknowledge it, commit himself to try harder to be more Adult-to-Adult in his relationship with her, have varying degrees of success for a week or two, and then revert to the same pattern, to her chagrin. Yet, their love for and commitment to each other were such that they kept coming back—to attempt to break the cycles, to sharpen the contract, to enhance the marriage, to practice and build the relationship strengths and skills. They had become a couple, prepared for their quest.

This part of the pilgrimage towards wholeness lasted for four years and four months, and involved 25 conjoint sessions, 12 individual sessions with Mary, and seven individual sessions with David. The first 15 conjoint sessions were held on an approximately weekly basis, just prior to and immediately following their marriage. The remaining 29 sessions were scattered throughout the following four years.

PHASE II: THE QUEST

The Myth: "Over the river and through the woods to mother's house we go. . . ."
The Reality: "Across the River Styx, through the gates of Hell, and into the Abyss."

The Seekers felt somewhat secure together, able to trust each other more, to commiserate with each other regarding career frustrations, and to celebrate the successes. They learned to share playful time together, and were gradually building an increasingly satisfying sexual intimacy. At times, each accused the other of working too hard and they negotiated changes in their schedules to "block in" time for each other on a regular basis. However, they were still unable to break certain repetitive cycles, cycles in which both felt pained, but which he would not openly acknowledge, and in which he responded with passive aggressive actions (e.g., "I forgot you were out late when I dead-bolted the door and went to sleep"). He described these actions in the office with shamed affect, but an almost gleeful smile on his face.

To these actions, she would respond with rage and pained withdrawal. In one sequence, she would schedule herself so fully that there was little or no time for togetherness for several weeks at a time. To this he would respond with a passive aggressive gambit and the game would continue, effectively blocking their attempts to deepen their intimacy and begin plans for a family. He would, of course, also overschedule himself so that she would be so pained as to withdraw from him, effectively abandoning him to himself, paining him, resulting in . . . , and the game continued. It was laborious, aggravating, painful and, at times, enraging. Both enjoyed the times between the cycles, but with a canny precision, one of these negatively charged explosions occurred whenever one of the two was ready to move the relationship to a deeper level of intimacy. In therapy, the Seekers sought the help of a Nurturing Parent, for they now knew that there was no magic, just the reality of the feared hard work.

Assessment during Phase II

In the second phase of treatment, both Mary and David had become convinced that something "deeper" was going on, because they were frustrated in their attempts to break the intimacy-blocking gambits and games. In the office, they could quickly get beyond the old linear attributions, and describe the circular interactions in exquisite and painful detail. The skill-building techniques, contracting process, and brief "peek" into each of their families of origin (to gain some appreciation of the effect of familial relationships and dynamics upon personal development and expectations regarding marriage) had been helpful to both of them. However, David and Mary indicated that they were both, in some ways, better able to use the learning and skills with other people than with each other. Clearly, something was "contaminating" their ability to relate more effectively together.

They sensed it was related to some parallel processes they were observing between the way they were relating to each other and the way people related in their families. Often, something like the following was said with anger and pain, "You're treating me just the way (*insert various family members here*) treats your (*insert other family members*)!" Each became determined to explore the family of origin in a deeper manner, to look at the pained realities without rose-colored glasses and the defenses of denial, avoidance, and projection. This exploration, in its latter phase, would reveal, for David, sexual abuse and sadism, and would add the Axis I diagnosis of Post-traumatic Stress Disorder, delayed onset (309.89) (PTSD) to his multiaxial diagnosis.

The PTSD impacted upon the relationship in several ways: the dissociative aspects kept him distant from his feelings, and, in turn, from her feelings as well (i.e., he "numbed out" in the affective domain). His previously repressed fear of being abused/killed left him hypervigilant and somewhat avoidant of close relationships (i.e., "If I get too close, I will get beat up or killed."). In order to get close to, and more intimate with, Mary, he needed to deal effectively with the repressed material with the therapist alone, as well as directly with his partner. It was surprising to the therapist that the PTSD did *not* impact negatively upon the relationship in the sexual area. No evidence of sexual dysfunction emerged at any point in the course of treatment.

Developmentally speaking, from an individual life cycle perspective, she had entered her "Age 30's Transition" (Gould, 1978), while he had successfully negotiated his "Age 30's Transition" and was entering a period of role stability.

Secure in their love for each other and their commitment to the marriage, challenged by their faith to seek wholeness, with the strength of the couple and the support of the Nurturing Parent, the Seekers engaged in serious reflection upon the family of origin.

Treatment during Phase II

In the descriptive section of Phase II, the therapist was referred to as the Nurturing Parent, in the belief that the Seekers had entered the second phase of treatment, Parentification (Rado, 1956, 1962, 1969). In this stage, the therapist is viewed as less godlike and magical, but significant transferences may still be present. If they can be utilized to permit the therapist to play the part of a needed Nurturing Parent who provides encouragement, belief in their abilities, nurturing support, and protection, then such transferences may be not only permitted, but encouraged at this point. This was the role of the therapist at this stage in the treatment process as they entered the "Land of the Giants," reflecting upon the past, experiencing the Inner Child feelings as if they were transported back in time to the early events that had contributed so greatly to the personalities formed in the present. Yes, there were fond memories of childhood and extended family gatherings. However, it was out of the other, darker memories that the growth would occur and the freedom would come.

The principles and techniques of family-of-origin work were utilized extensively. The genogram, developed by Murray Bowen (1978) and extensively discussed by McGoldrick and Gerson (1985), was adapted to include the history-gathering aspects of Guerin and Pendagast (1976); the relationship/family "mapping" features of Minuchin (1974); the impact, internal images, and "story" aspects of Duhl (1981) and Hof and Miller (1981); and the projective emphasis of Wachtel (1982). The sharing of each other's story increased their understanding and trust, paving the way for deepened intimacy.

Both wrote several "letters" to their respective individual parents, some of which were sent or read face to face, others of which were primarily for the benefit of the writer. In these letters, they dared to put into words the forbidden thoughts and feelings of the Inner Child, and to speak them out loud to his/her partner or to the therapist (James & Jongeward, 1971). Transactional Analysis and Gestalt "empty chair" and role playing techniques were utilized to deepen the affect, enhance memories, and learn and practice new ways of relating to family members with assertiveness and personal power.

Each made several visits to their family—to parents and to siblings—to attempt to retrieve the past, to connect in new ways with the family, to redefine the family relationships in the here and now. The goal was a slow, non-confrontational connection, beginning with requests for information and clarification of family experiences. Respect for self, parents, and siblings was stressed, and time for thoughts and feelings to settle and be worked through between contacts was always planned for. Confrontation and expression of painful feelings was done only when deemed safe and necessary. Issues of loyalty, betrayal, entitlement, indebtedness, and justice were addressed (Boszormenyi-Nagy & Spark, 1973), as well as the issues of differentiation, individuation, and possible restructuring of family alliances and relationships in the present (Bowen, 1978; Framo, 1970, 1976; Nerin, 1986; Paul & Grosser, 1981; Williamson, 1981, 1982a, 1982b).

Early in this Phase II of therapy, David had an extremely significant experience, one in which he reframed certain aspects of his experiences in his family. In his own words:

> One of the critical turning points in my own awareness about my life came after reading an assignment on family masks [the Sanford, 1974, reference noted above]. After my reading had incubated for some weeks, I was sitting in the therapist's office describing my mother and father and their particular actions in an incident, (I can't recall just what), when suddenly the good masks I had given them were burned away like melted plastic. Their good masks became distorted and revealed a darkly shadowed sinister look. The feeling was frightening, and yet revealing, for me, as it automatically filled in gaps in family events I could not previously explain.
>
> This unmasking further unfolded to me with the recognition of my parents action in helping me to continue to smoke. I had previously viewed my parents' gifts of cigarettes, lighters, and other smoking material as kindly gestures. But, this did not square with the fact that I was a frequent victim of bronchitis and had severe respiratory problems, with a family history of "weak lungs." Often, when I would attempt to quit smoking for health reasons, they would subtly draw me back, saying, "Oh, just one won't hurt." The truth was that it was killing me and enslaving me in their addictive, abusive system. The sad truth was that I was as expendable as a cheap cigar. This first awareness, centering around a seemingly small vice, was the beginning of my unmasking process in therapy. This unmasking, or recognition, process was the first step in my deepening awareness of my sexually sadistic family of origin.

Shortly after this experience, David decided to stop smoking and accepted a referral to another therapist for autogenic training regarding smoking. After two sessions, he stopped smoking and has not smoked since. In addition, he joined a health club and began a personally satisfying exercise program.

Mary found the letter-writing experience and home visits extremely helpful.

In her words:

> Since my husband could not make up for the lack of love and acceptance of my mother, Larry asked me to write a letter to my mother so that I could bury my fantasy mother, and grieve over what I will never have from my mother, and learn to live with my real mother. Every sentence in the letter caused profound sadness, and at times, rage. The repulsion my mother felt when I was born, because I was dark-skinned, made me feel powerless, Larry asked my to read *The Velveteen Rabbit*, by Margery Williams, and I cried bitterly when I read what the Skin Horse told the rabbit: "Real isn't how you are made, it's a thing that happens to you. When a child loves you for a long, long time, not just to play with, but really loves you, then you become real."
>
> I was not real as I began the letter, but as I concluded it, I touched my skin, and for the first time, I felt beautiful. I went home and read the letter to my mother, in the presence of my father, and the tears cleansed my skin and my soul. This was the first time I ever claimed myself in front of my parents. Soon after, David could hold me and I no longer wanted to run away. I did not find ways to alienate David, so that he would find me unattractive, like my parents. This was the beginning of breaking a very destructive cycle inherited from my family of origin, which was infecting my marriage.

During this second phase of therapy, Mary was able to move much closer to the resolution of her differentiation and individuation issues *vis-à-vis* her family. Prior to this period of her life, she had overidealized her father and vilified her mother. She was able to develop a more balanced view of the total family system, and to set effective boundaries for herself. In her words:

> Dad was very sensitive and attentive to me whenever Mom was not around, but in my mother's presence, Dad could never take a stand, because he preferred to keep my mother happy, rather than have close and fair relationships with his children. Dad became extremely ill, and his life was threatened . . . All the unresolved issues between my siblings and my parents became critical in the intensive care unit of the hospital. Who will take care of mother, in case Dad dies? Who will take care of Dad, if he lives as a virtual "vegetable," and is unable to care for himself at all? What are my parents entitled to from me, since I am the only child, out of all of the children, who paid for her college, her own wedding, and all of her own living expenses since being a teenager. All of the others had those things paid for by my parents.

My siblings wanted me to share all the responsibility for the care of my parents equally. I was enraged by this mandate. It was very clear to me that I was being used. The guilt practically paralyzed me, as the illness had my father. Larry told me to write down a list of what I believed my parents can legitimately expect from me. I wrote the following: a phone call once or twice a month, and an occasional visit. My list included nothing else. My siblings were furious, because they always counted on my overfunctioning to attain my parents love and approval, and I guess I contributed to them having such a belief system. But, I held on to my position of what I was going to offer to my parents. I was no longer paralyzed from guilt and responsibility. My marriage was no longer driven by my loyalty to my parents and the intensity of guilt, but by a sense of relief and calmness.

However, the Child within is slow to accept the reality of what was and is, slow to relinquish the fantasies, the unrealistic expectations and dreams. Mary notes:

I always thought that I should spend holidays with my family, and when my father came home from the hospital, David and I decided to have a "Hallmark Card" kind of Christmas, in gratitude to God for my Dad's recovery. We cooked for days, and sent out formal announcements and set up for an elegant dinner. My family was two hours late, because they stopped by to visit friends, and my parents criticized my cooking and my choice of gifts. My older sister brought a bag of frozen vegetables and asked me to cook them as the side dish for the elegant roast my husband had prepared. My younger sister asked for my wrapping paper, so that she could wrap my present. My brother never even bothered to show up. My tears felt blood-filled, because I knew that I would never experience a "Hallmark" Christmas with my family. Larry asked me why I continued to set myself up for this pain and rejection, and I knew that it was familiarity with pain, and an unending hope that things would be better, if only I would try harder, that caused me to dream of a "Hallmark" Christmas.

David's initial family-of-origin work focused on trying to be honest with his parents regarding his father's alcoholism and his sense of being triangulated and parentified by his mother. He spoke with each of them individually, and, for a while believed he had been heard. He realized that he had learned to depend upon himself to escape the enmeshment at home, and to vicariously care for himself by caring for others, namely, his mother, his siblings, and his childhood friends, a style of relating he carried into his adult life.

During this second phase of treatment, Mary took a new, highly visible, and powerful position within her denomination. This led to significant marital stress. David's fears of abandonment were "hooked," and after a brief period of denial, he took responsibility for his feelings and shared them directly with Mary. In one sense, the marriage had come full circle. Now David could overtly disclose his fears of abandonment. Supportive therapy to reassure Mary concerning the normal nature of her anxiety in the face of a major life transition (an effective reframe), along with a renewed use of the relaxation techniques and the exercise regimen, brought the anxiety quickly under control. Several conjoint sessions to explore the expressed fears and to renegotiate marital roles and expectations demonstrated conclusively to each of them the extent and nature of their growth as individuals and as a couple.

Shortly after this event, David had a "breakthrough" experience regarding his rage and pain at being an ACOA. Flashes of incest, guilt, and shame exploded alongside of his intellectual awareness; yet, he was still desirous of avoiding the deeper, "secret sins." He accepted a referral to an ACOA group, and began the process of sharing himself with others, and learning that he was not the only one to have had such experiences.

Throughout Phase II, the principle of "safe person, safe place, safe time, safe material" was practiced, stressed, and reiterated (cf. Courtois, 1988; Dolan, 1991; Maltz, 1991). In other words, nothing was to be done regarding any of the more repressed material that was breaking through into consciousness unless all of those criteria were met to the satisfaction of the person dealing with the issues, be it David or Mary. This is an example of a "go slow paradox," as discussed by Weeks and L'Abate (1982). That meant, as is so often the case with family-of-origin work and incest/abuse survivor work, that weeks and even months would pass between sessions. However, the therapist/Nurturing Parent/Guide was always available for phone consultations, and the Seekers always made an individual or conjoint appointment when they felt they needed to delve into material that was beyond the resources they had as individuals or as a couple.

In this phase, and all of the phases of treatment, the therapist was keenly aware of the important role that appropriate self-disclosure and "use of self" could play in the therapeutic process (Baldwin & Satir, 1987; Jourard, 1971). He freely shared his personal story with Mary and David: his history; his own family of origin; his own struggles with painful feelings; his growth, successes, and struggles in his own marriage. They laughed, they worked, and they shared sadness and tears together, the three of them, in a fashion, all "seekers."

Now that Mary was somewhat at peace, it seemed that David was becoming more tense and stressed. They took a trip to her homeland, and while they were visiting one of the largest Asian cities, the pressing of the people, the chaos, and the squalor all around led David to a panicked sense of being overwhelmed. His obsessive/compulsive defenses could no longer control the anger and contain the intrapsychic material that was pushing into his consciousness. The internal sense of losing control led to a veritable flood of long-repressed material, in his awake state and in his dreams, with flashes of memory and affect, relating to living in a dysfunctional, alcoholic family with severe incest and physical abuse.

Prior to the trip, he had ceased going to his ACOA group, and had cut himself off from his family. In effect, he was trying to deal with his issues by not dealing with them. However, the denial, the avoidance, the repression could no longer stand in the face of his pursuit of wholeness.

He sought out his siblings to discuss with them their memories of the past. His 35-plus years of "loyalty," rage, abuse, denial, loss of childhood, helplessness, fear, and so forth broke free, finally to be dealt with in a more thorough fashion. When his father demanded the return of a prior gift of land, he confronted him regarding the long history of abuse and incest. He was met with stonewalling denial.

Therapy during that time focused on enabling him to slowly recapture and reconnect the memories, thoughts, images, sensations, and feelings of the past. He realized how he had tried to atone for his parents' sins—the victim feeling guilty. He touched the deep sadness, pain, and loneliness behind the family myth of "David, the wonderful child." The dissociative processes were beginning to be replaced with a sense of an integrated past.

Throughout this process, the Nurturing Parent provided support, protection, and encouragement, along with a clear, firm, reality-based affirmation of what the responsibilities and entitlements of children and parents are in healthy families. Slowly, David internalized his "rights and entitlements" as a child.

At one session, "Little David" fully appeared, with all of his loneliness and fear. The session was spent nurturing the little, lost child, and "getting to know him." David was assigned the task of purchasing a stuffed animal, as sort of a "coming out" present. He bought a tiny, faceless, bear-like animal, "nondescriptive," as he himself felt. It reminded him of the pain of being a "throwaway child," and having his pets killed by his father.

In and between subsequent sessions, the memories, sensations, and feelings came together. He remembered the sexual abuse by his mother, including the stimulation, wanting to be loved and not be a nonperson, how "not right" it was, and feeling literally suffocated. The shame, the guilt, the anger, the depression, were all intensely felt. And slowly, with rage, came the emerging new frame, with the words, "I was the victim!"

He risked telling Mary his story, and let her hold him as he cried. He met with one of his siblings and shared with him the story, and each supported the other. This was a relief for David, because he had feared denial and rejection. And then, more memories came, of what his father did—the burns with the cigars and cigarettes.

Releasing the emotional pus permitted the healing process to continue, and he began to open himself to the caring and love from others, but still with the fear that the "the other shoe would fall," that they would turn on him and hurt him or use him. He also remembered his preadolescent fear that his father would kill him if he caught him with his mother.

His sense of responsibility towards his siblings emerged, along with his guilt at not being able to protect them and save them from similar abuse. The grief he felt at the loss of his family was deep and profound. He and his siblings accepted a referral to another family therapist to begin to deal with the issues openly, and he even expressed the hope that perhaps the parents could eventually be involved. Over five months, they had six sessions, and talked about the issues directly and indirectly. His siblings were still very much enmeshed in the family system, and, while not denying David's allegations, could not share in his expressions of rage and desire for "justice." When the family therapy ended, he felt cut off, with little hope of reconnecting with his parents (who still denied his allegations and just wanted him to return to the family as if nothing had happened) or with his sister. He still had some bruised hope regarding his brother that required some healing time before it could be acted upon.

During this time, he shared increasing intimacy with Mary, including a prolonged, relaxing, "not in control" vacation. He was learning to take control by not needing it so badly. The death of an elder pastoral associate felt like a death in his "family," like the loss of a "father," and the feelings he experienced reinforced his sense that his extended surrogate "family" was the source of his genuine nurture, support, and love. Towards his own family, he could feel only anger and the need for distance. It was necessary and real, and a way of coping with the sadness and the loss. Still, he had the sense that something deep within him had changed. He still feared closeness somewhat, and feared his father would seek him out and kill him. However, there was also a sense of increasing calm at times, a sense of being "over the top" of the mountain, a sense of better, more intimate times ahead.

At this point, Mary and David still had to wrestle with the occasional regression between them, and the "meanness and viciousness" of which each was capable, especially when their pain and need for caretaking/nurture were not addressed directly. These "regressions" were normalized and reframed as expressions of the system trying to maintain a familiar homeostasis, and as attempts at self protection. Skills that facilitated direct expression of the need for nurture, and direct, empathic, verbal and physical responses were practiced and continuously reinforced.

They also had to deal with the Guide regarding the occasional family-of-origin incident—maintaining the boundaried contact with her family and dealing with the self-imposed cutoff with his family and the second-hand, indirect messages passed to him by other family members. For now, they had each other, and their many genuine friends. There was a letting go of fantasies regarding the family, a sense of acceptance of the limitations, and careful attention to the resolution of the grief and loss. The Quest was over.

This part of their pilgrimage towards wholeness lasted for two years and three months, and involved 10 conjoint sessions, 25 individual sessions with David, and eight individual sessions with Mary.

PHASE III: COMING OF AGE IN THE PROMISED LAND

The Myth: *"When you wish upon a star, your dreams come true."*
The Reality: *"It ain't over until it's over"; "The road to Heaven is Heaven."*

The Seekers were genuinely happy together. Mary and David had quite successful careers and they were able to purchase a new house, one in which they could raise a family. Anxiety increased when they considered becoming parents, especially when they reflected upon their individual histories. But, the Guide had them reflect upon the reality of who and what they were in the present, renegotiate some sex-role stereotypes regarding parenting expectations (a change in definition), expose and resolve the fears about being abusive parents (a change in predictions), and deal with the cognitive distortions in a straightforward manner (a change in interpretations).

For the most part, it was a quiet time for Mary, happy in her career, her marriage, her local church, and her doctoral studies. For David, it was also a more gentle time, with the rage being resolved and replaced with more of the sadness, and even some pity for his parents. He began to share his story with more of his friends in order to facilitate his healing. He revisited the house in which he grew up and the grove of trees where he used to find solace from the abuse in order to "close out" some chapters of the past.

They assessed with "whom" in each family they could have "what," while continuing to build their friendship networks. Each of them reached out to the extended family, to seek new connections—she, with cousins and one sister and a brother, he, with a grandmother, his brother, and a long-lost uncle, who was delighted to hear from him. Mary gave him the gift of a visit to the uncle, and the experience was wonderful for both of them, finding a relative who genuinely cared and who could shed much confirming light on the family dynamics. Several cousins responded positively and were incorporated into their newly developing "family." The meetings with the siblings were more tentative, with a curious blending of hope and sadness; however, the proverbial door was left open.

David wrote another letter to each of his parents. They were well integrated, focused on personal expression rather than on blaming, and even left open the possibility of reconciliation. His reading of *Victims No Longer* (Lew, 1990) give him a further feeling of comradership with other victims of abuse, and contributed to his sense that this portion of his work was nearing completion.

After a rather long hiatus, Mary had one last opportunity to confront her "unending hope." Her parents had returned to their Asian country to sell the family home and settle the estate. When they returned, her mother called her and explained that each child was to receive from her a piece of jewelry or an artifact, as a share of the estate. In her words:

> I was once more filled with hope, and I drove down and picked my share, a gorgeous piece of jewelry that looked absolutely stunning on my golden brown skin. I sang with joy all the way home. I knew exactly what outfit would highlight the jewelry, and I would wear both for the upcoming holiday. That Easter Sunday morning, I felt like a bride, and felt that perhaps my parents did love me.
>
> That afternoon, I went to visit my parents, and friends and siblings alike complimented me on my traditional attire and jewelry, and I could literally hear my mother sigh. She called me to a private room with my Dad at her side and asked me to return the jewelry. My father was silent. The mask of my mother's pretentious love fell off and I *knew* I could never again receive a gift from my parents, even upon their death. I had a nightmare that night, and in it my white pearly teeth were smashed by someone, after many people had admired them. The jewelry was snatched from me and smashed. I wrote to my parents that I will no longer participate in gift-giving with them. It was painful and difficult, but in retrospect, as I write this, I feel such a relief at not living in a world of fantasy or pretension!!!

The Seekers had settled in to a more open and intimate life together and with those around them. Problems were dealt with directly and with increasing skills and decreasing lag time between awareness of the problem, addressing it, and resolution. Talk of having a family increased dramatically. Each was less fragile and more responsible when "hooked." The vulnerabilities in each of them were occasionally touched in a painful manner, but they were generally able to respond with empathy to each other and give each other the needed nurture. David's desire for "revenge" regarding his parents occasionally flared up, and their continued refusal to acknowledge the abuse frustrated and enraged him—and hurt deeply.

It was the best of times for them, but for each of the Seekers one more demon needed to exorcised.

Assessment during Phase III

In this phase of treatment, Mary and David were quite self-reliant and relied also on their "coupleness" and friendships for support and nurture. There was a tremendous increase in self-responsible behavior, self-nurture, effective couple problem-solving and conflict resolution, and a deepening intimacy between them. Interactionally and intergenerationally speaking, treatment was almost completed. They were each functioning in a developmentally appropriate fashion in most areas.

For Mary, individually speaking, it was a time of role stability, and there was also a sense of completion. For David, as his "Mid-Life Transition" (Gould, 1978) approached, there was a genuine desire to accept his personal authority and responsibility for his life, as he began reviewing and revising his personal, relational, and career values, goals, and priorities. It felt like an orderly transition, and not the "Mid-Life Crisis" he had heard about so often. But, before the transition could be completed, and the relevant tasks accomplished successfully, there was one other task that took precedence, a task that would require him to enter the world of his Object Relations (Scharff & Scharff, 1987, 1991), and resolve the projections and the introjections that had helped to mold and shape his personality.

Treatment during Phase III

Towards the end of the Phase II treatment section, and in the Phase III descriptive section, the therapist was referred to as a Guide, in the belief that the Seekers had, in fact, entered the third phase of treatment, Self-Reliance (Rado, 1956, 1962, 1969). Much of the treatment experienced during this phase was included in the descriptive section to affirm that the "treatment" was, for the most part, in their hands, with regard to form, content, and process. Much of what the therapist did was to affirm, confirm, support, and encourage. Interpreting, action planning, and the verbal processing of the relationship and the various experiences were done mostly by the clients.

This third phase of their personal and couple journey lasted for two years, and involved 26 conjoint sessions, and seven individual sessions with David.

On the occasion of Mary treating herself to a stuffed animal, a bear, David responded towards it with what Mary called, "sadistic behavior." He, at first, dismissed her accusations as ridiculous, "I was just being playful." But, with a little further introspection, he revealed that his behavior towards the bear triggered primitive (age four to five) memories of physical abuse. He concluded that he was fearful of being vulnerable and playful, jealous of the affection she showed towards the stuffed animal, and fearful of being hit or burned. These issues were projected onto Mary, and he protected himself with his "sadistic behavior."

When the issue arose again, this time with the behavior directed towards Mary, in public, while they were dining with a new friend of Mary's, David's realization of what was occurring deepened. His pain was emerging as rage whenever he saw Mary receiving love. He realized his father's lifestyle and rules of living were to "intimidate, subjugate, humiliate." His "Bully Child" had learned the rules well, and used them whenever he needed to protect himself from further pain. A letter to this part of himself was quite revealing:

> Dear Bully. The purpose of my letter is to tell you that I do not need you anymore. Yet, it is with some reluctance and fear that I let you go. I am not entirely sure, or perhaps the word is secure, without you. We have been together from my earliest memory, when I needed you. It is only recently now that I know why I needed you and who called you into being to protect. In my self-discovery of the truth about my abuse, I focused for most of the time on protecting myself from Mom and remembering about her abuse. But, the truth about you, Bully, is deeper in the past. You were called into being by my father, who is also your father. It was actually he who began my abuse, and who taught us how to protect ourselves by hurting, teasing, humiliating those around us. Yes, it was Dad who showed us, and how. It was he who, at about age 3, took us and our little friends behind the garden wall and "taught us," sexually abused us, made us act out sexually, and then gave us pain, shame, and a bitter heart, like punishment. It was he who taught us never to trust friends—and keep those around us off balance with the occasional jab, whack, pinch, or kick.
>
> Yes, Bully, it seems that only in subjugating those around us we can be secure. But, as both of us can see, it doesn't work. Not now. Because, we will end up alone, sad, broken, dishonest souls, like him, a master with no slaves. I, the Real Child, have begun to see another way to live. I like it better than the old way, because I want to be free, whole, honest, a real child, like others I have met. I want to let go and not have to attack, hurt, or subjugate to be safe. I've tried without letting

you go or remembering all. Now, *at last we meet to send you back* to your father, the father of my Bully, a sadistic father! This is where you belong, not with me, a Real Child. I want to be soft, trusting, playful, honest, and real. I'm going to try to make you go home, with help. It's the last part of becoming whole. I do not want you or your sadistic father to hurt anyone else, not me, my wife, or my children. So, you must go! I'm letting you go, afraid of what I'll be left with.

It's sad to think, why, even you came to be, but you were born in the sadistic abuse somewhere more than my lifetime ago. Your dark roots may reach very deep, your umbilical cord goes somewhere far. I'm sad for you, but our time is ended. I will struggle to make you die, even as I remember your birth with me. Go back! I do not want to enslave people and hurt to control them, although you like this. I want them to love me because they feel a loving child near them, not a sadistic bully. I have managed to keep you underneath my "good" veneer and just barely from abusing others. I hate struggling with you for control. I want to make you leave *us* alone. With help I will. Now that I know where you came from and what you do, your power is shrinking. Thank God for my new awareness. David.

The letter was read aloud to the therapist, and afterwards David and the Bully (played by the therapist) had a talk together. As treatment progressed, David slowly realized that he could "reform" the Bully and reframe some of his actions as having served a protective function for many years. He realized that he did not have to "kill" him, and that, in fact, the Bully was also a part of himself. More memories emerged and were worked through, and the experience led to a gentle reconnection with his brother, and the emergence of a much kinder, gentler person in relationship to Mary. He was fearful of his "shadow side," but also aware that when it was contained, the deep sadness and depression were more likely to emerge. But, along with them came an increasing desire for closeness and intimacy with others, including men.

In the subsequent months, the anger towards his parents virtually disappeared, to be replaced by an emptiness that required filling with genuine interpersonal relationships and intimacy. He started a men's group and arranged several outings with men with whom he chose to relate. Mary felt the gentleness and appreciated the genuine increase in warmth and overt affection he demonstrated towards her. He knew there was still growth to be experienced and wounds to heal, but there was also a sense of completion emerging.

As a last gasp, the old system sought once more to pull them back to the place from which they had come, to the old homeostasis. Mary was invited to give a keynote address at a national convention of her denomination, and in the session prior to their leaving for this experience and a subsequent vacation, they both exuded happiness and glowed with warmth, excitement, and anticipation. Towards the end of the session, the therapist reminded them to be careful, that "too much" happiness might be unbearable, and that they might speculate together regarding "who and how" it could be "screwed up." They both laughed at the paradoxical prediction, as David suggested that he could be mean, and Mary suggested that she would "stumble" and make a fool of herself in front of her colleagues. In retrospect, she wrote:

> I was invited to give a keynote address in Orlando (full of coconuts like my native land), and I worked on the presentation for six months. I wore a stunning red dress and gave the best address of my life. My husband was so proud when I received a standing ovation, and he told me that I had done a *perfect* job in my delivery. Perfect . . . success . . . totally new feelings for me. I was euphoric; the smell of my perfume, "Joy," and the smell of the newfound success permeated through my whole system.
>
> The next day my husband and I were planning on our second honeymoon in the Magic Kingdom. The night of my success and joy, we went dancing to a place called The Pit (how ironic the name was). A drunken man asked me to dance with him in the pit. My husband despises alcoholics, since he comes from an alcoholic family. The smell of success and joy were so intense that I never smelled the alcohol on my dance partner. My husband was so humiliated and saddened to see me dance with this drunken, falling down man. I fell down from the ladder of success and perfection in the pit, and took all of the magic out of our forthcoming trip to the Magic Kingdom.
>
> When I got up from my fall, I called Larry. He spoke with me and with David and with the two of us, helping us to express and understand the pain, the anger, the shame, and the humiliation. He reminded us of the warning and prediction during the last session. We were reminded that our marriage was not used to success and perfection and magic, and that I made sure that I gave away my "jewelry" before it was snatched away, by dancing with the drunken man in The Pit. Since David didn't do it for us, I did it. We talked together, and forgave each other, rather easily, in spite of our vulnerability, and with this new insight, we went to the Magic Kingdom with a renewed smell of success and joy as a couple.

When they returned from their vacation, it was with genuine humility, caring, and affection that they processed the experience. There was also a reconfirmed belief regarding the power of the system to try to protect against too much change too soon.

CONCLUSION

Therapy with this couple needed to be done from a truly integrative perspective. It is difficult to conceive that the growth, change, and wholeness experienced by Mary and David could have emerged from the utilization of a single model. A dialectical perspective was needed, a flowing back and forth between surface and depth; between past and present; between him and her; between affect, cognition, and behavior; between the individual, the interactional, and the intergenerational.

The vilification, blaming, and linear attributions were replaced by self-responsibility and an appreciation of circular causality. Each learned to attribute self-responsibility and positive intentionality to the other, as well as to the self. Mary learned to view David as "David" and not as David *plus* a conglomeration of projected images from her past; and, David did the same *vis-à-vis* Mary.

Many changes that occurred were the result of hard work, practice, and positive reinforcement. Others appeared to be classic examples of spontaneous compliance on their part. The conditions that contributed to all of the changes included the following: David and Mary's love, hope, faith, motivation, determination, and willingness to change; the congruence that existed and was created between the clients and the therapist, which permitted the therapist to work implicitly (e.g., using metaphors, stories, and personal self-disclosure) and explicitly (e.g., using a specific contracting process and letter writing); the therapist's attention to their respective learning styles and the creation of a safe learning environment; and, the willingness of all three to attribute positive intentionality to each other, and to view each intervention as a provisional try.

At this point in time, the Two Seekers are truly celebrating, and they continue the integrative process. David's vulnerability is still being healed, and he is still wary of the limelight. Mary is learning to embrace her "demonic side" and integrate it into her personality. The process continues for each of them, as they move towards and into that last stage of the therapeutic process, the one that is so often traversed with the *Self* as the Wizard, the Nurturing Parent, and the Guide—the Self-Aspiring stage (Rado, 1956, 1962, 1969). As individuals, as a couple, as a "family," they have prepared themselves well.

Part II

CASE STUDIES FROM THE INTERSYSTEM PERSPECTIVE

This section of the volume consists of chapters that illustrate the application of the Intersystem Model. All of the chapters were written by staff members of the Marriage Council of Philadelphia, who are active as clinicians and involved in the training of marital and family therapists. Authors were invited to select a case that would exemplify the complexity of the Intersystem Model. Such a case would ideally be one in which assessment and treatment were multidimensional, i.e., include the individual, interactional, and intergenerational aspects of the client-system. Contributors were asked to highlight the concepts from the Model that helped to understand or treat the case. While the editors could have written explanatory statements to accompany each chapter, we chose to have the authors weave our ideas into their chapters. We hope this technique will help the reader understand the concepts as they were immediately applied.

Contributors were asked to use the Case Formulation Form for Assessment and Treatment that is routinely used at Marriage Council. This form is reproduced on pages 26 and 27 in Chapter 1.

CHAPTER 3

Too Old to Go Steady: The Case of Marcia and Barry

April Westfall

OVERVIEW OF METHOD OF ASSESSMENT

My initial work with couples tends to follow the Intersystem Model, in that I conduct a fairly lengthy and thorough evaluation of the couple before making a decision as to whether to see them in conjoint therapy and, if I do see them, as to how to proceed with treatment. The evaluation process consists of the following: one or two sessions initially focused on current problems and couple dynamics and then on gathering a relationship history; at least two sessions exploring the individual history and family background of each partner; and, lastly, a general feedback and review session leading to goal-setting and developing a preliminary treatment plan.

In the first session, the couple and their relationship system are the primary focus. With both partners present, I am able to get a picture of their interactional style at the outset of treatment, how they each define the relationship problems and their reasons for coming to therapy, and their stated treatment goals. I also want to gather information that will help me to understand how the couple system has evolved over time, so that their present difficulties can be placed within the larger historical context.

In the more individually focused sessions, I get a detailed developmental and family history of each partner (i.e., gathering information about developmental milestones, academic performance, peer relationships, and relationship with parents and siblings, as well as their perception of their parents' marriage). This gives me the kind of information I need in order to understand the individual needs and expectations of each partner at the time of couple formation and, for some, marriage. In addition, I believe the individual sessions are critical to developing rapport with each partner, conveying the message that the therapist understands and cares about each of them as individual persons, as well as caring about them as a couple. I prefer to conduct these sessions with both partners present, because their having an understanding of each other's history is critical to a full participation in the assessment process. Each partner's position as "outsider" also permits them to see and to comment on certain things that their partner may be unable to notice or may selectively forget.

Finally, in the feedback and review session, I share with them the results of my initial assessment, including what I believe to be some of the contributing factors to their current distress. This session tends to be more of a dialogue between the couple and myself, rather than a one-way presentation by me. I look for what they have done with what we have previously discussed (e.g., What difference has it made to their understanding of their problems? How have their feelings about the relationship changed through our earlier discussions?). I also want to know what they have felt or thought about discussing such intimate matters with me? During the earlier sessions, I assess individual motivation to work at the relationship and explore any factors that might inhibit their desire to do so (e.g., one partner's known involvement in an active affair). In the feedback and review session, I deal explicitly with any such impediments to treatment.

If we can all agree on a preliminary treatment plan and goals, I will make a recommendation for them to come in for conjoint therapy on a regular basis for a specified period of time. On occasion, I have recommended individual therapy for one or both spouses as an alternative to, or precondition for, couples therapy (e.g., when one partner is having an active affair and unwilling to end the affair in order to participate more fully in couples therapy, when one partner appears too emotionally fragile to tolerate hearing the other's complaints, etc.). More often, I prefer to begin with conjoint work on their relationship problems, even if I believe there may be significant individual personality or background factors that may complicate treatment later. I would rather consider individual therapy only as the couple work seems seriously stalemated or when it could effectively support a somewhat tenuous effort by the couple. In this feedback session, I will also make a recommendation for further professional consultation (e.g., psychiatric or other medical evaluation, psychological testing, etc.) if I think this is necessary for a more accurate and complete evaluation of their problems.

CASE FORMULATION

I chose the case of Marcia and Barry for inclusion in the book because it aptly illustrates the kind of dialectical process engaged in by a therapist working from the Intersystem Model. The couple entered therapy with a very specific presenting problem, and change strategies were initially targeted to remedy their complaint. Yet, as the therapy unfolds, the definition of the problem is considerably broadened to include both inner and outer dynamics, and interventions flow back and forth from affect to cognition to behavior. It is the fluidity of this approach and the move, back and forth, from the particular to the general that captures the spirit of the Intersystem Model.

Initial Presentation of Problem(s)

Marcia (age 29) and Barry (age 27) initiated couples therapy the week after they decided to live together for the first time. This action seemed to produce a crisis, whereby all their previous relationship difficulties were brought into bold relief. Foremost among their concerns was their sexual relationship and, more specifically, the fact that they had not been able to consummate their relationship through sexual intercourse. An earlier diagnosis of vaginismus had been made by Marcia's gynecologist, who was initially consulted about the problem and found no gynecological abnormalities. Vaginal dilation exercises were prescribed by her physician, but not carried out, before a referral was made for couples sex therapy.

Relationship History

Marcia and Barry met each other for the first time two years previously through an introduction by a mutual friend. They were both lawyers, and part of their initial attraction to each other had to do with their common career interests. They also spoke of their similar backgrounds—both from upper-middle-class Jewish families—as an important factor in their decision to continue dating. On a more personal level, Marcia spoke of liking Barry's easygoing manner and positive outlook on life. She also enjoyed his sense of humor, finding him quite funny at times. Barry spoke of finding Marcia pretty and of respecting her serious-minded approach to her career.

In reviewing their sexual relationship, both stated that they had felt an initial physical attraction to the other and felt somewhat nervous as a result. Both described having had fairly limited sexual experience prior to their first meeting. Marcia was still a virgin at the time and felt embarrassed by this fact, regarding it as a sign of immaturity. She was calmed and reassured, however, by Barry's easy acceptance. Marcia reported being orgasmic through self-stimulation prior to meeting Barry, but the couple had not been able to incorporate this behavior into their sexual activity together. For his part, Barry reported only slightly more sexual experience before meeting Marcia, leading to sexual intercourse on a few occasions. Those episodes were initiated by more sexually experienced women, who would take charge of the sexual relationship. He described those occasions as enjoyable, but short-lived.

The couple described their initial sexual involvement with each other as fun and mutually pleasurable, with each feeling increasingly open in their sexual explorations during the first several months. Sometime after the first six months, however, things began to change for the worse, setting a negative tone that was to continue and eventually led to their seeking outside help. Having attempted sexual intercourse on a few occasions and having failed, they quickly became disappointed and frustrated. This disappointment seemed to affect their sexual approaches to each other in a more generalized way, with Barry's initiations soon being met with angry refusals by Marcia. She criticized Barry's sexual approaches as so tentative and ill-timed that she could respond only with annoyance.

When asked about other problematic areas, Marcia identified Barry's relationship with his parents as a frequent source of contention. She viewed him as too childishly dependent on his parents for someone his age. She spoke of feeling relegated to second place, with his first loyalties still being to his parents. She also said that she had never felt welcomed by his parents on visits to their home. They showed no particular interest in her, preferring to reminisce about earlier times with Barry.

For his part, Barry complained of Marcia's negative attitude and frequent fault-finding. They had previously sought out therapeutic assistance for these problems and continued in couples treatment for several months before terminating. They described feeling reasonably satisfied with the results of that therapy, as evidenced by their most recent decision to live together. They were not able to address any of their sexual complaints in that setting, however, as their therapist lacked expertise in this area.

When questioned about their level of commitment to each other and possible plans to marry, they reported having no plans to marry anytime soon, but might do so at some future time. They described their relationship as sexually monogamous, and neither expressed any desire to date other people.

Initial Impressions and Reactions

Marcia and Barry presented as an attractive, articulate young couple, with much in common in terms of family background and educational and career goals. They also appeared well matched physically, not too dissimilar in stature or style of dress, both garbed in professional attire. If anything, I wondered if there might be too much sameness in the relationship, indicative of an intolerance of differences that might prove troublesome in other areas.

Marcia assumed a rather rigid posture throughout much of the first session, and her manner of sitting with her hands folded neatly in her lap suggested a kind of primness. Barry appeared more relaxed, but tended to fidget in his chair and scan the room, especially when Marcia was being critical of him. At those moments, he looked rather childish, and I found myself agreeing with her depiction of him as immature.

Both of them were able to talk openly, with only slight embarrassment, about their sexual problems during our first session. I felt encouraged by their candid and thoughtful presentation of their difficulties in this area and their mutual determination to resolve the problem.

Marcia's Individual History and Family Background

Marcia grew up in a Midwestern city, St. Louis, the younger of two daughters (three years apart). Her father was an engineer by profession and quite successful in his work. She remembered him at home as being busy with various household projects, always fixing things. Her mother acted as home-maker and was never employed outside the home. Marcia described her as a giddy, hysterical type, who could be quite childish at times. She pictured their marriage as warmly loving, with clear and traditional sex-role distinctions between husband and wife. She described herself as being on good terms with both parents throughout her child and adolescent years. Always a very good student, she readily received the approval of both parents, who prized academic accomplishment.

Marcia's father died suddenly two-and-a-half years ago of a heart attack. She spoke of having developed a close, confidential relationship with him during the year prior to his death. Only a year out of law school and in her first job, she would frequently phone home to discuss with him issues pertaining to her professional functioning and her problematic relationship with her boss. She greatly missed these conversations, becoming tearful in speaking about her father and his untimely death.

Following her father's death, Marcia found herself becoming more annoyed with her mother and her flighty, emotional style. She spoke of her with condescension, and seemed to relate to her and her apparent neediness over the loss of her husband in an almost parental manner. Her current relationship with her older sister was described as cordial, but distant. She expressed some jealousy toward her over the fact that her sister was married and had two children. Both mother and sister still lived in St. Louis, a considerable distance from Marcia's new home in Philadelphia. Neither of them had visited Marcia in Philadelphia, nor had they met Barry.

Barry's Individual History and Family Background

Barry grew up in New York, the younger of two sons (a year and a half apart). His father was an accountant, and his mother a homemaker throughout his child and adolescent years. She would sometimes assist her husband in the office during the busy tax season. He believed that they had a good marriage, as evidenced by the fact that they seldom fought. He described his relationship with both parents as good, with his mother being especially nurturing. He could remember no particular traumas in growing up, other than his mother's giving birth to a stillborn child when he was four years old. This child was female and he remembered his mother later voicing regret that she had lost her only opportunity to have a daughter.

He spoke of feeling close to his older brother, if somewhat competitive with him at times. When his brother had married a year ago, Barry was pleased that he had been asked to be Best Man. He believed that his brother now shared a closer relationship with his parents, which he attributed to the fact that they lived in a nearby town and could socialize with them on a regular basis. The fact that his brother was an accountant and shared a common profession with his father permitted a level of discussion between them unavailable to Barry.

Since Marcia had spent time with Barry's family on numerous occasions and had firsthand knowledge of them, she was able to add to Barry's picture of the family in important ways. She described a rigid demarcation between parent and child generations in his family and enumerated various ways that the "adult children" were kept in a childlike position (e.g., not being permitted to pay for long distance phone calls, being expected to spend all holidays at the parents' home, being expected to seek out and listen to the parents' advice on major decisions). Barry responded with nervous laughter to Marcia's descriptions of his family, yet was careful to point out that he did not share her annoyance with regard to his parents' expectations. Instead, he preferred to think of their wishes as a continuation of the same nurturing quality he had always felt and enjoyed from them.

Barry did acknowledge that his parents, both in their mid-fifties, were quite youth-conscious and overly concerned about aging. Again, Marcia was quick to bring in supporting evidence critical of Barry's parents, mentioning a remark made by his mother at his brother's wedding to the effect that the new couple should take their time in starting a family and that they were not in any hurry to become grandparents. While Marcia viewed this remark as one more indication of his parents' selfish disregard for their children's more age-appropriate desires, Barry said that he found his mother's comment rather amusing.

Intrapsychic/Interactional/Intergenerational Assessment

Individual system(s)

In terms of defense mechanisms, Marcia tended to project her own unmet dependency needs onto Barry. She would then respond to to him in a belittling, contemptuous way. Barry resorted to denial in defending against any negative thoughts or emotions, especially anger, adopting a "peace at any price" attitude. He was able to protest, if only gingerly, against Marcia's excessive fault-finding.

Both seemed somewhat uncomfortable with their bodies. Marcia appeared ill at ease and rigid in her body movements; Barry moved about nervously and aimlessly, using his body in a clowning way. In addition, they both were inclined toward perfectionism, which only complicated their first attempts at sexual experimentation and interfered with their ability to learn from these experiences.

Interactional system

Marcia and Barry presented as bright, highly verbal people, who had no trouble putting their thoughts into words. I was more concerned about their ability to communicate affectively with each other. Marcia seemed more comfortable expressing anger, and voiced strong feelings of sadness and grief when speaking about her father's death. When unable to talk Marcia out of her negative feelings, Barry tended to withdraw or to resort to a distracting silliness in the face of strong emotion. Both seemed rather inept in expressing tenderness toward the other, although their liking for each other was readily apparent in our sessions.

Their decision-making and conflict-resolution skills seemed strong in some areas, weak in others. They were able to agree to enter couples therapy early on in the relationship and, more recently, with me. The decision to live together for the first time seemed to have been made rather effortlessly, and with real enthusiasm. Both pledged sexual fidelity to the other, in spite of their difficulties in this area, pointing to further congruence in their vision of the relationship. Still, the obvious tension in discussions about Barry's parents pointed to continuing problems and irresolution in this area, despite their frequent debates over the issue.

Intergenerational system

Several factors at the intergenerational level seemed to impede the couple's developing a greater level of intimacy, both emotionally and sexually. I wondered how Marcia's meeting and becoming involved with Barry so soon after her father's premature death—only six months later—had confused and confounded her initial feelings about their involvement. Her still strong feelings of loss in discussing her father suggested that she might fear moving toward a closer intimacy with Barry, perhaps anticipating another loss.

Barry's parents' difficulties in negotiating a life-cycle transition—to one of middle-aged parents of adult children—seemed intensified in their attitude to their younger son. I speculated on the effect of his mother's losing a child through stillbirth, around the time that Barry was about to start school, in fostering a close, mutually dependent relationship between mother and younger son. Nor did he seem too eager to give up his cherished role as "the baby" of the family for the dubious distinction of being recognized as an adult. Yet, if he were to develop a more adult relationship with Marcia, such a sacrifice would be necessary.

Finally, both Marcia and Barry spoke of feeling closer to their opposite-sex parent. Both voiced mild feelings of envy toward their older siblings, because of their closer identification with the same-sex parent. I was left with the impression that each of my clients had missed out on some important aspects of the relationship with their same-sex parent. For Marcia, the loss seemed more exaggerated due to present circumstances, by the physical distance now separating her from her mother and by her overly critical attitude toward her mother since her father's death.

TREATMENT

Preliminary Treatment Plan and Strategies

Following the individually oriented sessions with Marcia and Barry, we met to review the results of our initial assessment and to decide whether or not to work together further. Both expressed feeling comfortable with me, and felt our earlier sessions had already been helpful to them in creating a less judgmental and more hopeful stance in dealing with areas of conflict. In keeping with their initial presentation of the problem, we made a joint decision to focus treatment on their sexual complaints and, more specifically, on Marcia's condition of vaginismus and on the couple's inability to engage in sexual intercourse. In accordance with generally accepted practices in the treatment of sexual dysfunction (Hof, 1987; Kaplan, 1974, 1983; Leiblum, et al., 1989) my initial interventions were designed both to assess more accurately and to treat the more immediate causes of the dysfunction. The fact that Marcia had failed to follow through with the vaginal dilation exercises prescribed by her gynecologist, combined with the couple's more generalized avoidance of any sexual contact, led me to begin the experiential work with a modified version of Masters and Johnson's (1970) Sensate Focus exercises.

Introduction of Structured Behavioral Exercises

Sensate Focus refers to a set of graduated, behavioral tasks frequently prescribed during the beginning stages of treatment of a variety of sexual dysfunctions. They are designed to permit a gradual introduction of touching and pleasuring between partners, while keeping the anxiety level effectively low. Such prescriptions tend to promote spontaneous compliance from the couple in sex therapy. They are also useful diagnostically, in providing a more detailed and accurate assessment of the couple's sexual interaction patterns (e.g., how they approach each other sexually, what the partner's emotional and behavioral response to the initiation is, pinpointing where in the process of sexual exploration one or both begin to feel anxious and their way of handling such moments, etc.).

Marcia and Barry both expressed an eagerness to get started with the exercises as they were explained to them in the session, and both laughed a little at the idea of such pleasurable homework assignments. They seemed comfortable with my directions, which were to have them take turns in giving and receiving all-over body caresses, with the exception of explicit genital and breast caresses. During our next meeting, the couple reported having set aside time to complete this first set of exercises. Both expressed feeling mildly "turned on" sexually by the experience and seemed obviously pleased and encouraged by this result. Marcia insisted on keeping some clothing on during the experience and refused to permit Barry to kiss her, but was otherwise cooperative. Barry did not seem bothered by this specific refusal in the face of Marcia's seeming openness to the experience more generally.

In reporting his responses to Marcia's touching him, Barry expressed pleasure, although he was somewhat vague in describing his experience. Toward the end of our session, Marcia voiced a desire to continue with the present homework assignments a while longer, before moving on to something else, so that the touching could feel more natural. Barry said he was in no hurry to move ahead, and was just glad for them to be getting along together in bed again.

The next two weeks followed a similar course, with the couple working cooperatively together and completing the assignment with no obvious difficulties. After only a month, however, the couple reached their first stalemate, refusing to carry out the prescribed tasks and retreating physically from each other once again.

His Way/Her Way or The Battle for Control

In reviewing what went wrong, there was an obvious quality of annoyance and irritability in Marcia's voice as she spoke of Barry's inept manner of going about the tasks and of his failure to really listen to her words as to how she wished to be touched. In part, this irritability seemed to extend beyond their sexual relationship and to be a function of their difficulty in adjusting to living together for the first time. Here, as in the sexual arena, there was frequent squabbling, with issues of control being predominant. Marcia, especially, seemed to have fairly fixed ideas as to how they each were to behave and did not hesitate to voice them. Furthermore, she would become quite annoyed with Barry when his actions failed to conform to her notions of appropriate male sex-role behavior (e.g., "Men should stay out of the kitchen"; "Men should be able to take care of any household repairs"). Many of her expectations seemed in direct conflict with Barry's own ideas about how he should be helpful (e.g., "Men should share responsibility for washing the dishes each night").

I pointed out that they each were clearly products of their parental families, with their own characteristic styles and traditions, and were simply behaving in ways that felt natural to them. Their legal training seemed to promote an argumentativeness between them as well, making compromise more difficult. I also suggested the possibility of Marcia's wanting to keep alive the memory of her deceased father by getting Barry to behave in ways that would more closely resemble his familiar style. Consequently, she felt frustrated and disappointed when he acted in a way that dispelled this image. Marcia was tearful and obviously upset during these discussions about her father, and Barry was able to move away from his usual defensive posture and to offer real support.

Marital Commitment vs. Sexual Consummation

After addressing some of these more general issues of living together, we were able to resume attention on the Sensate Focus work. Just as the couple had progressed to the point of including more direct sexual touching and genital caresses, a conflict emerged centering on the issue of relationship commitment. Although the issue of marriage had originally been presented as a nonissue, it proved to be a critical barrier to further sexual intimacy. The couple had reached a deadlock, with Barry refusing to think realistically about marriage with so little sexual satisfaction in the relationship and Marcia unwilling to become more sexually intimate without reassurance from him of a commitment.

In analyzing the problem more carefully, Marcia traced the onset of their commitment struggle to a much earlier time, around six months after their first meeting. Marcia described feeling very happy with Barry and enthusiastic about the prospect of a future life together. It was in this spirit that she proposed that they become engaged. She spoke of being extremely hurt by Barry's lukewarm response to her proposal and his definite reluctance to move forward with marriage plans. Not surprisingly, it was around this time that they both began to notice significant sexual problems.

Barry's recollection of these earlier events tended to confirm Marcia's story. He spoke of having been very surprised by Marcia's marriage proposal, thinking such a serious step to be premature. Six months later, he felt more ready to consider marriage after being together for almost a year. Yet, by this time their sex life had become so unsatisfactory that he was reluctant to go forward with such plans.

Following the initial commitment crisis, a pattern subsequently evolved that drove them even further apart. Every few months, one of their friends would become engaged or married, causing Marcia to become upset all over again and to threaten to leave Barry. Eventually, she would calm down and resign herself to remaining with Barry. Still, she would belittle herself for not having the gumption to end the relationship. Sometimes her anger would surface in hostile remarks or verbal harangues directed at Barry. He responded to her badgering him in a way that suggested he was unaffected, countering with a statement to the effect that he knew that she had not really meant what she said. At times there was an enactment of this pattern in the therapy, with Marcia attacking Barry in a belittling, sarcastic manner. When I challenged Barry to respond more directly to Marcia's attack, he replied that it was not his style to become angry.

At this point, I chose to have a session with each of them individually in an attempt to break the deadlock. These sessions were very useful in allowing me to explore certain issues from their individual histories without their becoming unduly defensive. With Marcia, I was able to deal with her rather special dependency on Barry early in their relationship, as a result of the untimely death of her father so soon before meeting Barry. Marcia was able to acknowledge her heightened vulnerability at that time, still grieving over the death of her father. She also saw it as the source of her intensely negative reaction to his reluctance to commit, which threatened further loss for her. I was also able to validate some of her more realistic concerns relating to her age and the encroaching biological clock, while suggesting that there still might be enough time for her to start a family. With Barry, I was able to examine the reasons for his need to deny and cover up anger and for his reluctance to be assertive and defend himself more directly to Marcia. We spoke of his parents' discomfort and intolerance of anger, which were first apparent to him in the way that they strongly discouraged any fighting between his brother and himself as children.

Following these two individual sessions, I resumed working with them as a couple. During the next few months, Barry's manner of dealing with Marcia did change, in that he was able to more readily defend himself against her constant carping. For her part, Marcia seemed to almost welcome this show of forcefulness from Barry, and she rather quickly backed off when he protested against her ill-treatment.

Eventually, the deadlock between them gave way, and there was an easing on both sides into less polarized positions. Marcia decided that she wanted to consummate their sexual relationship, even if they were to eventually separate. After over two years of continuous togetherness, she wanted a more normal sexual relationship, regardless of their long-term prospects as a couple. Barry did not so much back away from his desire for a better sexual relationship, but he was able to look at his reluctance to commit in a more complex fashion. He began to acknowledge and accept responsibility for his anger and dissatisfaction as a result of Marcia's incessant criticisms.

At first, Marcia was threatened by Barry's disclosure, viewing it as one more obstacle to a future together. Within a short period of time, however, she was able to use this information to get more control over her anger. Barry reported feeling so heartened by the lessening of her hostility that he was now ready to become engaged. Marcia responded by saying that now was not the time for this to happen, preferring to concentrate on their sexual relationship instead. Still, she clearly seemed pleased with his proposal, and they both seemed amused by the reversal in their characteristic positions.

Sex Is Hard Work vs. Child's Play

At this point in the therapy, they were both quite conscientious in their approach to the genital pleasuring and vaginal dilation exercises. They carried out their routines, however, with an apparent clinical detachment that seemed devoid of pleasure. Interspersed with these prescribed exercises, the couple admitted to "fooling around" in a manner that hinted at a more spontaneous, feeling quality to their exercises. Still, they were careful to avoid any genital or breast contact at those moments. With some embarrassment, they described a rather routinized habit of childlike play, during which they would engage in baby talk and silly games together. They referred in detail to one such game with the coined name of "Letters," consisting of them each taking turns writing alphabetic letters with their fingers on the other's back and the other then trying to guess the letter.

These games seemed to set a tone to their bedroom activities that was incongruent with adult sexual behavior, including sexual intercourse. Nevertheless, I reframed this play-acting as beneficial to their relationship as a whole in that it permitted a cooperative and lighthearted joining together, in contrast to their more typical contentious, lawyer-like style. I also speculated that it might have allowed them to feel less discouraged over what they had so far not been able to make happen in the bedroom, namely, sexual intercourse. Thus, it might be difficult for them to let go of these bedroom games, not knowing whether anything as pleasurable could replace them. I also predicted that things might become more difficult between them if they were to terminate the games too quickly—losing out on a gentle, fun-loving way of being together.

I encouraged them to explore new ways that some of the "silliness" of the games could happen outside the bedroom setting, but in a manner that would not embarrass either of them. I also suggested that they think of ways to impart more romance into their living together as a way of infusing a different kind of positive feeling into their lives, one more consistent with their stated goals. At a more behavioral level, I had them each take turns planning an evening or weekend activity together that might generate such feeling between them.

Individual Therapy Work

Because of the difficulty that both Marcia and Barry experienced around the notion of generating romantic feeling in their relationship, and their way of dealing with this difficulty through mutual blame, I moved to see them each individually for a more extended period. The change in format of the therapy came at a point when we were all feeling some impatience with the progress that had been made in the sexual area. The couple had been in treatment with me for almost seven months without a clear resolution of the presenting problem. I had been impressed by their willingness to deal with issues more openly and responsibly in my earlier individual sessions with each of them. Consequently, I believed it might be productive to use this format for a more sustained period. I chose not to refer them to different individual therapists, in order to prevent a loss of continuity of treatment and to permit a better coordination of their individual therapies toward their common goal. Initially, I proposed that I meet with each of them bi-weekly for a period of one month, at which time we would review the situation and make a decision as to whether to continue with this format for a longer period.

In contracting with the couple for the individual therapy sessions, I raised the question of client confidentiality for discussion among the three of us. We all agreed that I should feel free to refer to any material from their individual sessions, if I so chose, except in those instances in which I was asked directly by one of them not to disclose something. Since the couple had been fairly open with each other in the past with no serious harboring of secrets, I was not unduly concerned about being placed in an ethical bind. In addition, I believed that each of them had sufficient confidence in my trustworthiness and even-handedness from our prior therapeutic work together to permit me to see each of them separately for a longer period. Even so, Marcia voiced some feelings of anxiety after my first session alone with Barry, which passed rather quickly once we had explored the nature of her feelings together.

Individual Sessions with Marcia

Much of my individual work with Marcia was directed toward a careful examination of her sexual self-image; the goal was to foster a more positive sexual identity. Marcia's approach to the Sensate Focus exercises had been quite clinical, as if she were carrying out a medical regimen. Although sometimes flirtatious, she behaved so in a rather childlike manner, drawing a clear line between such behavior and sex, which was regarded as serious business. In our sessions, Marcia was encouraged to do some reading of erotic/ romantic material in order to more fully develop her sexual imagination. Rather than recommend specific books, I suggested that she visit certain book stores in the area known to carry such material and peruse their shelves, but in a leisurely, exploratory manner. I also had her begin to fantasize what it might be like to have sexual intercourse with Barry and to see if she could imagine herself feeling pleasure. As a result of these experiences, she spontaneously began to have sexual dreams. At the same time and on her own, she began to freely involve herself in various feminine activities, (e.g., buying perfume, dressing more provocatively than usual in the evenings with Barry).

The individual work with Marcia also focused specifically on the important issue of body-image, and her view of her body as somehow defective in ways that might cause her to be more susceptible to injury and pain. We looked at this view historically, as grounded in her initial misgivings about her body around the onset of menstruation. She related how her older sister had instructed her in the use of tampons, saying how it was a "snap" to use them. When she was unable to insert them easily, she felt quite frustrated, and was left with a vague sense of being abnormal in some way.

In addition to this more analytical examination of the historical antecedents to her fears, I worked with her at a behavioral level as well (e.g., having her perform a genital self-examination with a mirror and prescribing exercises designed to relax the musculature surrounding the vagina). Although she followed my instructions without fail, she continued to have vague misgivings about her body and to wonder if the sensations of "tightness" or mild discomfort in the genital area were normal. At this point, I encouraged her to recontact her gynecologist for an appointment, so that she could describe her sensations in detail to her physician and get a clear explanation as to what was happening. She followed through with the appointment and was reassured about her physical health, reducing her anxiety still further.

In our discussions of Marcia's relationship with her mother, it soon became apparent that she lacked a positive identification with her mother as a woman, viewing her as childish and narcissistic. Nor could she imagine her mother as someone with sexual feelings and interests. She was able to relate to her mother more easily at the level of maternal feeling, and she readily acknowledged her own desire to have a child someday. During this period, Marcia made a visit home to her mother in St. Louis, with the expressed purpose of getting to know her better as a woman. She questioned her directly about prior pregnancy and birth experiences, and specifically, about her manner of coping with the attendant discomfort and pain. Marcia returned from this visit feeling elated, both by her own courage in willing to risk talking with her mother about such intimate matters and by her mother's helpful and serious response to her questions.

Marcia also recontacted a friend living in a nearby city, who had experienced a problem of vaginismus similar to her own sometime in the past. She had previously lied to the woman about having resolved her own sexual difficulties, too embarrassed to admit to still having a problem. Her willingness to acknowledge her continuing sexual difficulties with her friend at this time seemed indicative of an important shift in her sexual self-image, a shift toward greater self-acceptance. I also viewed both the visits to her mother and her friend as somehow reflective of a positive transference to me as an older woman professional.

Individual Sessions with Barry

Our individual work began with Barry's anger and generally negative feelings toward Marcia, causing him to be turned off sexually much of the time when they were together. He spoke of no longer experiencing her as sexually attractive, not due to any lack of physical appeal, but because of her manner of controlling and criticizing his every sexual move. In addition, Marcia's rather clinical approach to lovemaking in the past had made it into a mechanical exercise. We explored ways that they might approach their sexual sharing in ways that might rekindle some romantic/erotic feeling, with Barry assuming more responsibility for their recovery. He was directed to deal more explicitly with Marcia as to his "turn-offs," and to begin to ask for those things he saw as "turn-ons."

More analytically, we were able to examine Barry's reluctance to make demands on Marcia as tied to issues with his family of origin. In the earlier sessions with the couple, Barry had consistently defended his parents' actions to Marcia, while seeming to enjoy Marcia's disparaging references to them. In our individual sessions, Barry was able to make a more balanced appraisal of his parents and to assume a more critical posture toward their infantilizing behavior. For example, on his 28th birthday, his parents had bought him underwear several sizes too small. On this occasion, Barry chose to challenge their choice of a gift and to suggest a more suitable alternative for future occasions. Another opportunity presented itself when Barry's father was put in the position of having to look for new employment, when his accounting firm decided to relocate elsewhere. His father confided to Barry his nervousness in having to interview for a new job at his advanced age. Barry was able to respond to his father in a reassuring manner and felt quite good that his father had turned to him at such a time.

We also discussed how Barry had chosen to confide in his parents, rather than turn to Marcia with his personal and professional problems. In part, this seemed the result of anticipated criticism from her. At other times, he was able to see how he had discouraged her from taking some caring action on his behalf (e.g., arranging a birthday party for him with friends), as a way of maintaining distance from her. This distance allowed him to continue to maintain a primary dependency on his parents, which he recognized as something he was reluctant to give up. As Barry began to recognize his part in the distancing process with Marcia, he was able to again risk sharing with her in a close, confidential way.

Sexual Consummation and Conclusion of Therapy

During the first six weeks of the individual sessions with each of them, Marcia became increasingly responsive to Barry's caresses, to the extent of experiencing orgasm with him for the first time. Both Marcia and Barry seemed heartened by these changes in their sexual behavior, and within a few weeks thereafter, expressed a readiness to attempt sexual intercourse. Marcia, in particular, seemed eager to move ahead, once reassured that her gynecological functioning was normal. After only a few attempts at penetration, they were successful, enabling them to experience sexual intercourse together for the first time. After conferring by phone, the three of us agreed to meet together again for our next therapy session. In this session, we reviewed the events surrounding their successful penetration and discussed how they might proceed from here. The tone of our talk was obviously happy and celebrative.

Finally, I spoke about the need for them to function more autonomously, without as much direction and continued input from me now that they had reached this important milestone. All of us seemed to agree about their need for more privacy in the sexual area, so that they could more freely experiment on their own. We agreed to meet the following week in order to address any emergent sexual concerns the couple might have with regard to their recent experiences with sexual intercourse and to discuss plans for termination.

In this next session, it was apparent that although they both were in agreement about ending the therapy at his time, Marcia was experiencing some distress around separating from me. After discussing different options for dealing with Marcia's feelings, the three of us agreed to meet together for two additional sessions—each spaced two weeks apart—to permit a slower termination of the therapy. In these sessions, I dealt directly with Marcia's feelings of attachment to me—and mine to each of them—and her sense of loss associated with stopping therapy. At the close of our final session one month later, she seemed visibly more comfortable with our ending.

Follow-up

I received a note from Marcia during the summer, four months after our final therapy session. She reported, with some relief, that things were continuing to go well between them sexually. They had recently bought a home together and were busy planning a wedding for that November. She thanked me for all that I had done, and thought it only fitting that I share in their good news. In the postscript, she added that she had finally gotten the courage, with Barry's support, to sever ties with her old boss with whom she had a father-daughter relationship. She had found a new job in a small law firm and was looking forward to working in a place in which she would no longer be the only woman employee.

CONCLUSION

Analysis of the Therapy from an Intersystem Framework

Diagnostically, the couple's behavior in response to the initial Sensate Focus exercises suggested a dysfunction at the level of a desire phase disorder (Kaplan, 1979; Rosen & Leiblum, 1988, 1989; Weeks, 1987), rather than a more straightforward problem of vaginismus. My therapeutic work in this case involved a multilevel approach—aimed at both the immediate and remote causes of the desire disorder—and utilized both couple and individual modalities of treatment. According to Kaplan (1979), the immediate cause of inhibited sexual desire (ISD) consists of an active, albeit unconscious, inhibition of sexual desire by a focus on negative thoughts about self and/or partner. Such action impedes the couple's first stirrings of sexual feeling and interrupts their initial sexual advances toward one another. In this instance, both partners contributed to the suppression of sexual desire: Marcia's preoccupation with Barry's childish mannerisms and sexual ineptness, Barry's anxious concern about pleasing Marcia and his failure to communicate his own sexual needs, and their continual bickering during sexual encounters—all served to dampen erotic feeling.

My initial attempts to address directly the immediate causes of the ISD proved insufficient to remedy the problem. Consequently, in the ensuing months, I directed my interventions toward the more remote causes, i.e., the "deeper" conflicts associated with sexual pleasure that would trigger the suppression response. To review, this included an initial therapeutic focus on their power struggle, intensified by the number of adjustments and accommodations required of each in their decision to live together for the first time. Marcia felt disappointed and irritated with Barry's hovering presence, due to his failure to act in ways that conformed with her notion of how men should behave. For his part, Barry was confused by her reactions, since he was only doing what he had been raised to do, trying to be helpful to Marcia by assisting her in various household chores and by remaining close by.

As the couple were able to construe their power struggle in light of the differences in their early socialization, their negative labeling of each other's actions lessened considerably. Marcia could begin to acknowledge her ambivalent and conflicted feelings toward Barry—on the one hand, liking his easygoing manner, but, on the other, missing the more direct, take-charge attitude that she had come to expect from her father. Barry could see how the passive, dependent stance, so pleasing to his mother, would not receive the same approval from Marcia. These discussions were helpful in permitting a perception of their partner that was more differentiated from that of these parental figures.

From here, I moved to deal with the anger generated by certain contractual disappointments, which posed a serious impediment to progress in the sexual area. Marital contract theory, formulated by Sager (1976), provides a convenient model for examining the original formulation of the dyadic system, concerning the needs, wishes, and expectations that each partner brings to the couple relationship. Here, the individual contract refers to this set of assumptions and expectations about self and partner— "I will give X, and you will offer Y in return"—and not to an actual legal pact. Although much of the individual contract remains unknown to the other (as well as to oneself, if grounded in unconscious needs), each behaves as if the other had tacitly agreed to the exchange. When the partner behaves in ways that violate the "terms" of one's individual contract, the person feels betrayed and conflict often follows.

In this instance, Marcia entered the relationship with Barry with an unverbalized and unconscious need to be in a secure relationship, protected from feelings of loss or abandonment. When Barry refused to consider marriage after their first six months together, Marcia felt betrayed. She did not consider ending the relationship at that time, not wanting to risk further loss. Still, she was unable to respond wholeheartedly to Barry's desire for a fulfilling sexual relationship with her, finding herself holding back for the first time. In addition to this disappointment in the sexual area, Barry's unverbalized and unconscious need for approval and his wish to assume a dependent role in relation to Marcia's stronger self were thwarted by her harsh, critical stance toward his dependent behavior. Although continuing to push for a more satisfactory sexual life together, Barry's ardor was dampened by Marcia's harsh words.

I chose to reframe the couple's sexual problems as an obstacle that signaled the presence of other important, if covert, conflicts in need of serious attention if their relationship were to flourish. As such, the sexual symptom served as the point of departure for confronting other control and commitment conflicts. I was careful to avoid blaming the couple for not completing their sexual assignments to the letter, effectively eliminating their need to blame each other for what might have been regarded as a failure. When they could view their commitment/passion struggle in less negative terms, they no longer needed to vilify the other, as someone deliberately trying to thwart their personal happiness. There was more flexibility in the way they each defined the relationship, with greater sensitivity to each of their individual needs and concerns and more overall congruence. With their individual interests no longer defined in terms of "my happiness versus your happiness," they were able to work together more harmoniously toward common goals.

It was at this point in the therapy, when they were both working earnestly to reach their sexual goals, that they revealed to me their longtime habit of engaging in childlike bedroom games. With some embarrassment, they described these games in detail, while laughing together at the silliness associated with some of their invented rules. I chose to frame these games as positive, in providing a needed contrast from their usual sober, disciplined bedroom routines and in permitting creativity and spontaneity and fun to enrich their life together. I asked them to continue with their games but, through a recontextualization of the symptom, moved to alter their meaning from something secretive and embarrassing to a more adult form of romantic play.

At a "deeper" level of causation, the couple's childlike bedroom games and sexually avoidant behavior could be seen as grounded in a fear of adult sexuality. Psychoanalytic theory would explain this fear in terms of unresolved oedipal conflicts, possible in both partners, as well as in terms of problems of sibling rivalry. Kaplan (1979) has described how such oedipal conflicts and/ or sibling competition can lead to an unconscious fear of sexual or romantic success.

In my individual sessions with Marcia and Barry, I chose not to explore directly the oedipal implications of their sexually avoidant behavior. Instead, I tried to circumvent the problem by fostering a more positive identification with their same-sexed parent. I had each of them renew active contact with their parents, but in a way that would permit more adult-to-adult sharing to emerge. In addition, I explored more directly with each, issues of sibling rivalry, looking at how their older siblings had acted as barriers to a closer relationship with their same-sexed parent.

Marcia's depictions of her mother and sister suggested a fairly negative view of women, discouraging her from forming a closer relationship with her surviving family members and with female friends. Although I suspected that this negative view might have come from her father, I chose not to confront this possibility directly, given her intense loyalty to his memory. Instead, I had

Marcia enter into more serious discussion with her mother, resulting in a revision of her earlier unfavorable appraisal. In addition, I worked to correct her many bodily distortions through assigned reading and the use of visual materials. These bodily distortions had contributed to her fearfulness of adult female sexuality and had also interfered with her developing more active sexual fantasies. As she became more relaxed about her body, she began to freely and spontaneously enter into more feminine behaviors and experienced erotic dreams for the first time.

In my individual sessions with Barry, we dealt with his need to actively suppress any anger toward his brother, his competitive rival, for the sake of family harmony. In similar fashion, Barry would hold back any direct expression of anger toward Marcia, but had become increasingly withdrawn sexually in the face of her critical and controlling behaviors. A pattern had evolved whereby Marcia would blame Barry for her inability to respond to his sexual overtures, which she criticized as too tentative and ill-timed. Barry would then respond to her criticisms with a kind of passive resignation, becoming ever more anxious and tentative a lover, infuriating Marcia all the more.

As Barry was able to confront Marcia with his anger, she could better understand the circular nature of the problem and began to assume more responsibility for her part in this frustrating interplay. At the same time, she became increasingly open and receptive to his sexual moves. Feeling rewarded rather than punished for this show of initiative, Barry, in turn, was able to bring a new forcefulness and confidence to the relationship, moving away from his earlier passive, dependent style. He also showed a greater willingness to turn to Marcia with his needs, thus furthering the couple's interdependence.

These combined therapeutic interventions permitted a sufficient loosening of their resistances so that they could resume work on the structured behavioral tasks toward a successful resolution of the problem. In the end, they were designing their own next steps, with minimal input from me. This contributed to their feeling of excitement when the desired change did occur, and to their ease in claiming this success as their own. They had effectively moved to a position of two differentiated adults, functioning with greater mutuality and satisfaction in their relationship.

CHAPTER 4

Work, Wine, and Thee

Diane Logan Thompson

INTRODUCTION

The case described below involved a couple who presented with problems related to substance abuse and over-extension at work. Therapy took place over a 13-month period of time and included 31 sessions, which can be grouped into four major phases: (a) *Reframing* individual problems as problems in the relationship and establishing a mutually agreed upon goal for therapy; (b) *Negotiating* for change by clarifying what each spouse was willing to contribute to the process of change; (c) *First order change* in the problem behaviors initially identified; (d) *Second order change* in the systemic emotional forces involved in the process of differentiation.

CASE FORMULATION

Identifying Information

Carol and Tim came together for the first therapy session. Carol was a 32-year-old Caucasian female who appeared slim, tidy, and well groomed. That particular evening she was dressed conservatively in tailored pants and a sweater she had worn to work. She was employed full-time in an administrative mental health position. Tim was a 33-year-old Caucasian male. Although he was also neatly groomed, he was significantly overweight and dressed in more casual attire. He was employed full-time as a draftsman. They had been married for seven years and had no children.

Presenting Problem

Although Carol and Tim were both courteous and pleasant, Carol appeared more eager to speak. She explained that they had been having frequent arguments about Tim's drinking. Carol believed Tim's use of alcohol was a serious problem, but she stated that the rest of their relationship was good.

History of the Problem and Solutions Attempted

A brief substance abuse history revealed that Tim had experienced blackouts many years earlier and received two citations for driving under the influence of alcohol (DUI's) before they were married. He completed a 28-day program and an associated 14-day jail sentence soon after they married. Marijuana and alcohol were his substances of choice. Upon completion of his treatment program (six years ago), it was recommended to Tim that he not use any substance. He followed no formal aftercare program but reported that he used neither alcohol nor marijuana for five years following treatment. However, he had been using alcohol (twice a week, up to eight drinks per occasion) for the past six months and marijuana (four times per week) during the past year.

Throughout their marriage, Carol and Tim never discussed Tim's use of substances, his treatment, or his jail term. Carol stated that she wanted to talk about these issues with Tim in therapy in order to gain a greater mutual understanding. Carol had been aware of Tim's use of alcohol, but had only recently "discovered" that he had been using marijuana during the past year. Carol reported that she drank alcohol approximately twice a month, no more than three drinks per occasion, and she and Tim both denied any history of problems associated with her use of alcohol.

In contrast to Carol's perception of the problems they had been having in their relationship, Tim believed that Carol's lack of trust in him was the primary issue with which they struggled. He wanted to put the past behind them and did not see his use of substances as a current problem. Tim explained that he had stopped using marijuana during the previous two weeks and he intended to not use marijuana again. Furthermore, he did not believe he had a problem with alcohol.

Carol agreed that she did not trust Tim, particularly after her "discovery" that he had been using marijuana for the past year. She also believed that he underestimated his use of alcohol. However, she was able to share some of the responsibility for their lack of communication by identifying a potential association between the increasing distance between them and the amount of time she was away from home at work. She reported that it was not unusual for her to work 12-hour days and expressed concern that her long hours at work may have allowed Tim to increase his use of alcohol and marijuana without her knowledge.

Intersystem Assessment

Intergenerational system

Carol described her father as "opinionated, domineering, and sarcastic." He was an uninvolved parent who spent his time working or drinking. Nothing Carol did was ever good enough for him. She described him as an alcoholic who was still using alcohol and in denial about his alcoholism. She reported that he drank to the point of drunkenness several times a week, had blackouts, and had received many DUI's. When he was drunk, he spoke often of painful times in the past and he sometimes became argumentative. Her father was the next to oldest in a family of eight children and had been cut off from two of his brothers since before Carol was born. He had a history of gambling and had had several affairs.

Carol's mother was an only child who attended private boarding school beginning in the seventh grade. Carol described her as "passive, dependent, depressed." She had never worked outside the home. When Carol was 14, her mother developed a serious medical illness which she self-medicated with alcohol. She eventually developed secondary physical problems associated with her use of alcohol and stopped drinking.

Carol described her parents' relationship as "very tense and dysfunctional." She recalled frequently waking up during the night as a child and hearing her parents arguing. In general, she believed that it was difficult for her mother to give to others or to confront areas of conflict directly. (For example, Carol believed her mother knew about Carol's father's affairs but never dealt with it.) Her father emotionally abused her mother and hit her once or twice. Carol generally took the role of a quiet observer in her family or intervened to get her father "to leave [her] mother alone."

Carol was the youngest of five children. She saw all of her siblings (three older brothers and an older sister) as very "opinionated" and stated that she tried not to be like them. She was concerned about the use of alcohol by two of her siblings.

When asked what she brought from her family of origin to her marriage, Carol explained that she saw herself as "sensitive and a conflict-avoider" like her mother, yet "unavailable and hardworking" like her father. In her marriage, she wanted to avoid being opinionated, sarcastic, and distant, and wanted to learn to be more intimate.

Tim referred to his father's family as the "lazy side of the family." He described his father as "outgoing with a loud roar but little follow-up." Tim's father stopped drinking the day Tim was christened, following the recommendation of his physician. He also stopped gambling, which had led to serious debts in the past. Tim described him as an involved parent who coached several sports in which Tim played.

In contrast, he referred to his mother's family as "the eager side of the family." He reported a close, satisfying relationship with his mother whom he described as "assertive and easy to talk to." She had worked full-time outside the home since Tim was a child and managed all of the family finances. Although Carol volunteered that Tim's mother may have a problem with alcohol, Tim quickly dismissed the issue.

As a young child, Tim believed his parents had a happy marriage with many friends and good times. However, they separated for nine months when he was 11 years old, which he later understood was due to stress associated with huge gambling debts accrued by his father. Tim reported that he believed his parents had been able to regain a stable, satisfying relationship.

Tim had an older half-brother from his mother's first marriage (her first husband died in an auto accident) and a younger brother. He reported no stressors or concerns in his relationship with either sibling.

Tim described himself as "lazy," like his father, with a similar history of substance abuse. In his marriage to Carol, he wanted to avoid being an underfunctioning person, but also wanted to be warm and nurturing, as he had experienced his father as being.

Individual systems

Carol and Tim each struggled individually with many Adult Children Of Alcoholics (ACOA) issues. For example, Tim described fear of abandonment, loneliness, all-or-nothing thinking and doing, and control issues. He attributed none of life's problems to substance abuse. Rather, he feared (predicted) that Carol would abandon him for her work. (Perhaps as his mother had done, although he denied this.) He explained that he frequently felt lonely in the evenings before Carol returned home. His use of substances showed an all-or-nothing pattern, i.e., he was either in control when not using or out of control when he did use substances. He defined himself an "adjuster," i.e., he was able to be flexible but rarely took charge or made decisions. He seemed to have little sense of direction, choice, or power, except when he used substances (Gravitz & Bowden, 1985.) He demonstrated low self-esteem through his difficulty in setting limits on what he would or would not do regarding his use of substances and what he would or would not tolerate in terms of Carol's work hours. When discussing his family of origin, Tim seemed to demonstrate dissociation by matter-of-factly reporting issues related to alcohol abuse, gambling, and marital separation while denying any associated pain or suffering.

Carol struggled with many related issues. In contrast to Tim, she attributed all of life's problems to substance abuse. She felt betrayed by Tim and feared (predicted) he would abandon her once again (as her parents had) through his use of substances. She defined her role as that of being responsible for controlling Tim's use of substances and expressed guilt for enabling him to use during her absence. She demonstrated all-or-nothing thinking by her belief that she had to continue to overfunction at work or leave her job, i.e., she had to be on top of everything or on top of nothing. She took care of her subordinates by doing the work they chose not to do. She appeared "overly serious, overly self-reliant, unable to trust or relax" (Gravitz & Bowden, 1985). Her low self-esteem was shown in her difficulty setting limits on what she would or would not do at work and what she would or would not tolerate from Tim at home. She feared being a victim of Tim's substance abuse and denied the clues of Tim's use of marijuana during the previous year.

Interactional system

The individual ACOA issues with which Carol and Tim struggled seemed to complement each other and together formed a powerful but destructive dance. They were trapped in an unhealthy interdependence. Tim's lack of direction, choice, or power was complemented by Carol's willingness to provide direction and assume control. Together they stepped to the dance "Don't talk. Don't trust. Don't feel." Carol defined love as caretaking; Tim defined intimacy as being smothered. Carol took care of Tim while ignoring her needs, and Tim cooperated by avoiding taking charge of anything.

Neither spouse had clear bottom lines and both seemed to fear that if they admitted personal needs, each would be hurt by the other and thereby lose power and control. Both felt trapped and unable to see options. Neither Carol nor Tim were able to be themselves and share control with one another. They each had dissociated from their painful experiences with substance abuse and now were cut off from significant parts of themselves. In this sense they were the same or congruent with each other. They colluded in order to avoid confronting their pain. As they continued to ignore their experience and deny their feelings, they tripped over the same relationship issues, over and over again.

Gender Issues

The assessment described above identified balance and control as key issues for Carol and Tim. In terms of balancing work and family, Carol and Tim each seemed to hold egalitarian gender ideologies (Hochschild & Machung, 1989). That is, they each wanted to identify with both home and work and to have equal power in the marriage.

However, within Carol there appeared to be tension between her egalitarian gender ideology and her underlying feelings about what she did. On the one hand, she wanted to be a driven career person (like her father), but she felt she should want to be more responsive to Tim (like her mother) and take more responsibility for their relationship. In addition, although Carol wanted to share the responsibility for home with Tim, she was confronted daily with the expectations of her supervisors that she continue to overfunction in her role as administrator. As she overfunctioned at work, it became increasingly difficult for her to carry an equal share of the responsibility at home.

Tim expressed minimal direct dissatisfaction with this arrangement. Rather, he continued to avoid taking charge or expressing his own needs. Indirectly, however, he may have been expressing his anger and regaining a sense of power and control by using substances while Carol was working long hours into the evening.

The beliefs about manhood and womanhood that were held by Carol and Tim were based, at least in part, on early childhood experiences. In each case, one parent had overfunctioned at home and the other had underfunctioned. Interestingly, in both cases it had been the opposite-sex parent who had underfunctioned in terms of emotional involvement at home. Carol knew she did not want to be like her mother (home full-time, passive, dependent, depressed) and did not want to be married to a man like her father (domineering, argumentative, unavailable). In contrast, Tim wanted to be like his father ("lazy," outgoing, involved with family) and he wanted to marry a woman like his mother (employed full-time outside the home, "eager," assertive.) In fact, in many ways Carol was the kind of woman Tim wanted to be married to and Tim was the kind of man Carol wanted to be married to. Unfortunately, their individual gender ideologies (what they thought) sometimes conflicted with these underlying desires (what they felt) based on feelings associated with early childhood.

Furthermore, the way in which Carol and Tim each individually wanted to approach work and family responsibilities influenced what seemed like a gift to the other and what did not. For example, Carol wanted to see herself as a driven career person. Therefore, coming home earlier in the evening was interpreted as a gift to Tim. Tim did not see this as a sacrifice as he assumed she would want to come home earlier. Carol also wanted Tim to compensate for her working less by his working more.

In a similar manner, Tim interpreted his behavior as easy-going and fun-loving. Therefore, he saw becoming less "lazy," carefree, or fun-loving as a sacrifice and gift to Carol. In return, he wanted her to become less serious and responsible to compensate for him becoming more so. Carol did not see his gift as a sacrifice, as she assumed he would want to become a more responsible person.

TREATMENT PLAN AND STRATEGIES

The first three sessions were devoted to assessment. In the first session, details surrounding the presenting problems were obtained from Carol and Tim. Three problem areas were identified: (a) Tim's use of alcohol and marijuana; (b) Carol's long hours away from home at work; (c) Carol's difficulty trusting Tim. The second and third sessions were individual sessions used to review family history and relationship dynamics in Carol and Tim's respective families of origin.

In sessions four through six, material obtained during the assessment was reviewed and the search was begun for a strategy that would integrate Tim's history of substance abuse and Carol's overextension at work into one interactive model that could be used to treat them as a couple. Our work followed a relapse prevention model, based on social learning theory (Marlatt & Gordon, 1985). In brief, the model views addictive behaviors as overlearned habit patterns rather than as addictive "diseases." Strategies are individually designed to change these "bad habits" through self-management and self-control procedures. The individual is not considered responsible for developing the habit or voluntarily controlling the behavior, but he or she is held responsible for changing the habit.

Conscious effort was taken to remain systemic and to consider the circular nature of Carol and Tim's interactions, i.e., how Tim's use of substances influenced Carol's functioning at work and was in turn influenced by it. The individual problems identified by Carol and Tim were therefore reframed as overlearned habit patterns that had developed in response to problems of balance and control in the relationship. Carol and Tim were each responding in unique ways to the same relationship problems. The task was to shift the couple to thinking in terms of circular attributions.

A dissociation of parts had taken place within Carol and Tim individually, as well as within their relationship. As individuals, Carol and Tim had both learned to dissociate outer events from inner meanings, thereby disowning much of their sensory experiences involving substance abuse. The result was that they were both cut off from significant parts of themselves. Our goal was to recover those lost parts and build a more complete identity for each. This involved learning to care for themselves (as opposed to being victims) and developing the ability to let go of the past (rather than denying it). They were each asked to read *Recovery: A Guide for Adult Children of Alcoholics* (Gravitz & Bowden, 1985).

Individual Contracts: Moderation at Home and in Work

Once the problem had been reframed, an affirmation paradox was used to help change their "habits." Individual behavioral contracts were signed stipulating what Carol and Tim were each willing to contribute to the process of change and the consequences they would agree to accept if they were unable to adhere to the agreement. Carol and Tim were each allowed input into one another's contract, but the final decision-making regarding the terms of each contract was handled by the individual who was responsible for fulfilling the contract.

A significant challenge in working with Carol and Tim was dealing with their disagreement regarding Tim's use of alcohol and marijuana. Carol defined Tim as an alcoholic and she wanted to deal with that directly. Her concerns were supported in a brief substance abuse history, which revealed significant problems associated with Tim's use of alcohol and marijuana. Tim, however, denied he was an alcoholic and wanted to put any problems he had with substances behind them.

Carol felt responsible for helping Tim remain in control regarding his use of substances. Tim, in turn, felt powerless and smothered by Carol's need to control, and he saw few options other than absolute restraint or overindulgence. It is not surprising that in such a "forced compliance" situation (as described in Chapter 1), Tim eventually began to behave, when he was not with Carol, as he had prior to substance abuse treatment. In that sense, his renewed use of alcohol and marijuana may have been a "reactance effect," i.e., a move to regain a sense of power and control as a reaction against Carol's attempts to control him (Marlatt & Gordon, 1985.) It therefore seemed critical for Tim to take an active role in treatment planning and decision-making in order to avoid generating the same reaction in him against perceived control by others (in this case, perceived control by the therapist).

Carol and Tim each made a commitment to work on the following goals: (a) increase awareness and options regarding the problem behavior (substance abuse and overextension at work); (b) develop improved coping skills and self-control capacities; and (c) develop a greater sense of confidence in terms of one's capacity to control one's life. With Carol's input, Tim established a moderation contract whereby he committed to consuming no more than four drinks a week for three months. If he was unable to fulfill the agreement, he would undergo a formal evaluation at a substance abuse treatment program.

It should be noted that the therapist did not expect Tim to succeed in following the contract for three months. Tim continued to express the belief that he did not have a problem with alcohol and he stated that he was agreeing to the terms of the contract only as an attempt to gain Carol's trust. In part, the contract was a way for the therapist to "join with the resistance," and paradoxically take control by giving it back to the client (as described in Chapter 1). It appeared that Tim would have to experience failure by being unable to drink in moderation before he could begin to break through his denial.

Carol established a similar moderation contract, with Tim's input, in which she committed to working only until 5:30 three evenings a week and until 8:00 the other two nights. If she was unable to fulfill the contract, the only consequence that was acceptable to Carol was a job change.

Interactive Outcome

Both spouses were able to follow their contracts for 10 weeks (sessions 4 through 6). In session 7, Tim reported that he had five beers on one occasion. At that point, despite our agreement, he was unwilling to attend a formal evaluation at a substance abuse agency. I therefore recommended that we take a break from conjoint sessions until he felt ready to work on the problem behavior we had agreed to explore.

Carol had also broken her contract by coming home later than she had committed to several evenings a week. However, she had begun to realize that by simply changing jobs she would not necessarily gain any greater understanding of the problem behavior. It appeared that no matter how much effort she put into whatever job she had, it would probably never seem like enough (just as nothing was ever good enough for her father). Carol therefore requested individual sessions to explore how her overextension at work possibly served some need of hers. Her request was honored since, unlike Tim, she was still asking to focus on the problem behavior we initially had agreed to explore.

During the next six weeks, Carol came in for five individual sessions. We explored her need to feel needed at work and her associated difficulty with saying "No" and establishing boundaries. We also reviewed the more general lack of balance in her life and she began to develop a renewed interest in exercise and other pleasurable leisure activities that she had enjoyed in the past.

However, as Carol learned to attend more to her own needs and feelings, she became increasing clear about how angry she was at Tim and how stuck she felt in dealing with that anger. She continued to work long hours and began to see this as a way for her to avoid dealing with her anger. As long as they continued to avoid conflict (i.e., to avoid talking about his substance use and abuse) she would never be able to predict Tim's behavior and therefore would continue to feel unable to trust him. She decided to ask Tim to come in to help her work on a new issue, namely, their lack of communication and her associated anger and difficulty feeling trust.

During the first conjoint session (session 13) under the new contract, Carol was able to clearly and assertively express her anger towards Tim and explain her lack of trust to him. Tim, in turn, stated that he felt "blamed" and he experienced a sense of helplessness when he attempted to respond to Carol.

During the following week, Tim continued to express his helplessness by drinking to the point of intoxication. This time, however, neither Tim nor Carol was able to dissociate or hide in denial. Carol's recently acquired assertiveness skills allowed them to deal more directly with his abuse of substances.

In the next conjoint session (session 14), Tim agreed to schedule an evaluation at a substance abuse agency. He and Carol completed the evaluation together. The result of the evaluation was that he was diagnosed as being in the early to middle stages of alcoholism and was strongly encouraged to participate in an intensive outpatient program. Tim agreed to stop using alcohol, but stated he was still not ready to define himself as an alcoholic and did not want to begin a treatment program.

Carol appeared relieved and quite pleased in our next conjoint session. She reported that she had been able to come home from work on time each night during the previous two weeks. She and Tim had spent more time together and Tim felt more able to participate in conversations with Carol. He agreed to develop an abstinence maintenance program and Carol agreed to attend several Al Anon meetings.

A balanced lifestyle centered on moderation became the goal of the next two sessions. An equilibrium began to be established for Carol and Tim between activities that they each perceived as external "hassles" or demands ("shoulds") and those that they viewed as pleasures or "wants" (Marlatt & Gordon, 1985). For example, we discussed: (a) replacing a problem behavior with positive addictions, such as aerobics for Carol; (b) planning periods of free time during the day; (c) allowing substitute indulgences, such as a massage; (d) removing as many tempting stimuli as possible from their daily environment; and (e) taking "time out," i.e., slowing down and stopping before saying yes to a request at work or a temptation to use.

During the next nine weeks (sessions 18 through 24) Carol and Tim once again distanced from one another. Tim continued to maintain abstinence, but Carol consistently worked hours that extended beyond her therapy contract. She also began to attend every other session alone, reportedly due to last-minute changes in Tim's work schedule.

Individual sessions with Carol during this segment of the therapy focused on changing the "recursive context" (as described in Chapter 1) of her problem with overextension at work. More specifically, she began to increase the number of people with whom she consulted regarding the problem in order to gain more control of her behavior. She initially approached her immediate supervisors with a new job description which she created for herself. She was given positive feedback regarding her performance to date, the new job description was accepted, and she was given approval to hire an additional staff person to relieve some of her responsibilities. Unfortunately, she was not able to significantly alter her hours despite the support she received from her supervisors.

Conjoint sessions with Carol and Tim continued to develop the theme of relapse prevention and a more balanced lifestyle. In addition, high risk situations for relapse and their cognitive antecedents were explored. High risk situations discussed included: (a) negative emotional states (e.g., frustrations, anger, anxiety, boredom); (b) periods of interpersonal conflict; and (c) social pressure to engage in undesirable behavior. Rationalization, denial, and the decisions or choices that precede relapse were highlighted. In particular, Apparently Irrelevant Decisions (AIDs), defined as "a number of mini-decisions over time, each of which brings the individual closer to he brink of the triggering high-risk situation," were identified (Marlatt & Gordon, 1985). Examples of these mini-decisions, which Carol and Tim were able to generate, included drinking nonalcoholic beer and going to bars with old drinking friends.

In the final segment of therapy (sessions 25 through 31), Carol and Tim were able to weave their goals and efforts into a more integrated dance. Both had gained control of their initial presenting symptoms (i.e., Carol was working the hours she contracted in earlier sessions to work and Tim was not using alcohol or other substances). The focus of the sessions therefore shifted away from specific behaviors and towards systemic emotional forces involved in the process of differentiation. Consideration was given to emotional forces within the nuclear family (Carol and Tim) as well as to those transmitted from previous generations. The application of Bowenian theory (Friedman, 1991) to the interconnection between work systems and family systems was also explored.

By the end of this segment of the therapy, Carol and Tim were each better able to: (a) regulate their emotional reactivity; (b) demonstrate a greater balance through the reciprocal processes of self-definition and self-regulation; (c) take a stand in intense emotional systems; (d) maintain a less anxious presence in the face of anxious others; and (e) know where responsibility for oneself ends and allow one's partner to take responsibility for her/himself. Carol stepped down to a clinical staff position, which allowed her more time at home with Tim. She also began to attend ACOA and Al Anon meetings to further develop her ability to turn over responsibility for Tim's use (or nonuse) of substances to him. Tim was able to undergo major surgery and a lengthy recovery without relapsing. They celebrated their individual growth and their growth as a couple during a week-long vacation and terminated therapy upon their return.

CONCLUSION

Carol and Tim entered marital therapy with problems related to substance abuse and overextension at work. Therapy continued for 31 sessions over 13 months and included individual (intrapsychic), interactional, and intergenerational components. The intrapsychic principles, described in Chapter One, that were explored/utilized in therapy included interpretation, definition, and predictions. The interactional interventions, also described in Chapter One, which proved most helpful in terms of movement towards change, were reframing and affirmation paradox.

At the time of termination, Carol and Tim had successfully learned to control the problematic behaviors. Tim was no longer involved in substance abuse and Carol had taken a different position at work that she believed would be less demanding on her time. They each appeared to be more differentiated from their families of origin, as well as from one another. Several high-risk situations associatied with potential relapse were reviewed during their last session and the importance of maintaining a clear relapse prevention program was emphasized.

CHAPTER 5

Nuclear Family vs. Family of Origin: A Paradox

Nathan Turner

INTRODUCTION

Mr. and Mrs. Jones, a couple in their early thirties, presented themselves for therapy with a "sex problem." As the reader will discover, their real concerns were traceable to their families of origin. Their concerns were complex intrapsychic, interactional, and intergenerational issues. Self-esteem, control, rescuing, independence/dependence, and lack of adequate marital boundaries were only a few of the key issues in this interesting case. Despite the complex interlacing of issues and their personal pain and struggle, Mr. and Mrs. Jones are a wonderful, real, and down-to-earth couple simply wanting a better, happier marital relationship.

CASE FORMULATION

Initial Impressions and Reactions

Mr. and Mrs. Jones came to see this therapist for problems with their sexual relationship. They had been married for three and one-half years and were childless. The first marriage for each, she was 34 and he was 30 years old. They had grown up in a southern urban area.

Initial impressions were of a sincere couple with significant family-of-origin issues impacting the marital relationship. Both were bright, attractive, and intelligent in appearance, yet casual in dress and manners. They each functioned well in their respective workplaces. Despite their initial attempts to be "polite" in the first few sessions, it was apparent that each harbored resentments, frustrations, and anger at the other. In sum, the initial impressions they made were positive with mixed affect, leaving the therapist with curiosity about what might be the deeper issues affecting them and their marriage relationship.

Presenting Problem

The presenting problem was articulated by Mrs. Jones when she complained that her husband was not a "passionate lover." He, in turn, accused her of being "inconsistent in desiring sex," refusing to have intercourse with him on many occasions. Clearly, each blamed the other for their "sex problem."

Early on in the therapy it appeared that they maintained their "sex problem" in the marital system as a defense against their fears of intimacy. "Sex" was a convenient "mask" for their latent control issues in the marital system, with roots in the family of origin for each partner. Although they tried to persuade the therapist that "sex" was their problem, it was obviously symptomatic of deeper issues.

Other problems, in addition to the fear of intimacy and control issues, were the projection on to her husband of messages/tapes from her mother, while he utilized a combination of genuine naivete and passive-aggressive responses that served to exacerbate their marital tensions. For Mrs. Jones, his passive-aggressive style triggered many deep and resentful memories of her father's similar style in her parents' marriage. She could not respect her father for not standing up to her mother.

Mr. Jones was the youngest of four children, with three older sisters who helped raise him and left him with the feeling that he was an "only child." His father was a professional man and a workaholic, leaving the son to be raised by his mother and three older sisters. Consequently, he always felt closer to his mother and to women in general. He grew up with a "rescuer complex," which meant he wanted to be helpful to women.

Mrs. Jones, as the third of five daughters, was the best student of all the children. Her mother was a very controlling personality who ruled through constant criticism and the withholding of love and compliments. Despite this background, Mrs. Jones had a loyalty issue related to the introjected messages/tapes that instilled scripted messages such as "Never trust a man," "Be a martyr," and "Don't be sexual or sensual even if it feels good, and be sure to keep your breasts covered." She had a history of being overly concerned with her appearance despite the fact that she was an attractive woman.

Mrs. Jones projected her irrational introjects onto her husband, and this triggered many of their arguments. She was easily triggered into "moods," temper tantrums, and had a tendency to act out a victim/martyr role. These tendencies led her to exaggerate many scenarios which, later, turned out to be minor scenarios when she relaxed. Her moodiness and temper often served as a quick trigger to turn on/off her sexual desire for her husband. In her attempts to control her husband and "win" him over in even small matters, she could be demanding and needy of large amounts of reassurance from him.

Interfacing with her temperament, Mr. Jones would act, at times, in immature ways. As a compulsive type of personality, he could get preoccupied with details, be overly conscientious in trying to please his wife, and direct lots of his energy into his work/career. Occasionally he showed an ability to be critical of authority figures. He was compulsive in high school and tried to become a perfectionist. He began to get top grades, achieve in sports, and excel in varied school activities. He had significant intrapsychic pain about his family-of-origin history, especially regarding a series of cut-off relationships. For example, he wanted to relate to his grandparents, but was prevented from doing so by his parents.

Both Mrs. and Mr. Jones were triangulated with their parents and/or families of origin. Essentially, the sex problem was being maintained in the marriage through denial, projection, unrealistic expectations, role-reversals (parent/ child), individual immaturity by both, and distorted thinking. For example, she saw him as a wimp and he believed he was small and weak compared to other men.

History of the Problem

Historically, this couple was trying to be a 1980's couple with a spirit of being co-equal in the marriage in nontraditional ways, while at the same time being enmeshed with very traditional sex-role models that were less than ideal and inadequate for the idealism which this couple placed upon their young marriage.

It appears that, unconsciously, Mr. Jones married his "mother or older sister" to replicate family-of-origin patterns comfortable to him, such as being most comfortable around women. Mrs. Jones unconsciously married her "father" by adroitly selecting a naive, passive-aggressive husband reminiscent of her father's pattern. Ironically, both had been more controlled/influenced by their mothers than they realized. He had learned to accommodate, please, rescue, kiss and make up in his family of origin as the youngest child who was basically raised as an "only" child. She, on the other hand, had been raised to be critical, angry, conflicted in sexual self-acceptance, guilty, and fearful of intimacy. Her sexual experience threatened his sexual inexperience when they first dated and even after they married. Her emotional neediness for reassurance and acceptance conflicted with his restricted ability to express himself emotionally. He feared her anger, while she loathed his indecisiveness, immaturity, naivete, and inexperience.

Their marriage appeared to be a case in which intergenerational system issues flowed directly through to the younger generation, whose marriage suffered from weak boundaries, weak identity, triangulation, scripts, and loyalty issues of closeness-distance.

Mr. Jones had no prior experience with psychotherapy, but Mrs. Jones had had approximately one year of individual psychotherapy prior to meeting her husband-to-be.

Changes Sought by Clients

The change the clients initially sought was to improve their sexual relationship. The wife desired for the husband to be more passionate as a lover. He desired for her to be more congruent and consistent in her professed desire for sexual relations.

Besides these overt expressions for change, it was obvious that they had some other, unexpressed, yet very desired changes for one another. First, both wanted to be understood and accepted by their partners for what they really were and where they had come from (family of origin) without the necessity of change. Though both feared intimacy, they desired change in one another without wanting to change themselves. They wanted to be controlled less by their partner even though they did not want to relinquish any of their control over the partner. While viewing the family-of-origin problems in their partner's family, neither was able to see how his/her own original influences were being played out. Clearly, the wife desired emotional support and reassurances from her husband, while he was emotionally constricted in his ability to express emotions or even identify his own feelings. Change was sought in the emotional realm by both in very indirect ways at first. Unconsciously, the wife wanted to change her view of men from mistrust to trust. Her husband, unconsciously, wanted to change his view of himself from a "nerd" to a more masculine type.

Recent Significant Changes

One major change for the couple occured when Mrs. Jones started full-time graduate work at a local university even though she was employed part time. The husband continued his full-time job in a technical field with a large corporation. The other potential change was how and when to decide to start a family. Each had different ideas about when to begin a family, but they did agree they wanted a family at some point. Otherwise, they had no other major psychosocial life stressors or changes.

Intersystem Assessment

It was apparent to the therapist viewing the couple from an Intersystem perspective that solutions would need to be attempted on the 1) intrapsychic level, 2) the interactional level, and 3) the intergenerational level.

Individual systems

The presenting issue was a marital problem focused on an alleged "sex problem." Based on the presenting complaint, the initial diagnosis on Axis I, in DSM III-R terms (American Psychiatric Association, 1987) was V61.10: Marital Problem. On Axis II, Mr. Jones had features of 301.40: Obsessive-Compulsive Personality Disorder and 301.84: Passive Aggressive Personality Disorder. However, there were insufficient criteria satisfied to utilize either diagnosis. Therefore, a diagnosis of 301.90: Personality Disorder Not Otherwise Specified was appropriate.

Mrs. Jones met the criteria for a diagnosis of 301.50: Histrionic Personality Disorder. On Axis III there were no findings since both mates were in good health. Axis IV was a "3" (moderate) for both partners, regarding psychosocial stressors, indicating that while they had some marital tensions and problems with their families of origin their stress level was moderate and not severe. For Axis V, a Global Assessment of Functioning (G.A.F.) rating of 80–90 was appropriate for both spouses regarding their highest level of adaptive functioning during the past year, indicating that the majority of the time each partner functioned well, absent of symptoms or with only minimal and/or transient display of symptoms.

In brief, this couple's marital problems were best viewed as an idiosyncratic blending of their individual personality dynamics into a confusing marital interactional system influenced by their respective intergenerational systems. Listed below are some of their more significant diagnostic behaviors, discussed in the narrative portions of the chapter:

Husband	Wife
· Denial	· Projection
· Perfectionism	· Irrational thoughts
· Preoccupation with details	· Overly concerned with appearance
· Overly conscientious	· Tendency to exaggerate
· Critical of authority figures	· Acts out victim/martyr roles
· Restricted ability to express emotions	· Easily triggered temper moods and tantrums

· Indecisive	· Easily turned off/on sexually
· Triangles with parents/ grandparents	· Triangles with parents
· Procrastinates	· Demanding and needs reassurance
· Acts immaturely (at times)	· Attempts to control husband and "win" over him even in small matters
· Sexually inexperienced	· Sexually experienced
· Fears intimacy	· Fears intimacy
· Functions well at work (to overfunctioning)	· Functions well at work (to underfunctioning)

Husband's individual system

Mr. Jones came from a family with an intergenerational system of emotional distance and cutoffs in the relationships between parents and grandparents, as well as parents and children. His mother was an adult child of an alcoholic parent and his father had a military background and later was self-employed in civilian life. Mr. Jones' parents prevented and forbade him and his sisters from relating to their grandparents due to historic family secrets and rifts they were never told about in any detail.

Against this intergenerational history, Mr. Jones tended to overidealize his parents and talk of their affection for him and one another and how happy his childhood had been. His denial mechanisms were strong and he was unaware how often he spoke in contradiction to his wife at home and in some therapy sessions. The lack of openness in his family of origin seemed to precondition him to seek a mate who had some desire for openness and sharing. Not surprisingly, he described himself as a "people pleaser" in his family, as well as in his marriage and even at work. Given this background, he was a good listener except when some of his defense mechanisms were operating without his conscious awareness.

Object relations theory (Nichols, 1987; Nadelson, 1978) holds that adults react to others based, in part, on how such persons resemble *internal objects* (mental images we form and carry within us which are intrapsychic representations of self and/or others which are split into "all good" or "all bad" categories, some of which are retained and others projected onto another individual). This process is termed *projective identification*. Mr. Jones seemed to project his "mother/sister image" of an idealized type on to his mate at times and then to be upset that she was, in fact, not that way at all. Indeed, he tended to project an idealized image of "wife/mother" on to his mate along with overidealized images on to his wife's parents which were not justified by the reality of how they actually were. His intrapsychic need to idealize, deny, rescue, and "get along" with everyone was a serious blind spot for him to confront in the therapeutic process. Ironically, he indicated that one reason he was attracted to his wife-to-be was for her "insight" into others.

A related intrapsychic mechanism in Mr. Jones was his self-description, using terms like "nerd," naive, sexually inexperienced, dumb, weak as a male, wimp, and a self-blamer. He would, at times, take full responsibility for triggering a fight with Mrs. Jones when, in fact, he was not totally to blame. It was his way of trying to reconcile with her and avoid more of her anger or moods.

Wife's individual system

Mrs. Jones came from a family in which her mother grew up fearing her father, even though the whole family said he treated her very well. Her mother saw sex as dirty and to be avoided, her body to be covered up and not exposed to a man, and gave out a powerful message that men are not to be trusted. Mother had very low self-esteem and covered it with a sharp, critical tongue towards others, with harsh discipline which at times appeared to be irrational. In contrast, her father was a loving, peaceful man who refused to lead, discipline, or be strong with a woman. He was passive, quiet, caring, and a people pleaser.

From this family-of-origin context, Mrs. Jones emerged with a plethora of issues: (1) low self-esteem; (2) conflicted in how to relate to her father; (3) difficulty in trusting men; (4) deep intrapsychic conflict about her own body image and how comfortable she felt in a man seeing her nude; and, (5) feeling triangulated into her parents marriage in dysfunctional ways over the years. At times, she felt parentified by her parents into a role-reversal wherein she acted out the "parent" role while they fought like two "children."

From childhood on, Mrs. Jones cried easily. Not surprisingly, she was the most rebellious child in her family of origin since it was one way for her to differentiate herself. She acted out in numerous ways over the years. Her mother had a lifelong issue of whether or not others "heard" her and whether she spoke "clearly" enough to others. Both of her parents seemed to have individual histories of feeling insecure about themselves and modeled this insecurity in the family home as the children grew up.

From adolescence on, Mrs. Jones dated widely and had numerous sexual partners. Further on in therapy, she admitted that she had a long history of sexual problems with most of the men she had as sexual partners. Her sexual problems included the following: "they were not passionate enough"; her lack of orgasms at times; her lack of pleasure; and, her lack of feeling close versus distant after having had sex.

Her intrapsychic mechanisms included her projective identification onto her husband-to-be that he was a wonderful listener and more caring for her feelings than he was able to be. Her idealized image of the strong father figure she had always desired was projected onto her husband who was, in fact, the opposite. Internally, she could not see that he was too much like her real father instead of like her idealized father image. Her enmeshment with her family of origin was carried right into her marriage, unconsciously of course. Symptomatic of her enmeshment was her irrational "loyalty" feelings to her family, although she could articulate her dislike of the original script messages and her desire to eliminate them from her life, she felt "guilty" and "disloyal" when she considered life without the negative messages.

Her distorted concept of her body image served as a powerful mechanism to defend against true closeness and intimate feelings with a man. Exacerbating this distortion were her moods, irritability, and even lower backaches or headaches when things approached being sexual in the relationship (unless she initiated the activity). Her need to control was modeled well by her mother. Mrs. Jones' control needs were greater than her verbalized needs to share control and feel closer in the relationship. Her ability to emotionally exaggerate a description of a scenario served well to defend against closeness and feeling vulnerable with her partner. When in doubt, she could quickly become a martyr or a victim in a given scenario.

Although she could function very well at work, when she came under any criticism, evaluation, or judgments from persons of either gender, she would project her parental-family-of-origin issues onto the person and feel devastated, doubt herself and her abilities, and be convinced she could not measure up to her lifelong script. At times, she would be either very irrational or cognitively distorted when required to think rationally about herself, whether at work or at home.

When her husband-to-be and she were dating, she got pregnant by accident and they agreed to have an abortion. Next, she moved into his apartment with him, and soon thereafter they married. Again, her issues with her own sexuality were heightened by this situation, and she took some resentment about having gotten pregnant into her marriage to further fuel her intrapsychic conflict about sex and intimacy. Once again, she had no conscious awareness of her intrapsychic issues with which she entered marriage.

Interactional system

The interactional system we call marriage is an intricate blending of two individual systems into a dynamic dialectic which knowingly and unknowingly interacts with the two intergenerational systems. The couple's marital contracts and communication patterns are two areas in which their dynamic interface became readily apparent.

Interactional systems are built on two or more intergenerational systems and the expectations of each individual lead to the establishment of a psychological marital contract on three levels: (1) conscious and verbalized; (2) conscious, but not verbalized; and (3) beyond awareness for both partners (Sager, 1976). Sager indicates that *first-level* contracts can lead persons into marriage, *second-level* contracts can lead to early marital difficulties, and *third-level* contracts with significant incongruities lie at the root of major problems as the marriage continues over the long term.

The most common contract with this couple was the third-level contract to play out parent to child roles, which was beyond conscious awareness for both partners upon entering marriage. For example, the wife's need to continue to rebel against her parents fitted perfectly with her husband's parentified need to parent her and rescue her at various times. This hidden contract served their intrapsychic needs, while consciously they complained about the amount of fighting they were doing (Turner, 1982).

There were three other hypotheses by the therapist about this couple's initial contracts: (1) a second-level contract for the wife to be strong while the husband was to be weak; (2) a second-level contract for the husband to act close while the wife acted distant; and (3) a second-level contract for the wife to control (win) while the husband protested her controlling ways (lose).

As these contracts are being developed and lived out, all couples and families form their own idiosyncratic communication patterns. Mr. and Mrs. Jones developed their own patterns over time, patterns that ran in cycles of clear to distorted, and from close to distant communication.

Their pattern, when viewed from the Intersystem Model, is best understood if one begins with the intergenerational history. Both partners had come from families of origin with parental models of distance and emotional cutoffs. Mr. and Mrs. Jones had been raised to be familiar with patterns of closeness-distance in their parental models.

When examining their individual systems, we see an interesting "fit" of her need for distance and his need for closeness. Their use of projective identification onto one another, which served as an original attraction to one another (because of their use of denial and rationalization), later served as a source of anger and conflict.

Not surprisingly, then, their interaction system ran a reciprocal pattern of closeness-distance for which their alleged "sex" problem was an accurate metaphor. Exacerbating their interactional pattern were annual visits to one or the other of their parental homes for the holidays. While there on the annual visit, one of them would regress to a childlike state while the other spouse complained and judged. Upon returning home, they would begin another round of conflict about the psychological defects in the spouse who had just regressed. The result was more distance. From the distance rift they could then begin afresh to move closer again and feel good about one another for a time—until the closeness became "too close."

After one holiday visit to the wife's parents, the husband gave her a vibrator as a Christmas gift. Upon returning home, she got angry with her husband for giving her such a "dirty" gift and refused to use it. Once again, she succeeded in creating distance, just at a time when he was promoting closeness and hoped for improvement in their sexual relationship. After an office visit in which this conflict was discussed, she was able to reframe the vibrator from a "negative" to a "positive" and make a connection to how her projective identification of her family script messages controlled her personal life. The vibrator seemed to serve as a neutral form of permission for the wife to enjoy sex since her script was that "mother" said, "don't enjoy it." Ironically, moving from person to object seemed to effect a change in the meaning of personal versus impersonal, meaning that Mrs. Jones began to reframe her old messages of "don't enjoy sex" (impersonal) to a new message of "enjoy sex" (personal).

They later reported that the vibrator had helped their sexual relationship and that sex had improved significantly. They began to be aware that sex was a metaphor for deeper issues with intergenerational roots for them both. From this insight, they began to increase the quality of their interaction, moving from their sexual relationship to the building of an improved verbal communication system.

Additional areas of needed growth and/or change in their communication patterns were a lack of conflict resolution skills, a clash in their cognitive styles, and an admixture of rational and irrational attributions they made to one another. Sager (1976) describes cognitive style as how a person takes in, processes, and then communicates information or data. People normally define, view, think, and problem-solve in distinctly different ways, i.e., their own, unique cognitive style. We know that extroverts and introverts process information differently, communicate differently, and can have sensory, intuitive, and thinking style differences; yet, both can be viewed as "normal." However, these differences can trigger serious interactional conflicts for couples who knowingly personalize the differences and view them as negative or self-diminishing, rather than valuing the differences as normative, impersonal, and potentially enriching. Figure 2 shows the dynamics of this couple.

Intergenerational systems

Mr. Jones' intergenerational system. As noted earlier, Mr. Jones was the youngest child in a family of four siblings. Three older sisters helped raise him

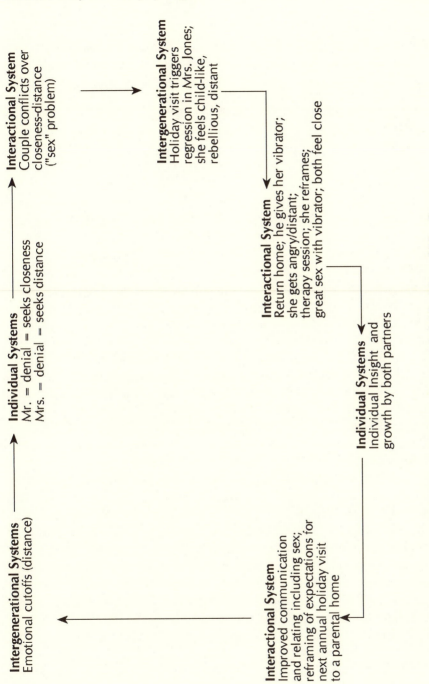

Figure 2. Intersystem Process Model for Mr. and Mrs. Jones

Intergenerational Systems
Emotional cutoffs (distance)

Individual Systems
Mr. = denial = seeks closeness
Mrs. = denial = seeks distance

Interactional System
Couple conflicts over closeness-distance ("sex" problem)

Intergenerational System
Holiday visit triggers regression in Mrs. Jones; she feels child-like, rebellious, distant

Interactional System
Return home; he gives her vibrator; she gets angry/distant; therapy session; she reframes; great sex with vibrator; both feel close

Individual Systems
Individual Insight and growth by both partners

Interactional System
Improved communication and relating including sex; reframing of expectations for next annual holiday visit to a parental home

and left him with a feeling of being an "only child." His mother was an adult child of an alcoholic. His father served in the military in early years and subsequently became self-employed in civilian life. He described his parents as "self-made types." His parents had a long history of feeling cut off from their respective parents and grandparents. It was so painful they forbade their four children to ever contact the grandparents or to respond to them. Mr. Jones believed there were family secrets in their history, but the parents refused to discuss them. Both of his parents were first-borns in their respective families. He indicated that most of his father's family had been divorced, even though his parents marriage was intact.

The more his family of origin was explored, the more he gradually began to drop his denial and rationalizations about the history. Finally, he began to allow himself to see an intergenerational history of secrets, mistrust of others, denial and rescuer scripts, lack of openness, value differences, alcoholism, probable physical abuse, and a stoic attitude towards life and relationships, especially in dealing with emotions. He felt lucky to not be around the older generation with what he termed their "closed-minded attitudes" toward many things in life, including the value of an education.

Mrs. Jones' intergenerational system. Mrs. Jones was the third of five daughters in her family of origin. While her oldest sister was called the "pretty one," Mrs. Jones was called the "smart one," since she got the best grades in school. She was also considered the "troublemaker" in the family because she rebelled in many ways, such as resisting her mother's controlling ways by arguing with her.

Her mother was never employed outside the home, and was viewed as overcontrolling, the family disciplinarian, critical of her and responsible for her being scripted to fear men, sex, and her own sexuality. Although her mother had an outgoing personality, her mother grew up fearing her father even though the family indicates her father treated her in very positive and loving ways. Her mother was the youngest in her family of origin, and always felt insecure personally and had low self-esteem. The way these issues were presented led this clinician to wonder if the mother had been sexually abused or raped in her early years.

Mrs. Jones' father was a passive, self-employed man who was not openly affectionate with anyone, including his own daughters. Her father claims he never got positive reinforcement from his own father and spent most of his life trying to prove his worth to his own father.

Her mother's family had many secrets and refused to discuss some family history. Family script messages impressed on Mrs. Jones while she grew up included the following: "Don't trust men"; "Be a prude"; "Don't be proud of your body, especially if nude"; "Don't be sensual or sexual"; "Don't enjoy sex even if it feels good"; and, "Keep your breasts covered up."

Combined intergenerational systems background. In summary, the combined intergenerational systems history for the two spouses reflects the following influences:

Mrs. Jones	Mr. Jones
· loyalty issues	· idealization of parents
· script messages (negative)	· rescuer script
· triangulated between parents	· triangulated between grandparents and parents
· distance issues	· closeness issues
· low self-esteem	· perfectionism
· weak boundaries	· rigid boundaries
· irrational thinking	· denial mechanisms
· anger used frequently	· anger avoided frequently
· attributes weakness to men	· attributes strength to women
· theme: "You can't do it."	· theme: "You can do it."

In looking at some of the key issues from the combined intergenerational backgrounds of this couple, it was predictable that they would encounter the marital problems that they did. The subtle influence of their second- and third-level contracts served to confuse many of their interactional attempts to understand one another. However, thanks to the fact that both wife and husband were good candidates for therapy and gained sufficient awareness of their unknown issues and influences, they were able to grow in therapy and benefit from an enhanced marital relationship. They were good candidates for therapy since they wanted to grow, avoid further pain in visiting their parents, and be the best potential parents whenever they had children.

Gender-Determined Issues

There are always gender-related issues in couples' and family therapy and there is a need for every therapist to be sensitive to those issues in the therapeutic process, including his/her own gender as part of the process. In the therapy process with the Jones's, the following gender determined beliefs/issues were particularly salient:

Mrs. Jones	Mr. Jones
· sex-role confusion regarding who is to be dominant in marriage	· sex-role idealization that his parents had an ideal marriage
· men are bad—don't trust	· women are emotional, nuturant,

a man	but need rescuing occasionally
· men are weak	· women are weak
· sex is dirty/bad	· sex is good
· women are to be emotional	· men are to be intellectual
(cry)	and unemotional
· women are to have low	· men are to have high
self-esteem	self-esteem
· women may use their	· men are to be providers
intellect and achieve in	and high-achievers
school	

For Mr. and Mrs. Jones, the gender determined issues contributed to the strong themes underneath the surface of the interactional system. A combination of genuine sex-role confusion, denial, naivete, inexperience, and script messages interacted to confuse issues and trigger anger, frustration and resentment. Blended in were aspects of their individual projective identification images onto each other to further heighten their tensions.

Given all of this individual, interactional, and intergenerational history, used for the assessment of this couple, let us now turn to the focused hypotheses of this case, prior to the discussion of the treatment plan.

Hypotheses Regarding the Clients

During the initial intake session with these clients, the initial hypothesis was that sex was a metaphor for other underlying issues. Believing in multicausality of many client issues that are presented in therapy, the assumption was that intergenerational and individual system issues were interacting to allegedly "cause" the presenting "sex" problem (Weeks, 1989).

Three further hypotheses were present: (1) each of their views of what was feminine/masculine might be an issue; (2) overt or covert closeness/distance issues might play a significant part in the couple's problem; and (3) dependence/independence/counterdependence issues might be operating in a manner to promote a closeness/distance cycle in the marriage.

TREATMENT

Individual Issues: Wife

As they entered therapy the wife originally demanded that the husband be a passionate lover. When the issue was reframed, relationship therapy was contracted for, instead of sex therapy per se, for an initial 10 sessions with an option to extend the contract if needed.

Therapy then focused on their (1) fears of intimacy, (2) control issues, (3) family-of-origin influences, (4) moods, anger, pouting, (5) indecisiveness, and (6) sex-typed roles. By the end of the 10 initial sessions, both partners were discovering latent and unconscious causes that were going to require more time to resolve. They were willing to extend the therapy contract on an open-ended basis, subject to periodic evaluation by the therapist as well as by themselves (Turner, 1985).

During the mid-therapy sessions they worked hard as a couple on their family-of-origin issues and influences and how they were impacting their marital interactional pattern. Both were amazed at how powerful their intergenerational influences and scripts had been for them individually. After being in therapy one and one-half years, the couple terminated with most of their issues resolved and relating very successfully sexually. They made steady progress with a few minor regressions during the term of therapy.

Change strategy

In addressing Mrs. Jones' complaint about her husband's lack of passion, the therapist reframed her complaint into a *metaphor* for warmth she had never received from her father (Weeks & L'Abate, 1982). Her linear attributions, namely that her husband was the cause of their poor sex life, were reframed to circular ones that suggested that her poor sex experience with prior lovers might be a viable causal factor as well. Most importantly, her projective identification of her father image onto her husband was challenged and identified. Once she became conscious of how her projective identification worked, she was able to begin to identify it and stop it before it was fully stated and acted out in the marital interactions.

Integration

As Mrs. Jones was *defining* her husband as a non-passionate lover, she easily began to *interpret* his behavioral style as passive, weak, and juvenile. Since she was more sexually experienced than he prior to marriage, she took a parent-to-child approach to him in the sexual area of the marriage. Her *prediction* was that her husband could not change and so she began to feel hopeless and discouraged about their relationship. It was difficult for the wife to see the *incongruence* between her actual interest in sex and her availability for sex compared to her verbal expressions about it. Her early insistence on her husband being to blame for their sexual problem prevented her from any real *interdependence* in the marital relationship with him. In summary, Mrs. Jones found it convenient to *attribute* negative motives to her husband, which made it convenient to judge him.

Client dialogue

The following client dialogue is a verbatim sample from one of the therapy sessions. This excerpt illustrates how the childlike behavior of Mrs. Jones, only in specific situations, served to confuse the roles of each spouse. Mr. Jones played an equal part with his own role confusion.

Therapist: How aware are you of how you're acting at a time like this?

Wife: Oh, I'm very aware. I know exactly what I'm doing!

Husband: Do you really? I didn't know that!

Therapist: You appear to know what you're doing.

Wife: I mean, to the extent that, I mean, it's not like O.K., let's do this deliberately, but I'm sure of it to the extent that in the back of my mind I say (to myself) "You're acting like a two-year-old."

Husband: The last time you started to...

Wife: I can't get out of it. I'm...

Husband: How can you be aware of it and say that?

Wife: What?

Husband: That you can't get out of it?

Wife: It's the sense of maybe when I was younger it was the only defense that I knew.

Therapist: Sure. That is understandable in light of your family background.

Wife: At that time. I didn't know what it was, but I knew how I was acting. I felt like a fool. I knew exactly how I was acting. I even said something poutish; you know, I pouted. I said, "All right, then, we'll go to your stupid party." I knew what you would say (to husband) ...but you laughed. You said, "What are you doing? You're acting like that whining little girl."

Therapist: What's the meaning of the word "can't"? How do we translate that word?

Wife: Right: I'm choosing not to is what I'm really trying to say with "can't."

Therapist: O.K. So, what are you really saying to (husband) at a time like that?

Wife: I don't know. That I don't want to change, or that I'm not willing. I don't know if I'm saying anything to him. I feel like I'm stuck.

Therapist: Well, are you saying it to yourself if not to (husband)? Who's being addressed?

Wife: I'm not sure what you mean. I'm aware that I'm acting like a child.

Therapist: I believe your statement was, "I can't." Remember what you said?

Wife: I can't change. I can't get out of it. That's what I said!

Therapist: "I can't get out of it" was your statement, correct? So, then translate that "can't get out of it" to "I won't get out of it." Then who's being talked to?

Silence

Husband: Me!

Wife: You? I'm saying it to you?

Husband: Yeah.

Wife: I'm not sure how you fit into this. I think it's something that is going on within me whether it's you or the "man in the moon" standing there. Anyway I'm not sure that I know who I am talking to.

Therapist: Well, if it's not (husband), who else might you be addressing it to?

Wife: My parents!

Therapist: O.K. And what does that make (husband)? Does he sound like your parents' stand-in?

Wife: Yeah.

Therapist: (to husband) So you are standing for her parents?

Husband: Yeah.

Therapist: Is that the translation of what you meant?

Husband: I was being very parental! (to wife just now ...)

Summary integration

As the reader may now see, the Intersystem theory of interaction provides an integrated way of working with the *intrapsychic* components of (1) interpretation, (2) definition, and (3) prediction, along with the *interactional* components of (1) congruence, (2) interdependence, and (3) attribution management. It brings together the relevant components that needed to be addressed with the therapeutic strategies of *reframing* and *highlighting* the wife's projective identification onto her husband.

At this early part in the therapy, the therapist was attempting to "plant the seeds" which would grow into *spontaneous compliance*; that is, a "change" the clients attribute to themselves and for which they take full credit and ownership. An early example was when the therapist suggested to them that other "messages might be encoded on their family-of-origin tapes which could provide them answers to their current problems" (Weeks, 1991).

Individual Issues: Husband

One of the husband's basic problems was his need to "rescue" and/or "help" his wife in various ways.

Change strategy

Mr. Jones, in his assigned homework, was asked to clarify what were his wife's needs and to request regular feedback from her about anything he did for her. In order to prevent himself from sliding into a "rescue" mode, he was asked to contract with his spouse for new, more acceptable ways to offer help that were considered helpful by her.

By taking on three new roles, Mr. Jones began a successful approach to more acceptable ways of offering help to his wife. The three new roles were (1) clarifying what were her actual needs, (2) requesting regular feedback from her, and (3) contracting with her for what was acceptable to her.

Integration

A key dynamic in their relationship was Mr. Jones' *interpretations* of his wife's needing to be rescued/helped even if she did not need to be rescued. Mr. Jones tended to *define* his wife as needy or helpless which enabled him to rationalize his "helping" interventions—needed or not. Related to his definition of his spouse's needs were his *predictions* that she really needed his help. Given the husband's incongruence in his internal dynamics, it was apparent that his combined *definitions* and *predictions* had been a trigger for anger and frustration between them. It appeared that Mr. Jones was seeking more *interdependence*, if not codependence, with his wife than she was comfortable with. Clearly, the husband was *attributing* needs to his spouse that were not always hers, but more likely were his own, even though he was not consciously aware of them.

Client dialogue

This section of client dialogue clearly illustrates the difficulties Mr. and Mrs. Jones had in making verbal contracts with one another. They were often surprised by one another's reactions and had never established ways to reduce their surprises and to lessen their emotional reactions to each other.

Wife: I mean that maybe I'm making an excuse for us, but in this particular occasion, and maybe there are others, I feel we are both turning around when one of us slips off and does the parent and child thing (to each other) and then we come back (on track again).

Therapist: O.K., then, if you want to make that part of the relationship, do you have a "contract" for that as to how that's going to work so the other person doesn't get bent out of shape so much?

Husband: No, we don't, and sometimes it comes as a surprise to me.

Therapist: Yes?

Husband: You know, that's when it's the worst. When it comes as a surprise (to me/to us).

Therapist: You still have to have a "contract" for that, you see.

Husband: Yeah????

Wife: What do you mean? A contract that we're going to do it, but we don't know when or where?

Therapist: Yes. An open-ended contract on that line that would make something work for you as an interlude or a change of pace or deviation from what your normal discourse is, you see. (Pause) And then you can assign yourself roles. You will know much more about what to expect from one another. Know that it may be time limited. It's not going to go on for weeks and weeks, and then, even though it may be a surprise in terms of the exact moment it starts, it's not a surprise as to what you both can expect from that point on, you see. I'm hearing there is a genuine surprise and then one or both of you aren't quite sure how the scenario is going to come out.

Wife: (to husband) I think for the most part you're expecting me to act like the adult that I normally do. So, when I start my pouting, you're kind of like, oh, boy, there she goes again ...

Husband: Yeah.

Wife: And I think you click into adult; I mean, I think you click into parent.

Husband: Well, I don't know. Parent is part nurturing, so I try to try that angle and sometimes that doesn't work, and then sometimes I get "Well, you should" and that doesn't work either. So, if we get a contract, I can say, "This is going on and this is what is happening and here's what my role should be and then let it take its course." You know, real surprises are the school times and sometimes when I come home from work or whatever and you're banging away at homework and say, "I'm almost done" or "It stinks" or "Life's horrible" ...

Therapist: It seems to me the two of you can do something in terms of contracting here. I'd like to see you give that some real attention and let me know what you come up with. I think you can discuss, for example, Mrs. Jones, whether you need to pout for awhile and what kind of role you need Mr. Jones to be in? Do you need him in a nurturing, parent role, or do you need him in an adult role, or do you need him to be silent? What are the expectations? What is most helpful and facilitative to you as well as to the relationship?

Wife: At that time? You mean I have to tell him at that time which one of those roles?

Husband: Yes, in advance.

Therapist: Contract in advance so he knows whether he should click into the parent, as he was saying a minute ago, or whether he should click into something else or just click off.

Wife: Well, I wouldn't know until I was doing it which of those I would want. Is that what you mean? I would never say every time I pout I want you to act like this.

Husband: Oh, then, how will I know?

Therapist: You mean there's a differentiation then for outcomes for pouting?

Wife: I think there are differentiations in terms of what's going on in terms of what I need from him.

Therapist: O.K., but, does the differentiation fall into several predictable categories?

Wife: I don't think it's predictable.

Husband: Well, I do.

Wife: I mean, I think there are several categories.

(The couple continued on and agreed upon some contract categories with which they were satisfied.)

Summary integration

Again, this couple responded very well to reframing interventions. A key to their steady progress in therapy was the therapist's continual emphasis on the power that they had to make their own choices. In this way, a *context* for change to occur was naturally implanted in the total process.

The therapist's emphasis throughout this case was on the couple's *process* of interaction rather than on a specific outcome per se. The use of the *affirmation paradoxic* strategy was utilized throughout this case. In repeated ways, the therapist facilitated the clients in defining and contracting for their desired behavioral changes (i.e., less conflict, more closeness, better sex, less rescuing, etc.), concomitant with an emphasis on their power to choose and the consequences of their choices. Such changes were then described as the result of internal processes indigenous to the client(s) (i.e., "messages," insights, answers already somewhere inside you). Finally, the therapist assisted them in identifying that the desired changes were either beyond their conscious awareness but within them, or beyond their immediate volitional control, such as situations and forces in other relationships or the environment or both.

Interactional System: Couple

A major problem in the interactional system was the poor conflict-resolution skills of the couple. Like most younger couples, this dyad had minimal skills for identifying and/or resolving their differences (Turner, 1982).

Change strategy

Since Mr. and Mrs. Jones were familiar with Transactional Analysis (T.A.) concepts, it seemed pragmatic to utilize their knowledge of and comfort with T.A. as a common knowledge base and reframe or modify the T. A. concepts as necessary. Specifically, many conflicts were Parent-Child transactions and the primary strategy was to change them to Adult-Adult transactions (Berne, 1961). Many of their conflicts were attacks on the person rather than on the problem itself.

The therapist provided them with a list of how-to-fight-fair skills from which they could select ones they believed would work for them (e.g., clarify the problem; contracts). It was also suggested that they might create their own fight-rules, since they already had good ideas within themselves that had never surfaced on a conscious level.

A further strategy was the therapist's suggestion that the husband had an *indwelling* ability to move beyond his procrastination pattern. Similarly, an additional suggestion was made to the wife that she had an *implicit* ability to control and decrease her use of anger while sharing, instead, her deeper feelings with her husband.

Client dialogue

The following verbatim client dialogue is an example of how Mr. and Mrs. Jones had a spat over whether to take more time to visit with her family or to go to a dinner with some of their friends. Even though Mrs. Jones had an opportunity to say "No" earlier, now she wanted to change her mind and they were beginning to disagree.

Wife: (to therapist) Except actually the way that I thought our argument started, but I could be wrong about it, I turned to him and said, "They were thinking of going to dinner, and it would be nice to stay with them." And I said it very Adult-like and he said, "We have to go to this party. I've made an obligation and you had your chance to say "No" to this party a long time ago.

Husband: Was I right?

Wife/Husband: (Both laugh.)

Wife: But obviously it felt very parental because I retorted with "Well, go." Our disagreement kind of then took off. So, I mean, I don't know. I'm not meaning to be difficult, but ...

Husband: I do that and I'm a Parent?

Wife: I don't know. There are times I think you are talking to a two-year-old, or you're pouting or you're putting your head between your legs and saying, "I don't want to go to work." But, I mean, I guess my confusion is we all have that in us and I guess I think you're allowed to let it come out once in a while as long as it's not for a real long unhealthy time.

Therapist: Had you considered sharing a deeper feeling than only a pout?

Wife: I really thought I wanted to be a little kid and pout and I didn't want to be an Adult at that point. I knew that he was right. And I knew that I was being a jerk and instead of turning to him and saying, 99% of the time, "You know you're right," and I do that most of the time.

Husband: Yeah, you do (lightly).

Wife: You know, "You've got a point, let's do this, " I really wanted to
            hold onto my pout because I was really upset and I knew I was
            not going to get my way.

Therapist: Oh, so there might have been some value in holding on and using
            your pout against Mr. Jones?

Wife: So, I kind of felt like I had to do it!

Husband: You had something at stake then.

Wife: I hadn't done it (pout) in so long and it was the one time it was
            really important to me.

Therapist: It was really important because ... ? (pause)

Wife: To hold on 'cause I knew he was right. So, we went to the party
            and didn't go with my family after all. In fact, an hour later I said
            to him, "It is not fair (to husband). You are absolutely right. We
            have to go." But it took me an hour to say that. I really wanted
            my time to pout because I don't get to be with my family very
            much. I really wanted to be with them another hour.

Therapist: So you had some really strong feelings there.

Wife: Yes. And he knew that and you could tell I wanted to stay and
            I could tell you were, even, you know, understanding enough that
            you were flexible; "well, if we hadn't said that we'd go, then we
            would have gone out to dinner. But we've made an obligation."

Summary integration

Through the use of *affirmation paradoxic* statements to each spouse, a
gradual process of *spontaneous compliance* was initiated (Weeks, 1991). In
addition, *reframing* was instrumental in utilizing their prior knowledge of
Transactional Analysis as a vehicle of change. As the interactional level of
their relationship was addressed, the couple began to *attribute change* and
improvement more and more to themselves or to forces within themselves that
they could not consciously identify. The more they took responsibility and
control for their *individual dynamics,* the more they felt in control of the
interactional dynamics, which they had believed were beyond their control,
thus leaving them feeling unnecessarily like victims.

A real key to their progress was their *attributions* to one another which,
initially, were their own unconscious projective identifications onto one
another. During the course of therapy, their unconscious projective identifications of personal insecurity, childlike roles, and need to control the other

were modified to feelings of personal security, adultlike roles, and a diminished need to control one another. Overall, as many of their unconscious projective identifications decreased, their marital interactions increased in stability, with the use of more conscious and positive ways of interacting and less fighting over small things.

Intergenerational System: Families of Origin

The most serious intergenerational problem for Mr. and Mrs. Jones was the annual holiday visit(s) to one or both of their parental homes. Each annual visit triggered major regression in both partners. Both dreaded the thought of each annual visit.

Change strategies

Each partner was assigned a specific role of observer and recorder of all behaviors, thought patterns, and emotions expressed by the parental system they were visiting. The spouse who was placed in the "child" role by her/his parents was asked to be a self-observer insofar as possible during such a visit.

The therapist *prescribed* their annual "symptom" of regression as one to be expected and normative during their visit, and *predictable* based on their history of such visits. A related part of the prescription was a lowering of their usual expectations of one another while on location at the parental home. An additional subset of the prescription was for Mr. and Mrs. Jones to practice using a *transition process* of briefing one another about their thoughts, feelings, fears, and anxieties travelling both *to* and *from* the parental home.

A final subset of the prescription was that the "child" visiting his/her parents ask more directly about family history, secrets, etc., than s/he ever had in the past.

One other change strategy was enabling them to *reframe* their criticisms of "self" during their regressed and angry times during and after the parental visit. For example, they learned to think of personal regression and childlike behavior as normative during a family visit versus judging self or other for the regression. This reframing strategy enabled them to erode some of their automatic projective identifications onto one another, and to find new ways to understand and support one another instead.

Integration

In their annual visit to one of their parental homes, the therapist prescribed that they use their "symptom" of regression to a Childlike state. The suggestion that they both observe self and parents in new ways created a paradoxical Childlike state. In affirming the values that might accrue from being in a

Childlike state, the client learned that the original negative Child-state could have a positive connotation and meaning as an Adult-state. Their *spontaneous compliance* occurred after the use of this *affirmation paradox*, as they had many spontaneous learnings and insights following the annual visit to her parent's home that fall.

CONCLUSION

The unique approach of this book was the plan to relate all cases presented through the constructs of the Intersystem Model. Our premise is that *paradox* is a universal aspect of psychotherapy. It is imperative that the clinician be able to think in *dialectical terms* about the dynamics occurring within the therapeutic process as well as in the lives of the clients. All the change processes are viewed as either *affirmation* or *negation paradoxes*. The couple's interactions are assessed for the *intrapsychic* components of *integration, definition,* and *prediction*. Their interactional processes were assessed for *congruence, interdependence,* and *attributions*.

A clear example of *dialectical conceptualization* in this case was their presentation of a "sex problem" as the initial symptom when, simultaneously, it was not a symptom. Ironically, it was their presentation of a paradox without being aware of what they were actually presenting to the therapist.

The wife's alleged lack of sexual desire occurred mainly when her husband desired to get close. When he was hurt, distant or withdrawn, she desired sex and criticized him for not being a "passionate" lover at such times.

One value of the *meta-formal dialectical approach* to therapy is the freedom provided the therapist to understand and work with the *implicit contradictions* and *paradoxes* comprising most human relationships. A key to such interventions, such as *prescribing the symptom,* is the role that disequilibrium plays in producing change (Weeks, 1991).

The *paradox* in therapy is built on the notion of taking control by giving it back to the client(s). Under this condition, the client learns to develop self-control and symptom-control by doing what is usually feared, avoided, or dreaded. The actual dread and fear of their annual visits to their respective parental homes was a major issue impacting this couple. Their lack of adequate boundaries between the couple system and the parental systems was evident even to them. When more control was given to them before, during, and after the annual visit, they began to develop a plan to observe, study, evaluate, discuss, and debrief their thoughts, behaviors, and feelings related to the holiday visits. Indeed, they began to act as scientist-practioners to self, the couple system, and their interface with both intergenerational systems.

The process of treatment occurred over one and one-half years for a total of 31 sessions. Other than six individual sessions for securing their respective intergenerational and personal histories (three each), all sessions were couple sessions. The therapy can be viewed in three major sections:

The *early therapy* focused on joining with the couple, assessing individual/ intrapsychic, interactional, and intergenerational aspects; developing goals; and securing a therapeutic contract.

The *middle therapy* took 15 sessions, during which a shift was made to examining their individual and couple systems in greater detail, forming new understandings of self (individual and family scripts, loyalties, self-esteem, power/control issues, closeness/distance issues, sexuality issues, and others), and developing skills in conflict management and fair fighting.

Finally, in the *later therapy*, the focus shifted for the last eight sessions to their interface with their intergenerational systems and to addressing the need to establish new, clearer boundaries separating their marriage from parents, friends, and even coworkers.

In point of fact, their alleged "sex" problem turned out to be a complex relationship issue rather than one of actual "sexual dysfunction." Mr. Jones' family of origin emphasized more independence; Mrs. Jones' emphasized more dependence. Their family-of-origin models clashed! As they discovered new ways to balance their respective dependence/independence needs, their counterdependence lessened and merged into a newfound interdependence.

Overall, this was a successful course of therapy with a couple who were highly motivated and with two individuals who must be given credit for making it a success. They became a "unified couple" in the therapeutic process and exciting growth occurred for both partners and for the marriage itself.

Major therapeutic changes included a new way of viewing one another (*definition*); fresh ways of listening, talking, and fighting (*interpretation*); and more specific and data-based ways of anticipating one another's reactions (*prediction*).

The distorted intimacy needs and behaviors, destructive control issues, her need to "pout," and his indecisiveness, all lessened or vanished over time, to their increased happiness. The increased congruence (that is, their behavior, thoughts, and words matched more frequently), fostered an easier interaction shown in fewer fights, fewer projections on to one another, and a new ability to contract for the meeting of their needs related to a new skill in reframing some of their own material. They appeared to be more creative, productive, and balanced in their relating.

As she changed her demands for him to be a "passionate" lover, he discovered a new ability to act more masculine in her eyes. In a rare move for the therapist, a prescription was given to the husband to consider taking Judo lessons and learn to control body, mind, and spirit in a unified but nonintellectual way. Interestingly, he did just that and grew in self-confidence more rapidly than one might have predicted. Since then, she has seen her husband as more masculine and sexy. At work, he has been given two more promotions and is in an exciting personal growth track.

Mrs. Jones has continued her growth in becoming more self-confident in her own career and learning to accept affirmations at work and home as real. Her self-esteem has improved at the same time while her professional skills have grown tremendously. What each partner attributes to self and to the other has shifted in a positive direction.

Finally, the reflections of the therapist are of a successful case with rewarding growth for both partners and for their marriage. Even their relationships with their respective parents have improved, to the extent that they have altered their expectations of all concerned during those visits and both sets of parents have lessened demands on them during the year as a result of their new marital boundaries. Typical of all couples, they will continue to grow in many ways in the years ahead because therapy is a process that continues for years beyond what happens in the therapist's office.

In retrospect, the therapist did numerous things that proved to be helpful, liberating, strengthening, and supportive to the couple during the course of therapy, both individually and conjointly. Considering the power of *paradoxical* therapy, it could be hypothesized that on some occasion a specific type of paradoxical intervention might have facilitated them, moving them along more quickly. Yet, who can say how fast anyone can or should move along in therapy, given the *power* of underlying emotions and cognitions (Amundson, Stewart, & Valentine, 1993). Perhaps it is appropriate to conclude by observing that the intriguing dilemma for the therapist is whether to use or not to use a specific paradoxical intervention—that is the paradox!

CHAPTER 6

In Quest of G-D's* Permission, or When the "Other Man" Is G-D

Bea Hollander-Goldfein

INTRODUCTION

Every therapy case is different, touching the person of the therapist in different ways. Although challenging in their complexity, the problems addressed in the case presented here were not particularly unusual. I liked Tom and Joanne and we worked well together. Rarely do couples stay in treatment long enough to address not only presenting problems but other significant relationship issues as well. This couple worked on many difficult issues, leading to significant changes in themselves and in their lives together. They entered therapy as two disconnected individuals; they left therapy as a couple.

The unique aspect of this case was the presence of G-d. Joanne's faith and her experience of G-d was a critical factor in both the etiology and resolution of the presenting problem. Since their faith in G-d was a primary force in their lives, the therapy was compelled to sustain constant focus on the clarification of their views of G-d's will and their views of His guidelines for human behavior. The incorporation of a spiritual dimension is unusual in outpatient practice conducted in secular settings, but its presence in this case undoubtedly enriched the process and broadened the treatment parameters. I was challenged to incorporate my understanding of their faith experience into my development of treatment strategies. "Answering to a higher authority" is an interesting, if not humbling, experience. Psychological principles of mental health were not the final word. With G-d as a partner in the process, mental health issues took on spiritual meaning. Therefore, the progress made in therapy was viewed as the combined result of all our efforts, achieved with the blessing of G-d.

---

* The name of G-d is printed in this way in fulfillment of the Jewish precept that reserves the full use of G-d's name for religious writings.

This case was selected for the casebook because of its breadth and depth. We certainly worked on the "three systems" (*individual, interactional, intergenerational*) to a successful outcome. *Congruence* with the couple, and struggling to understand their individual points of view were important in order to gain their trust. Trust was critical in working with their religious beliefs, especially since they needed to guide me in the process of helping them find permission from G-d to be sexual. It was precisely this posture in the therapeutic relationship that created an *interactional context* for change. In other words, I constantly emphasized the importance of *personal choice*. The issues of personal choice and personal accountability were critical due to the lack of choice that characterized their childhoods and adult lives. This process facilitated *spontaneous compliance*, which fostered change within them as individuals and as a couple.

Helping the couple achieve an interactive pattern of healthy interdependence took a long time. The exploration of *interpretation* (how each partner understood the relationship, their families of origin, and their personal experiences), *definition* (how each partner defined the relationship based on their interpretations), *attribution* (the meaning each partner assigned to events in the relationship), and *prediction* (the expectations each partner had of the other based on interpretations, definitions, and attributions) had to be accomplished first. Once I gained an understanding of their three systems, the meanings they ascribed, and the language they used, I was able to *reframe* their marriage, based on intergenerational and individual issues, as one of mutual protection as opposed to illness vs. health, or control vs. passivity.

Accepting the *systemic reframe* as a realistic way of describing their difficulties, they were able to accept mutual responsibility. As the frame of *circular attribution* evolved and they were better able to take mutual responsibility, I began to press for mutual accountability. This was intended to pressure Tom to become "visible" so that Joanne would have to deal with his real feelings and needs. It was this pressure that brought them into an interdependent mode where they began to take each other's needs seriously and to negotiate solutions. The cooperative way in which this couple worked with me and with each other, in spite of the strong undercurrent of resistance, enabled me to guide them through the therapy with *affirmation paradox*.

CASE FORMULATION

The following case presentation utilizes the format of the Intersystem Assessment: Case Formulation Form. It summarizes two years of accumulated data and experiential information, including knowledge of the outcome.

Working with this approach over the course of treatment generates a number of working hypotheses. In this case, with treatment already completed, the formulation includes treatment strategies, the reformulation of treatment strategies, and the actual outcome. The length of this case formulation exemplifies the commitment of the Intersystem Model to know client couples from the inside out and the outside in.

Initial Impressions and Reactions

When they entered marital therapy, Tom was 45 years old and Joanne was 42. They had been married for 15 years and had known each other for 17 years. They had two children, a girl 14 years old and a boy 11, at the time they initiated treatment. Tom was a manager in a district office of a national firm and Joanne was a homemaker. They are white, comfortably middle class, and practicing Catholics. For Joanne, her faith is a deep and important personal commitment. For Tom, his involvement in Catholicism is more a matter of connection and affiliation than deep personal faith. Irrespective of these differences, religious practice and affiliation are important parts of their family life, including the enrollment of the children in a Catholic private school. Their religious involvement did not seem rigid, but rather comfortable and meaningful.

The couple initiated treatment as a joint decision. A little nervous, they were eager to begin. Joanne's prior involvement in two therapeutic relationships and Tom's adjunctive involvement in these therapies had brought both of them to a point where they were prepared for the process, even if not always comfortable. Their prior experience gave them some measure of sophistication about the exploration of psychological and relationship issues. So, while I had to establish a therapeutic relationship with them, I did not have to socialize them to the therapeutic process. Understandable comparisons were made between me and the previous therapists who had helped Joanne enormously. This passed relatively quickly, and they did come to accept me as "their" therapist, in contrast to the recent past when therapists were "hers."

Tom and Joanne presented as personable, easy to engage, motivated, and seeking help. Tom is pleasant-looking, of average height and build, with a mild middle-age spread, neat and well-dressed. Joanne is a slim, attractive woman, well dressed in modern, casual fashion. While Joanne is more outgoing and conversational, Tom tends to be more reserved and passive. Joanne's personality initially predominated. This stylistic difference, which also characterized their communication patterns, was apparent during the early sessions. It was easier to engage Joanne than Tom, and therefore it took focused interventions to involve him.

Another pattern immediately apparent was Joanne's tendency to speak factually and with emotion, but always to me and never to her husband unless directed to do so. Tom responded willingly to any questions or comments directed to him, but he rarely spoke from his own needs, desires, or perceptions. He never spoke about his own feelings except in vague terms presented as secondary to Joanne's feelings.

While this interactional pattern was automatic for the couple, it had been reinforced by their prior therapeutic experiences, which had mostly been individual therapy for Joanne. Tom had come in only to give or get information. They started the couples therapy at Marriage Council with the awareness that during the three to four years preceding this contact, the metaphor for their relationship had been that Joanne's "plate was full." With the additional responsibility of the children, she had no psychological space for Tom. Due to the nature of her difficulties, this perception was accepted by both partners, although Joanne did feel some guilt. Her level of pain, the seriousness of the problems, her growing sense of entitlement (stemming from healthy individuation), and the support of the individual therapists sustained this framework for the relationship. Although Tom admitted and Joanne acknowledged that this framework was difficult for him, Tom's experiences in his family of origin and his own protective mechanisms had made him perfectly suited to be "off the plate." Equalizing their involvement in therapy, and balancing their disproportionate experience of entitlement to being taken care of, became the predominant long-term process goals of treatment.

An equally significant long-term goal was the introduction of circular attribution. In other words, it was important for both partners to take responsibility for the phenomenon of "the plate." A therapist may have coined the phrase "my plate is full," but the "plate" was jointly experienced by Joanne, who needed to be on it, i.e., in control, and Tom, who needed to be off of it, i.e., invisible. The more Joanne needed control, the more invisible Tom became; the more invisible Tom became, the more control Joanne needed.

Presenting Problems

They both agreed that the presenting problem, inhibited sexual desire (ISD), was Joanne's problem. For many years their sexual relationship consisted of infrequent contact, perhaps five or six times a year. When these contacts occurred it was only out of Joanne's sense of obligation and her fear of losing Tom.

The sexual problems dated back to the beginning of the marriage. Joanne reported that she felt attracted to Tom while they were dating, and that when they petted she felt aroused even without direct genital stimulation. They were not fully sexually involved because of their religious beliefs. Once married, they both reported that the sexual relationship changed drastically. Joanne pressured Tom to have intercourse, but only in order to get pregnant. Once she was pregnant, she became totally uninterested in sex until she was ready for the second child. She did not report experiencing pain or any physical discomfort, but her lack of interest did generate uncomfortable feelings in her during sexual involvement of any sort.

Tom responded by backing off and accommodating to her wishes, because Joanne was very emotional and clear about her discomfort. He did not want to hurt her or force himself on her. He has always been a "nice guy," according to Joanne, the "nicest guy in the world." Moreover, the constant rejection had left him unsure of himself, which only served to reinforce feelings of insecurity and inadequacy. He was not only a "nice guy"; in actuality, it became a lot easier not to pursue sexual contact at all. When she did indicate interest, he accommodated to her once again by making the experience quick and focused on intercourse. He had certainly relinquished his own need for self protection against the constant rejections. He had successfully modulated his own feelings of desire and had effectively shut down, turned off, and repressed his own sexual feelings. When we met for therapy, Tom and Joanne were in this state of homeostasis: exquisitely and painfully STUCK.

During the early stage of therapy, Tom admitted to feelings of frustration and to a desire to resume a normal sexual relationship. He was not in any way indicating that he harbored "angry" feelings. Joanne, on the other hand, was speculating that he must have been feeling angry and resentful, but that he was too frightened of her intense responses to admit these feelings. Frightened by his total lack of sexual initiative, she began to suspect that he must have been having an affair, but also felt guilty for putting him through this kind of deprivation. She expressed a desperate desire to change the situation, but the bottom line was that she had no feelings of sexual interest or desire and she felt very uncomfortable being involved sexually. She saw and admitted quite openly that she knew she had put him in a catch-22, sexually and emotionally. Therefore, playing everything in a low keyed fashion seemed to be his only option. This he did well, due to the survival mechanisms he had developed as a child.

History of the Problem

Historically, the couple did not report a particular event or apparent reason for Joanne's sexual inhibition, except the act of getting married. Since they were not sexually active before marriage, except for some petting, it is probably fair to say that the sexual inhibition was latent, and only became apparent once sexual contact became a real option. When Tom was forceful sexually, a few months after their marriage, Joanne experienced his actions as rape. This negative event, however, was not the cause of the sexual aversion already present. In fact, it is probably more accurate to say that the sexual inhibition precipitated this event due to the buildup of sexual and emotional pressure. Although not a cause of the ISD, this event served to reinforce Joanne's negative feelings.

The more profound impact of this incident was on Tom. He was so frightened by his behavior and use of force that he avoided any possibility of repetition. This meant both physical and emotional withdrawal. Joanne's ISD served not only to protect her, but also to protect him from his own sexual insecurities and lack of self confidence, as well as from his own strong feelings. Therefore, they each developed a personal investment in the symptom, ISD, due to the secondary gain of self-protection.

Accepting "mutual protection" as the shared meaning of the ISD meant the abandonment of their old frame of the problem. They initiated therapy with the view that Joanne was a caring person, but exceedingly controlling, perhaps "neurotic," the victim of her childhood and unable to help herself although she really did not want to be this way. Tom was seen as a nice guy, tolerating the intolerable in their sexual relationship, but otherwise not accommodating enough. The systemic view of the ISD as "mutual protection" reframed the problem with a more positive, sympathetic connotation and acknowledged the circular attribution, i.e., the joint responsibility of each partner for sustaining the symptom. In addition to viewing their problem(s) differently, Tom and Joanne were confronted with profoundly different definitions of themselves as people. From this new perspective they could be more sympathetic to themselves and to each other.

The meaning of the presenting problem, as described above, took time to emerge for Tom and Joanne. Accepting the new systemic reframe, that the ISD served to protect both of them from painful emotional issues, took many months and the intensive exploration of family-of-origin issues. It was equally hard for both of them to come to grips with Tom's investment in the problem until he began to talk about his insecurities and vulnerabilities This therapeutic step was dependent first upon Tom becoming "visible" in the therapy and then upon the couple's acceptance of joint responsibility. Their emerging understanding of circular causality and their realization of the importance of ascribed meaning helped them focus on the meanings they were attributing to particular events and experiences.

Joanne's attitudes had been shaped largely by the traditional Catholic view of sexual pleasure and the implications of this view for the role of sex in a marital relationship. In addition, as a young woman, Joanne had wanted to be a nun. Not achieving this goal had a profound impact on her life and most certainly on her marriage.

Solutions Attempted

Joanne had initiated individual therapy four years earlier because of the sexual problem and the guilt she felt for being the cause. She initiated therapy at that time ostensibly because Tom had completely stopped expressing sexual interest. Consequently, she began to fear that he was having an affair and that she would lose him. That therapy lasted one and a half years and was reported to be very helpful. To some extent, the therapy was focused on desensitizing Joanne to her own body, self pleasuring, and working with sensate focus.

Tom joined that therapy only periodically. The predominant focus was to enable Joanne to look at her life experiences more realistically and to understand their impact on her life in the present. Joanne's major problem with bulimia emerged in that therapy and she transferred to another therapist, a woman, who specialized in the treatment of eating disorders. That change proved to be an even more positive therapeutic experience. Although it was extremely difficult, it was during that therapy that Joanne acknowledged, for the first time in her life, the deeply imbedded, intense rage she felt for her mother. She came to see more clearly the negative aspects of her life that she had repressed and, therefore, had never owned as a part of herself.

Significant progress in this therapy occurred both in terms of family-of-origin work and symptomatic relief of bulimia. Issues of control were predominant in the therapy, and Joanne was taking major steps in taking control of her relationship with her mother. That new responsibility allowed Joanne to need and take less of a controlling posture in the other significant relationships in her life, specifically with Tom. Once again, Tom was only an adjunct in that therapy, receiving no special attention for himself and his own needs. The focus on the sexual problem had fallen by the wayside, because both Tom and Joanne recognized the emotional imperative to confront the negative impact of Joanne's relationship with her mother. That was accepted because it was clear to both of them that the therapy was critically important for Joanne and she was changing in very important ways. When therapy ended, because of the death of the therapist's husband, the therapist made the referral to me with the specific goal of focusing on the marriage.

Changes Sought by Clients

Tom and Joanne presented as wanting resolution of their sexual difficulties and as seeking a normal, mutually satisfying sexual relationship. As with most issues in the therapy, Joanne was more outspoken about her desire for this goal than was Tom. They were both sincere, not only in their wish for the fulfillment of this treatment goal, but also in their emotional ambivalence about how this change would happen and what its impact would be on their relationship. They did not focus on any other relationship difficulties as presenting problems or as treatment goals. Only as the therapy proceeded did it become painfully clear that other difficulties present in their relationship had to be addressed if they were to make any gains in their sexual relationship.

Recent Significant Changes

At the time of initiating therapy with me there had not been any significant life stressors for this couple. As stated above, their initiation of marital therapy at the particular time that it occurred was due to the inability of Joanne's therapist to continue working with her and the obvious need to focus on relationship issues if any further progress were to be made. During the course of the marital therapy, numerous stressors and life cycle events occurred, which they weathered fairly well. In certain cases, the external events were precipitants for growth.

Family of Origin—Joanne

Joanne is an only child. Her parents had significant marital problems and separated when she was 10 years old. Mother depicted father as "no good," even though Joanne never saw the arguments, beatings, and drunken binges that her mother claimed occurred. When her father was home, the atmosphere was very tense and Joanne preferred it when he was on the road. She does report that her father did try to have a relationship with her, but because of her mother's negative portrayal of him, Joanne completely rejected her father. This led to a complete cutoff after the marital separation, until Joanne initiated contact a few years ago, one and half years before her father's death.

During the marriage and after separating, Joanne's mother was involved with a married man whom she met while her husband was in the army, just before Joanne was born. At some point, her mother told her that the man was, in fact, her biological father and Joanne was happy to believe it. That relationship was a constant in Joanne's life, but certainly strange in many ways. The affair became more open after the separation, but never became a committed relationship, even after the man's wife died. Spending time in the household as if it were a family, he served as a father figure for Joanne, who remembers enjoying his presence despite the arguments and bickering that spilled over onto her.

Joanne later found out that the mother's claim about this man was a lie and that the man she had known as her father was truly her biological father. The discussion of Joanne's realization that her mother had robbed her of a relationship with her father emerged, along with the realization of deeply felt rage at her mother for the constant manipulation and control she experienced in her childhood. Both issues generated deeply painful, emotional responses during the therapy.

Joanne described her mother as "nosy, domineering, critical, and smother-ing." She described her father as a nice man, once she had gotten to know him towards the end of his life. Her mother's lover seemed to leave no long lasting impression on her in her adulthood. He was a shadowy figure who had another life, another family, and shady business dealings. He was a "sugar daddy who could not be counted on." In the end, he did not matter to her.

Joanne never resisted her mother's manipulative, narcissistic, self-serving control until she came to the painful realization with her individual therapist that her childhood was a "nightmare." The repression of this reality was quite pervasive and the acknowledgement of it came to her as an emotional flood. Due to her mother's continued attempts to control Joanne and Joanne's intense rage and vulnerability, the individual therapist guided her through a renego-tiation of the relationship by helping her set limits and boundaries. Joanne did that in written form because of her fear of verbal confrontation. The letters enabled Joanne to say what she needed to say from a safe distance and in manageable steps.

Although her mother was not religious, Joanne was sent to Catholic school. Inspired by her exposure to nuns and the religious life, Joanne felt called to a life of religious service in dedication to G-d and spent three years with a missionary order preparing to become a nun. At the end of that time, however, she was counseled to leave the order because "she had so much love to give that she should give it to a family." Joanne reported that she did not really understand why she was turned away, but acknowledged that she had begun to sneak food from the kitchen. Although she believed that the nuns did not know about the behavior, it was certainly a sign to her that something was not right. At that time, she could not accept that it may have meant that she was not suited for a religious life. For her, the failure of not becoming a nun was the biggest disappointment in her life, and represented a punishment and/or rejection by G-d.

Joanne went home to her mother and started to work and date. Mother was the same as always, controlling, critical, manipulative, and intrusive. Joanne did anything she could to be more separate and distant, but it was difficult to do so with her financial limitations. The ironic twist to Joanne's return home was her mother's constant allegations of sexual misconduct, when, in fact, Joanne was not sexually active until marriage. Rather, it was her mother who had been "cheating" with another man for decades. Joanne took her situation in stride, as she had been trained to do, for the sake of her psychological survival.

Joanne met Tom, a friend of a friend, a few years later. Her words to describe her impressions of him were, "polite, gentle, and macho; a gentleman, not a sissy." She was "comfortable with him, talked about everything, and shared religious feelings." She saw him as the "neatest guy in the world." She fell in love at first meeting, felt that he was sexually attractive, and they were married within two years. Children came right away, and so did the sexual inhibition.

Joanne married the opposite of her mother—someone who would put up with the controlling and critical parts of her that were like her mother.

Family of Origin—Tom

Tom comes from a poor, rural, steelworker family, one of eight siblings. They lived in a home with only two bedrooms. The males slept in one room and the females in the other room. He is unclear how his parents engaged in sex. He recalls his father knocking on the door of the females' bedroom and often being turned away. Lots of turmoil characterized his parents' marriage. Although he does not remember their arguments, Tom knows they were often about his father's drinking. He does not remember any violence, although his siblings report that there was. It was a poor life, with no vacations and few conveniences.

Nevertheless, it was not completely bleak; Tom reports good feelings about the family life with his mother and siblings. Striking about Tom's situation are his descriptions of coping with the cramped conditions by sitting at the table reading, doing his homework, etc., while being able to shut out the noise and chaos in order to concentrate. This mechanism of withdrawing into himself as a means of coping and self-preservation, while being able to concentrate on the task at hand, continues to characterize Tom today.

Three siblings are single and three are married; most of them never left the hometown. Tom is the only member of the family who moved away, went to college for a profession,and established a comfortable middle-class life style. The accomplishment seemed significant, even though Tom didn't see it as such. Family-of-origin issues came up frequently in the marriage because of the varied demands of his large family, including a brother who dropped in and out of their household and family events that took them back to his hometown periodically.

Prior to meeting Joanne, Tom had a short, tumultuous marriage that was obviously a mistake and was later annulled. He reports the same positive feelings about Joanne upon meeting her as she reports about him. He described her as "very sincere, warm, made me feel important, nice, friendly." The sexual feelings were there, but not brought to fruition because of their religious convictions. They seemed to have a strong, emotionally engaged relationship. For Tom, Joanne's outgoing, vivacious personality certainly made him feel important, and got him out of his standard mode of coping by withdrawing into himself and being invisible. Already primed for coping and adaptation, he easily slipped into accommodating to her needs and ignoring his own.

After getting married, Joanne put on the pressure to have a baby. After the baby, Tom was traveling a lot for his new job, which they hoped would ultimately become a stable, well-paid position. Tom's lack of availability to help Joanne with childcare generated resentment, but it also provided the opportunity for the sexual distance that Joanne wanted. As soon as he came home, Tom was sent out to do the grocery shopping, and as soon as he was in bed, there was avoidance of any sexual reunion. As described above, due to his fear of potential sexual violence, and his automatic coping mechanism of withdrawal, Tom backed off from initiating sex or even from feeling bad about the absence of physical affection in his marriage.

Intersystem Assessment

Individual system—Joanne

Diagnostically, it was evident that Joanne would receive the diagnoses of Inhibited Sexual Desire, Axis I—302.71 and Bulimia, Axis I—307.51. One year into marital therapy, when the obsessive preoccupation with food resurfaced, Joanne was referred for a psychiatric evaluation. At that time, the differential diagnosis (or concurrent diagnosis) of depression was explored and Joanne was placed on antidepressant medication, which helped her a great deal. It is not unusual for there to be an underlying depression in cases of eating disorders.

Although Joanne's interest in joining a religious order when younger was genuine, it also seems reasonable to connect her desire to be a nun with her need for a loving home and family. She also needed, although she did not realize it at the time, someone, something, more powerful than her mother to get her away from her mother's control over her life. She also needed unconditional love and she certainly viewed G-d as loving her, and vice versa. G-d has certainly served as her father in heaven and on earth and filled this void in her life. As a nun, the relationship would have been framed as a marriage complete with the symbolism of a wedding ring. She spoke of this with great emotional intensity when telling me about her great disappointment when she was asked to leave the convent.

Hearing her describe the rejection from the convent brought to mind the sense that she had married her second choice because her first love (G-d) had rejected her. Although this emerged for me as a metaphor for her dilemma, I never referred to it in the therapy, in quite this way, because I thought that she would hear it as a diminution of her religious feelings. Nonetheless, it did have the ring of emotional truth to me, and it helped me conceptualize the sexual problem in relational terms.

From whatever vantage point we understand Joanne, one cannot avoid the complexity of working with the juxtaposition of her family-of-origin dysfunction, her particular defensive pattern, and her deep and abiding faith in G-d and Catholicism.

Individual system—Tom

Tom is certainly a complementary match for Joanne. For all of her complexity, he is fairly straightforward. As a consequence of his defensive style of withdrawal, he has repressed his feelings and almost any awareness of his emotional needs. This developed as his primary psychological defense because his emotional needs were rarely met as a child. In order to survive and not experience constant pain and disappointment, he was best served by repressing his feelings and needs. Learning to concentrate on the task at hand certainly helped him to do well in school and "get out" of the family-of-origin system. Therefore, there is not much to say about him, because there is not much that I knew about him until the final stage of therapy. In fact, there was not much that he knew about himself. However, it is certainly possible that Tom was more aware of his inner self than was readily apparent, and that what I was seeing was his unwillingness to articulate his thoughts and feelings. Even when it was safer for him to communicate about himself and I had approached him in many different ways, he could not do it unless I was feeding him questions.

Tom's unwillingness and inability to talk about himself and share of himself during much of the therapy made it hard to diagnose him. He did not fall into any of the major categories, except, V Code—Marital Problem—V61.10. The only possibility that exists for describing Tom diagnostically is to say that he has some "dependent features" of the Dependent Personality Disorder—specifically, that he subordinates his own needs to those of a person on whom he depends in order to avoid any possibility of having to rely on himself, tolerates abuse, and lacks self confidence. While this may be true in the marriage, Tom is much more independent, self-reliant, and even self-confident in the world of work.

Except for outward appearances, this confident, competent person within the domain of work is not the same person who came in with Joanne for marital therapy. When asked about this discrepancy early in therapy, Tom acknowledged, without a great deal of upset, the schism within himself and explained that this is the way it had to be for Joanne to get the help she needed for her sake and for the sake of the marriage. He did not see himself as needing a whole lot until the changes that occurred in the final stage of therapy. The schism was most apparent when we were focusing on tasks, decision-making, assertiveness, etc. In the emotional realm, Tom was just as out of touch with himself at work as he was at home.

While it is a possibility that Tom could have been sexual with another woman, at least functionally if not satisfactorily, Joanne's inhibition, painful and rejecting as it was, served him well by protecting him from facing his own deep insecurities and anxieties. He felt the pain of his insecurities, but he never had to test whether or not they were true. His fear was that if tested, he would find out that he was not attractive, a poor lover, and therefore worthy only of rejection. Tom entered the marriage with these deeply imbedded and hidden feelings.

Interactional system

Other than being young and in love, Tom and Joanne came to the marriage with unresolved family-of-origin issues and emotional baggage from other life experiences. The match was a match made in heaven, so to speak. Joanne needed to be taken away from her mother and provided for. She needed a kind man who would be nice to her and be there for her, forever, no matter what. She needed someone who could accommodate to her in her needs for control, distance, and reassurance. She needed someone who wouldn't challenge her fundamental relationship to G-d, and who would be undemanding sexually. In all these ways, Tom took care of Joanne and accommodated to her control issues and symptoms.

Joanne, in turn, took Tom out of small-town U.S.A. and made him feel important. Being with Joanne was congruent with his early childhood training of accommodation and self-denial, which served to spare him from the challenge of relating. In exchange, Tom's insecurities were conveniently masked by Joanne's more serious problems, so he got to look good and leave his insecurities unchallenged. All of this formed the basis for the emotional contract of mutual love, devotion, and loyalty; mutual protection against external dangers like alcoholism, overt conflict, marital disintegration; mutual protection against the exposure of deeply imbedded feelings and needs; and the ability to stay as they were without the challenge to change, i.e., she could be controlling and critical (in a nice way), and he could be accommodating and emotionally withdrawn while physically present.

Their communication style followed the same pattern of "mutual protection" against the pain and the threat of change. Joanne was more forthcoming and communicative about her needs. Her engaging personality and sense of humor made this palatable. Tom was more guarded, uncommunicative about his needs, but articulate about the myriad of ways in which he accommodated. His pleasant, friendly manner and genuine caring for Joanne made this more palatable. They astutely avoided direct expressions of anger and subverted all direct conflict. It took many months before they were able to have an argument in the therapy session, and even more time before they could fight at home without fearing that their delicate balance would disintegrate. Many individual and interactional shifts had to take place before they could express anger and engage in a joint struggle over an issue. This possibility then paved the way for greater intimacy and trust.

From the pattern described above, it is easy to understand why some of the typical tactics of couples in conflict were not present for Tom and Joanne. They rarely blamed or vilified each other. There was no brinkmanship, with threats of lawyers or divorce. Although they had polarized roles, they never argued over who was right or wrong, or who would win and get his or her own way. All of this was predetermined by their fundamental emotional contract. While they appeared to function in a satisfactory manner, and to be responsive to each other's needs beyond the specific problem areas, their apparent interdependence (i.e., the amicable ways in which they worked together to deal with life) actually masked an unhealthy interdependence (namely, the joint effort to block awareness of each other's needs).

Their conflict avoidance, as evidenced by the lack of these destructive tactics, provides another explanation for the sexual problem of inhibited sexual desire. The psychodynamic and intergenerational explanations for the etiology of the problem are provided above. The interactional explanation is imbedded in their conflict avoidance and polite, cautious manner with each other. Along with their repressed and inhibited expressions of anger were their repressed and inhibited expressions of all strong affect, including desire and passion. The result was an emotional whitewash of the entire relationship, which was incompatible with the energy and tension of sexual attraction. The dynamic is reciprocal, i.e., the lack of sexual involvement suppresses the emotional life of the relationship and the suppression of affect within the relationship inhibits sexual interest. It was clear that a change had to be made in this vicious cycle.

By dividing life into inside the home and outside the home, Tom and Joanne managed to avoid conflict in their decision making. They were actually fairly compatible on the big decisions. The smaller decisions they divided up according to traditional roles. This process was not challenged until Tom began to articulate his unhappiness with not being involved more in the day-to-day life of the children.

Intergenerational system

The unresolved emotional issues stemming from childhood experiences in their respective families are discussed above, within the framework of intrapsychic functioning, defense mechanisms, and psychological adaptation. In this section, the same childhood experiences have different meanings within the framework of the family system and the intergenerational sequelae. Tom and Joanne did not, in either case, recreate the marriages of their parents. Both, in fact, have consciously rejected the role models of their parents. In many ways they have actually succeeded in creating a different marital system, but while intact as a couple unit and cooperative as partners in the venture of caring for their children, they have had significant problems in the domain of intimacy, sexuality, trust, and mutual caretaking, which were the predominant limitations in their families of origin. The differences lie mainly in how the issues get played out.

Inhibited sexual desire protects them both from the threat of intimacy, be it emotional or physical. The threat of intimacy encompasses not only the fear that the other person will be rejecting or abandoning, but also that the closeness would generate strong emotional reactions, be they passion, neediness, or anger. Joanne's ISD, her bulimia, and her mother have "kept her plate full" and have effectively shut out Tom. Being the nice guy that he is, Tom could be nothing else but supportive (which in his view means non-demanding, self denying, disconnected) when Joanne is dealing with so much difficulty and pain. The need for control that serves as Joanne's predominant adaptive strategy stemming from her family of origin keeps Tom out of a collaborative effort to negotiate life, while the withdrawal into self that serves as Tom's predominant adaptive strategy stemming from his family of origin enables him to tolerate the distance and demands set up by Joanne's problems. Tom's passive posture, which is what Joanne ostensibly wants when she places demands on him, also serves to generate feelings of contempt for him. These feelings of contempt keep Tom distant and unwilling, even if he were able, to be more emotionally available and more engaged. This interactional pattern describes the unhealthy interdependence that has kept the marital system together but dysfunctional. It appears as if they are taking care of each other's needs, but in fact they are denying their deeper needs in order to sustain the status quo, the only way they know to be with each other.

Gender-Determined Behaviors

The sexual drama played out in a rather stereotypical gender-based manner. Joanne withdrew sex, predominantly for her own deeply imbedded psychological reasons, but also, as the therapy bore out, because Tom was invisible to her. To whatever extent that they were sexually involved, Tom approached Joanne tentatively due to his own insecurities. The bottom line, once Joanne could admit it, was that she saw him as a poor lover. Religious beliefs made it hard for her to reconcile within herself the needs she was experiencing for more satisfying sex. The result was that it took a long time to bring these issues out into the open.

It is also true that the repression of anger and the avoidance of conflict short circuited their sexual arousal. This was clearly their style. While the shutdown was going on for both partners and each enjoyed the relative benefits of the safety provided by lack of sexual contact, Joanne took on the stereotypical role of the woman with ISD. In this way, she took care of both of them. When Tom finally admitted to his own naivete and insecurity, the bubble was burst and they had to share the problem.

TREATMENT

Hypotheses

From an intrapsychic perspective, Joanne was in the constant pursuit of gaining control over her life as a repetition compulsion of her attempts to escape the control of her mother. However, no matter how much control Joanne actually exerted, she never experienced being in control and therefore had to demand more. The need for control was also the outward manifestation of unacceptable and frightening feelings and impulses. From an interactional perspective, much of what Joanne wanted was actually congruent with Tom's family-of-origin experience, i.e., social isolation, accommodation to avoid conflict, and self-protective invisibility.

The parallel experience for Tom was the repetition compulsion to find someone who would finally "take care of him." This deeply felt need was doomed to be frustrated by his marriage to someone who needed distance from him as a way of maintaining her sense of self, and by his characteristic pattern of putting other people's needs first. From an interactional point of view, this pattern suited Joanne, who needed to have her needs put first. By continuing the lifelong pattern of "not being taken care of," Tom could fall back on his old familiar coping mechanism of withdrawal into self, which is the only way he knew how to feel safe. Joanne's inability/refusal to pay attention to Tom's needs gave him good reason to find refuge in the safe place within himself.

Seems like a perfect match! But, things are not always as they appear. What looked like accommodation, dependency, and invisibility actually enabled Tom to be in control, distant and safe. Joanne, knowing this, was driven to control what she could not even emotionally touch. His withdrawal served to fuel her ever-increasing demands and, of course, her demands and sexual rejection fueled his withdrawal. The only impetus to get out of this vicious cycle arose from Joanne's feelings of guilt and shame over how she was treating him. In order for something different to happen, Tom had to begin to take responsibility for himself and to stop acting only in response to Joanne. Then Joanne could stop acting in response to him and start taking responsibility for herself.

From the perspective of the couple, they saw Joanne as "sick," coping with a lot, and therefore "unable" to respond to Tom's needs. They attributed to Tom the perception that he was a "nice" guy who would do anything to help Joanne.

Based on these attributions, they shared the belief and made the prediction that things would get better. This process is called interactive constructivism and reflects the jointly created perceptions of the partners as individuals and of their roles in the marriage. In reality, the nature of these attributions could not have predicted any other outcome but a dysfunctional relationship. Viewing Joanne as "sick" continually reinforced her self-centered need for control and lack of responsibility for the marriage, and viewing Tom as "nice" continually reinforced his invisibility and lack of responsibility for the marriage. When things did not get better, and Joanne's fear of losing Tom and her guilt for how she was treating him became too intense, they came for help. More accurate attributions as to how they were really functioning, and more accurate predictions based on greater interpersonal knowledge, paved the way for significant changes in the couple relationship. Coming to grips with their need to protect each other from experiencing their deeply imbedded fears, vulnerabilities, needs, and desire for love and connection offered the couple a new and more emotionally congruent way of understanding themselves and each other. Coming to view their relational difficulties as manifestations of all the contributing factors creating the need for "mutual protection" enabled them to view the relationship with different interpretations, attributions, and predictions. In so doing, they changed the fundamental nature of their relationship.

Conceptualizing the multiple interactive influences in their lives that led to the problems they were experiencing made it painfully clear how deeply they needed to protect their vulnerable feelings of love, affection, desire, need, and longing. For Joanne, the blocks, i.e., her defense mechanisms, were fighting against such strong impulses that she actually became symptomatic to the point of developing bulimia and ISD. For Tom, the block expressed itself as accommodation and dependency. They both feared their anger because of the underlying rage and pain that fueled it, and therefore gave it no opportunity for expression, even at the expense of their happiness.

Treatment Plan and Strategies

Problem #1: Inhibited sexual desire.

    Change Strategies:

        Exploration of religious issues and religious context for sex therapy—Getting PERMISSION to be sexual and experience pleasure (INDIVIDUAL–INTERGENERATIONAL–INTERACTIONAL).

        Sensate Focus Program for the couple (INTERACTIONAL).

        Body exploration and self-pleasuring training for the wife (INDIVIDUAL).

Exploration of sexual issues and self-concept for the husband
(INDIVIDUAL-INTERGENERATIONAL).

Sexual Genogram—family learnings and legacies
(INTERGENERATIONAL).

Bibliotherapy—*For Yourself* (Barbach, 1976); *For Each Other*
(Barbach, 1982); *My Secret Garden* (Friday, 1973)
(INDIVIDUAL-INTERACTIONAL).

Problem #2: Dysfunctional communication.

Change Strategies:

Establishing a joint agenda for the couple, i.e., creating a
shared view of the following: (1) sexual problem is a
shared problem, (2) both partners' needs are equally
important in the problem solving and negotiation process, and (3) both partners' need for support, related to
individual issues, is equally valid (INTERACTIONAL).

Fostering communication about anything with any meaning
to the couple and engaging both partners in as balanced
a way as possible (INTERACTIONAL).

Facilitating the husband's expression of personal difficulties, including work, extended family, social
(INDIVIDUAL-INTERACTIONAL).

Facilitating the husband's awareness and expression of dissatisfactions with the marriage as a counterbalancing weight to the
wife's dissatisfactions, in order to make her equally accountable for change (INTERACTIONAL-INDIVIDUAL).

Fostering emotional awareness and affective expression by
working towards congruence between affect and verbal
content (INDIVIDUAL-INTERACTIONAL).

Facilitating verbal arguments with expressions of anger
congruent with verbal material (INTERACTIONAL).

Heightening affect to access underlying feelings and then focusing the emerging feelings on the appropriate family-of-
origin/historical material (INTERACTIONAL–
INTERGENERATIONAL).

Renegotiation of marital interaction (INTERACTIONAL).

Problem #3: Family and social relationships.

Change Strategies:

Renegotiation of relationships with children
(INTERACTIONAL-INTERGENERATIONAL).

Renegotiation of relationships with extended family—reestablishing connections with husband's family—clarifying

relationship with wife's mother (INTERAC-
TIONAL–INTERGENERATIONAL).

Renegotiation of social relationships—building friendships
(INTERACTIONAL).

Problem #4: Eating disorder (wife).

Change Strategies:

Referral to Overeaters Anonymous (INDIVIDUAL).

Negotiation within the marriage of how the husband can
help the wife with this problem at home
(INTERACTIONAL).

Fostering open communication and affective expression
(INDIVIDUAL–INTERACTIONAL–
INTERGENERATIONAL).

Facilitating expression of anger/rage (INTERACTIONAL-
INDIVIDUAL).

Neutralizing the power struggle for control in the marriage
(INTERACTIONAL–INTERGENERATIONAL).

Referral for psychiatric evaluation—Rule out depression—
medication (INDIVIDUAL).

The treatment plan presented above outlines the broad framework of the
couple's therapy. Due to the need for a concise account that best presents the
Intersystem Model, problem areas #3 and #4 will not be discussed at length.
The role of therapeutic intervention in those areas was important in the big
picture and they will be referred to in order for the reader to be able to track the
progression of issues within the therapeutic process, but the primary focus of
the discussion will be the Intersystem approach to problem areas #1 and #2.

Treatment Process

While the treatment strategies described above were all utilized in the
therapy over a two-year period, they did not necessarily occur in the order
outlined above, nor did they take equivalent amounts of time, nor did they
occur in discrete units. Everything was on the therapeutic agenda simultaneously. As stated in Chapter 1, the therapist "thinks about the client system
at multiple levels while directing the treatment at one issue at a time."

The overarching treatment goal was to get Tom onto Joanne's "plate." The
metaphor of the "plate" which Joanne brought from her individual therapy
worked well as the systemic reframe for the couple. Striving to be "on the plate
together" meant viewing each other as equally important in the process of
working on their marriage and, at the very least, meant confronting their

mutual responsibility for their individual and joint well-being. Helping them achieve healthy interdependence required many individual and interactional shifts. Their lack of blaming and basic accommodation to the process enabled the therapy to proceed based on the principles of affirmation paradox.

The predominant issue during the early stage of therapy with Tom and Joanne was the "permission to be sexual." It is common sense to say that without it the therapy would have been directionless and any attempt to address the sexual problems would have been met with overt and covert resistance, if not alienation from therapy. It was also true that Joanne had to tell me how to gain this permission. In order to be truly congruent with the couple and to co-create a meaningful change process, I needed to know not only Joanne's personal history with her faith, childhood experiences, etc., but also the generally accepted theological position (which seemed not to be clear cut), her view of the theological position (which was confused and guilt ridden), what attempts she had made for clarification (unfortunately, there were conflicting views), and what path was possible to gain clarification and, therefore, permission. She had already heard priests in various contexts, which was part of the confusion, but most importantly, it seemed in our discussion that the priest's word was not as meaningful to her as was G-d's word.

An exploration of Joanne's faith in G-d and what she truly believed was His intention about human sexuality, pleasure, and marriage brought to the surface her experiences in the convent and her profound disappointment with the rejection from the religious life. It is difficult to describe Joanne's face while she talked about her love of G-d and her desire to serve Him and be wed to Him as a nun. Marriage to a man was obviously secondary to this ultimate experience. At the same time, her love of G-d and her view of His love of people led her to articulate the belief that G-d had given and granted pleasure to people in order for them to sanctify and to enjoy their marriages.

During the time we discussed these issues, the image of "another man" came into view as a metaphorical encapsulation of the conflicted emotions that were very apparent. It was after this discussion that I asked her if we had permission to work on bringing sexual pleasure to her relationship with Tom. She said and felt that we had permission. And we did! Never again in the therapy did Joanne question the appropriateness of the sex therapy and never did she experience guilt about self-pleasuring, which she had come to view as a necessary aspect of the treatment, nor guilt about sexual pleasure,which she had come to view as G-d's blessing. With religious permission to pursue the sex therapy, the difficulties that arose in response to the exercises could then be viewed in psychological, emotional, cognitive,and behavioral terms, and could then be treated from whatever vantage point was deemed to have the greatest potential of succeeding.

The only residual problem was the reality that Tom was Joanne's second choice and that he always would be. I also found out that she did not think of him as attractive any longer. While the analogy of "another man" really does not hold, it is fair to say that it stuck with me and seemed to fit the difficulty of revitalizing the sexual life of a woman who could not be with "her lover" and who could not deal with her ambivalent feelings towards her husband. In many ways, ISD was the perfect solution. Tom's withdrawal in response to her rejection fueled the problem.

When this was probed further, it became apparent that Tom had his own sexual problems. Tom admitted to feeling insecure sexually, that he was inexperienced when he married, and that his approach to her has always been awkward, hesitating, and cautious. He also had no sense of romance, and Joanne needed romance even more than she needed physical contact. It did seem to be a matter of trying to help her fall in love with him sexually, as well as to wake him up! Putting their joint responsibility for the existence of the problem, and for its solution, on the table made it easier to understand the ISD as a means of mutual protection as well as self defense. This acknowledgement enabled Joanne to feel less guilty and less deviant and enabled Tom to feel less victimized and less frightened.

Another issue that dominated the early stage of the therapy was clarifying and coming to a common agreement about what was "on the plate." Joanne has had a large number of personal difficulties and life events to sort through, which is why she and her former therapist coined the phrase, "My plate is full." Once in marital therapy, it was absolutely necessary for Tom to jump on the plate before they could work on their joint problems. Moreover, for a long time, the operational view of the marriage placed Joanne as "the patient" who has always needed "help" and Tom as the partner who has always been okay. In order to equalize their engagement in the therapeutic process for addressing their sexual and marital problems, they needed to accept joint responsibility for the problems and their solutions. Because of the historical imbalance, it took some time for both Tom and Joanne to accept Tom as a working partner, entitled to compassion, understanding, and support for his personal needs and desires.

Within the first two months of the therapy, the sex therapy began with sensate focus exercises that were specifically designed to be safe and as anxiety-free as possible. The Med-Pro Productions (1976) sex therapy video series, Sensate Focus I–IV, was utilized in the therapeutic sessions. Tom and Joanne were generally cooperative, but we had to take the increments in the exercises very slowly, and we took many detours into individual, marital, and family-of-origin issues, an expected route considering the complexities of their "interrelated systems." Concurrent with the relationship focus of the sensate focus program, Joanne worked on exploring her body and becoming comfortable with self-pleasuring. There were many rationales for this work including (1) expanding behavioral options; (2) desensitizing herself to touch and thereby having greater receptivity to Tom's touch; (3) overcoming the sexual inhibition, first in private, where she would have complete control and mastery over the experience; and (4) fostering an appreciation of the pleasure that is part of sexual expression.

Joanne worked well with the Lopiccollo and Heiman (1976) films entitled *Becoming Orgasmic*. We worked back and forth between these two behaviorally oriented sex therapy programs. The assigned books about male and female sexuality, which Joanne read selectively, did not seem to have a significant impact. Careful contracting of each sensate focus exercise was critical, due to the many overt issues related to Joanne's sexual shutdown. Careful contracting was also essential because of their individual insecurities and anxieties. Frequency remained an issue throughout. They would engage in one definite and one optional sensate focus exercise session each week, depending predominantly on the children's presence in the house. Joanne much preferred a time during the weekend when the children were with friends or involved in activities. However, while Joanne's need for complete privacy was very rigid in the beginning, she did become more comfortable as time went on to engage sexually during other times of the week. Even with the increased flexibility, however, she persisted in preferring times when the children would not be home if this was at all possible.

The next challenge became to facilitate access to their sexual, erotic, passionate feelings and desires. Towards this end, we pursued romance and sexual fantasy. By romance, I mean the engagement in romantic experiences that were separate from any kind of actual sexual contact, but stimulated feelings of love, affection, sexual desire, and anticipation. This included special celebrations, nice dinners in quaint restaurants, candlelit dinners, holding the chair for her, holding the door open for her, flowers, etc. Joanne specifically proposed each of these activities, which Tom readily agreed to, except that at first he really did not know how to "do them right." This was not a matter of resistance. He really did not know how to bring a sense of romance to a quaint dinner, etc., so he had to be taught with Joanne and me as guides. There was some measure of success, and these "romantic" experiences became enjoyable for them, and creating some measure of increased sexual interest and anticipation.

Despite all the work and guidance, creating romance was difficult for Tom. They accepted this with good humor, and with a little regret on Joanne's part, but did not let this difficulty interfere with their pleasuring exercises. Unfortunately, this particular goal placed a lot of pressure on Tom to change, without a concomitant demand on Joanne. She was pretty good at being demure in the romantic setting and he was not very good at exuding charm. The unequal expectations could have been viewed as unfair, but, in fact, the stereotype that these behaviors represented was very emotionally compelling for both of them, and it was a joint goal to try and bring more romance into the relationship.

Joanne was more successful with the exploration of sexual fantasy than was Tom, and she derived tremendous benefit from it over time. Through fantasy, Joanne was able to access, to experience, and to express sexual interest and sexual pleasure. We began with a discussion of which performers and public figures were attractive to either Tom or Joanne. They were then encouraged to allow themselves to fantasize about these individuals, as a means of accessing and enhancing sexual feelings. The entire experience of fantasizing sexual material, during and not during sexual involvement, was discussed repeatedly and normalized as a common and often helpful experience.

This strategy was enormously liberating for Joanne, helping her to access her sexual desire when she felt blocked. Reading Nancy Friday's (1973) book, *My Secret Garden*, opened a new world for Joanne and she was very excited about it, almost girlish in her enthusiasm. Once again, Tom was compliant, and while he enjoyed the playfulness that was part of this exploration, he never utilized it to any great extent. Seen as the one who did not have the sexual problem, initially he did not experience himself as under any pressure to make changes, except as an accommodation to Joanne. What became obvious, however, was that while Tom was and always had been sexually functional, he has probably always been emotionally flat in his sexual expression. Therefore, I engaged him in a parallel process with Joanne in order to explore what turns "them" on. In so doing, I was facilitating greater congruence within the couple. The ultimate goal of mutual pleasure was dependent on the couple achieving a level of intimacy that could occur only within a more congruent relationship. Another strategy was the exploration of film as a means of stimulating arousal, excitement, and interest. The use of film became part of their routine.

While the sexual issues were addressed throughout the course of the therapy, communication about anything and everything was a constant focus. To accomplish this goal was critical, in order to engage Tom as an active participant in the therapy and in their relationship. The approach was straightforward and basically consisted of asking Tom a lot of questions about himself, his feelings, his thoughts, his beliefs, etc., much as one would do in an intake and or in individual therapy.

Helping them to engage in direct, spontaneous, verbal communication was a gradual process and seemed dependent on working though a number of other issues. Firstly, Tom did not budge on the communication issue until the connection was established to his family of origin and how he had coped with his family by learning to withdraw into himself. He experienced an emotional connection with a memory of himself at the kitchen table doing homework and successfully shutting out the chaos and noise around him. Experiencing how deeply he had buried himself and his needs, and how much he had missed in life, helped convince Tom of the importance of both self-exploration and communication with Joanne. Secondly, although Joanne repeatedly claimed that she did not want to hear about Tom's thoughts and feelings, partially because her plate was full, partially because she did not want anyone making demands of her as her mother had done, and partially because of her need for control, it was also true that she just did not want to be bothered. But, even Joanne had to admit that Tom's invisibility made him unattractive to her and irrelevant in her life, and that some contact with him was better than no contact. She also came to admit that, in fact, she needed contact with him.

Communicating feelings was a much more difficult therapeutic goal, especially the expression of anger. Due to their respective backgrounds and individual psychological makeup, the expression of anger was clearly "dangerous." In spite of the danger, the expression of anger was critically important to the preservation of their marriage in any healthy form. The unexpressed, underlying anger related to the marriage, combined with the unexpressed rage from their childhoods, kept the emotional life of their relationship frozen. Finding appropriate ways to express their anger that would allow for the release of pent-up feelings and even partial resolution of issues was necessary in order for them to gain access to their more vulnerable feelings of pain, neediness, sadness, intimacy, love, and passion.

Recognizing the intrapsychic and interactional barriers to communicating anger clearly and directly, I deliberately allowed Joanne to speak to her husband through me, i.e., by looking at me, not him. Once she did this, I directed her to make the same statement to him, not to me. This she did by looking everywhere else in the room other than at him. She was then directed to say it again and sometimes again, each time with gentle prodding to look at him, which she eventually succeeded in doing.

Once Joanne was able to express her anger directly to Tom, his anger began to emerge and come out more and more directly, and vice versa. Once this change had occurred, it became clear that Tom's accommodating, "helpful" style had contributed to Joanne's sense of guilt about her angry feelings and had reinforced the emotional prison that she had experienced with her mother. Tom's anger freed her to feel "normal" and to express her anger more freely. They could then discuss their vulnerable feelings. They were both able to loosen control over their emotional lives once they came face to face with the "danger" that they had feared and discovered that sharing their feelings with each other actually helped them to feel better and safer within the marriage.

The return of romantic feelings soon followed. At the end of treatment, the couple reported their view that their improved communications was 90 percent of the cure. I certainly agree that communication was at the heart of the therapy. When they ended treatment, they felt closer and knew more about each other than they had ever known before.

Tom and Joanne changed in many ways, and this was most certainly a successful case. While acknowledging that they worked hard and rebuilt their relationship, it is important to note that even with the gains that they made, Joanne never "heard bells" with Tom. I put this in terms of Joanne, because Tom is not the type to hear bells, but Joanne is. This is certainly a systemic issue, and we could say that it takes two to "hear bells." But, taken out of the systemic context for a moment, it was the "lack of bells" for Joanne that made the therapeutic effort even harder.

Underlying the religious issues, the intrapsychic, the intergenerational, and the interactional systems was Joanne's lack of attraction for Tom. Her sexual self was suppressed when she met him and her attraction to him was based on other aspects of him and their relationship together. These kept them together and enabled her to explore her sexual self and discover a deep affection for him, but nothing she described about her feelings and reactions to Tom matched the affective tone that characterized her description of wanting to be a nun.

Nothing in the therapy changed the sense that this life was her second choice, not her first. The situation was entirely different for Tom. He was blocked in many ways, but he was very aware of his sexual attraction to Joanne. His marriage to Joanne was a happy beginning for him that buried his painful past. In spite of entering the marriage from these divergent emotional experiences, Tom and Joanne were able to establish a meaningful and loving relationship.

CONCLUSION

When Tom and Joanne entered treatment, they were two disconnected individuals who were coexisting within a marriage and a family. When therapy ended, they were an interconnected couple with all of the ups and downs of what it means to be a couple. This journey took close to two years and involved almost every aspect of their relationship. ISD was their presenting problem, which turned out to be the tip of the proverbial iceberg, the symptomatic expression of many problems. The early work involved finding permission for sexual pleasure within Joanne's faith that was congruent with her relationship to G-d. A common agenda and joint responsibility for change had to be established and experienced. The primary goal of therapy was engagement, not just sexual, but verbal and affective. As their couplehood emerged, they addressed many significant problem areas in addition to their sexual problem. Their verbal communication improved significantly, and along with learning how to negotiate, they learned how to fight as well as how to achieve a mutually satisfying sexual relationship. There was greater affective awareness, as well as expression, for both. By the end of therapy, they could be mutually supportive. They renegotiated their relationships with their children and extended family, their roles in the home, the extent of their social involvement, and the ways in which they could help each other.

Second-order change was achieved by the working through of a number of pivotal issues. These can be summarized as (1) permission to be sexual, (2) satisfying sexual engagement, (3) joint responsibility, (4) affective verbal communication, (5) trust, (6) softening turf boundaries, (7) negotiating control issues, and (8) making friends. The exploration of family-of-origin issues was essential in the accomplishment of these goals. Individual changes enabled the interactional changes to occur and vice versa.

The changes outlined above reflect work within the three systems of the couple's experience, *the individual, the interactional,* and *the intergenerational. Congruence* with the couple and the experience of trust contributed to the *interactional context* for change. The emphasis on *personal choice* and personal accountability as part of the process of exploration facilitated the experience of *spontaneous compliance.* Helping the couple achieve an interactive pattern of healthy *interdependence* took a long time. The exploration of *interpretation, definition, attribution,* and *prediction* was essential in understanding how Joanne and Tom viewed their relationship. The exploration of the "three systems" was essential in understanding how to *reframe* their marriage based on intergenerational and individual issues. The *systemic reframe* of mutual protection, as opposed to the *attribution* of "sick vs. nice" or "controlling vs. passive," fostered a deeper sense of empathic understanding between the partners and a greater sense of mutual responsibility within the couple.

Coming to grips with their need to protect each other from experiencing their deeply imbedded fears, vulnerabilities, needs and desire for love and connection offered the couple a new and more emotionally congruent way of understanding themselves and each other. Coming to view their relational difficulties as manifestations of all the contributing factors creating the need for "mutual protection" enabled them to view the relationship with different interpretations, attributions, and predictions. The therapeutic pressure on Tom to become "visible" so that Joanne would have to deal with his real feelings and needs successfully created the experience of *interdependence.* The cooperative way in which this couple worked with me and each other, in spite of the strong undercurrent of resistance, enabled me to guide them through the therapy with *affirmation paradox*.

At the end of treatment, there was a strong sense of satisfaction about the gains made, along with some trepidation about the challenge to sustain the gains. It was my sense that many of the changes that Tom and Joanne experienced had changed them forever. Whatever the future would bring, they would approach the issues that arose differently. They changed their present, and in so doing, created a brighter future for themselves and for their children.

CHAPTER 7

Treating Inhibited Sexual Desire: The Intersystem Model

Stephanie Brooks

Inhibited sexual desire (ISD) has become one of the most common presenting problems for which couples seek treatment. The author has found useful the typology suggested by Kaplan (1979) for categorizing this sexual dysfunction. People who have never experienced sexual desire are said to have *primary* ISD. Individuals with *secondary* ISD are those who have experienced desire at some point, but presently have no desire or diminished desire. Individuals with *global* ISD are those who lack desire in all situations and with all partners. Individuals who experience inhibited desire in some situations, or with a specific partner, are said to have *situational* ISD.

The etiology of ISD is multicausal. In general, it can develop as a result of many factors, including past sexual trauma, stress, illness, fear of loss of control or rejection, conflictual relationships, and lack of sex education (Weeks, 1987; Knopf & Seiler, 1990). Other factors that seem to predispose couples to ISD are incompatible levels of desire in the respective partners, being upwardly mobile and achievement-oriented, anxiety regarding sexual performance, depression, strict religious backgrounds, and avoidance of intimacy and commitment (Knopf & Seiler, 1990).

According to Kaplan (1979), only a small number of ISD patients respond to traditional, behaviorally oriented, sex therapy. She suggested a "psycho-sexual" therapy approach as the treatment of choice, a model that combines a psychodynamic approach and behaviorally oriented sex therapy. Knopf and Seiler's (1990) work provides a number of exercises that focus on making personal and relationship changes and sexual enhancement. Although they discuss the impact of intrapsychic and intergenerational issues on ISD, their approach is essentially behavioral.

Leiblum and Rosen's (1988) book, *Sexual Desire Disorders*, offers a comprehensive overview to the assessment and treatment of ISD. In general, it illustrates treatment from psychodynamic and interpersonal perspectives, as well as cognitive-behavioral, systems, and medical frameworks. However, the most integrative approach to treatment described is Lazarus' (1988) Multimodal perspective. He advocates an assessment of strengths and weaknesses, in the following aspects of the individual's lives: *B*ehavioral, *A*ffect, *S*ensation, *I*magery, *C*ognition, *I*nterpersonal relationships, and the use of *D*rugs (BASIC I.D.). His BASIC I.D. approach is similar to the Intersystem Model in that the assessment phase is systematic and multilevel, which enables the therapist to identify barriers within the BASIC I.D. framework and shape specific interventions to meet the particular needs of the clients.

The following case illustrates the Intersystem Model (Weeks, 1987; Weeks, 1989) and how it can be utilized as an approach to treating inhibited sexual desire. It demonstrates the fluidity of the model and its applicability to a variety of presenting problems, including the treatment of sexual dysfunction.

CASE FORMULATION

Cynthia, age 31, and Ricky, age 30, were a young upwardly mobile, middle-class, Caucasian couple who had been married for 14 months when they entered treatment. Both partners were employed as educators in the creative arts. They lived alone, with two dogs, in a large metropolitan area. Initially, Cynthia presented for treatment alone, with complaints of a lack of sexual desire for her husband.

Initial Impression and Reactions

The therapist sensed that Cynthia feared intrusiveness and loss of self in her relationship with Ricky, which led to her seeking distance from him. Ricky, to the contrary, desired closeness and feared rejection, which led him to the desperate pursuit of his partner. This repetitive pattern generally fostered conflict about intimacy, sexuality, and control.

Presenting Problem(s) and History of the Problem

Cynthia came to the first session alone, reporting a history of lack of sexual desire and pleasure, which had resulted in feelings of guilt and in fights with her husband. The guilt stemmed from her belief that she denied Ricky pleasure that he was entitled to; therefore, she was a "bad wife."

At the therapist's request, the two were seen together for the second interview. Ricky reported that he initiated all of their physical intimacy. He attempted to please Cynthia, but frequently "felt like a failure." Over the past few months, he had experienced premature ejaculation, which led to feelings of embarrassment and helplessness. Ricky said he often found himself feeling guilty after requesting sex, but reported having no anger toward his wife. However, he did feel "used and unloved" by her. Four months prior to entering treatment, his requests for sex had escalated, and Cynthia perceived the requests to be abusive, believing that he had insatiable needs. She also reported that Ricky "grabbed" her body, which further angered her and reinforced her avoidant behavior.

Although Cynthia's health was good, she reported a number of somatic complaints—specifically, terrible menstrual cramps, headaches, and chronic fatigue. She was frequently stressed about demands placed upon her at work, which left Ricky to take care of their new home and their two dogs. Cynthia believed that if Ricky "really" cared about her, he would not expect her to keep a spotless house. Ricky worked full-time and attended school part-time, and the responsibility for the care of the house and the dogs contributed to his feelings of being "used."

Sex had been pleasurable and without any problems before they moved in with one another eight months prior to treatment. Cynthia had lived in New York and Ricky had lived in Philadelphia. They had a "commuter relationship" for approximately two and a half years, which helped to maintain a functional equilibrium regarding intimacy. The ISD was maintained by pursuer-distancer behaviors, which increased after they moved in together and after their marriage. For example, when Ricky requested sex or made affectionate overtures toward his wife, he believed he was trying to recreate the pleasure they had in their relationship prior to marriage. Cynthia, in turn, would withdraw from Ricky by becoming angry and complaining of poor health or fatigue. Reciprocally, sometimes when Cynthia felt guilty for not being sexual with her husband, she would initiate sex or some affectionate behavior. At those times, Ricky would respond by becoming angry or critical of her.

Solutions Attempted

Ricky had discussed their problems in his individual therapy with another therapist. At one point in the past, they had agreed not to have intercourse, in order to reduce their anxiety. This contract was short-lived, because Cynthia would approach Ricky and pleasure him by using oral or manual techniques. As a result, Ricky would want intercourse and Cynthia would become angry at him for wanting to break the "contract."

Changes Sought by Clients

The couple desired a pleasurable sexual relationship in which Cynthia would want sex and begin to initiate physical intimacy. They hoped that Ricky would focus on his needs, instead of worrying about pleasuring her. They also wanted to improve their communication skills, because they felt inhibited from being open and honest with each other about their feelings.

Recent Significant Changes—Stressors

Cynthia had moved from New York to Philadelphia eight months prior. Their new identity as a recently married couple posed adjustment difficulties for each of them. Cynthia had recently started a new job, and they had purchased a new home. The couple had an abortion a year prior to marriage, but at the start of treatment Ricky wanted children as soon as possible.

The Individual System

Cynthia used projective identification, denial, and predictions to protect herself. She predicted that she could not please others and that Ricky would be unable to give her pleasure if she allowed herself to be vulnerable. Although she reported that she never had pleasurable intercourse, there was conflicting information about her ability to enjoy sex. Specifically, once Cynthia was past the Desire Phase of the sexual response cycle, she experienced no problems in experiencing pleasure. She had a positive past history of sexual desire and enjoyment with Ricky, as well as with previous lovers. She was thus diagnosed by the therapist as having secondary ISD.

Cynthia projected her feelings of inadequacy and control onto Ricky. Often she felt that Ricky was harsh, unappreciative, and demanding, and that he lacked an understanding of her efforts, and that he was "inadequate" and "controlling." Cynthia disowned her sexual desire and gave up the idea that she could have control over her sexuality. She believed that she was "a sex object" for Ricky, and his pursuit of her for sex reinforced this belief, made him a perfect receptor of her projections, and perpetuated the ISD (cf. Feldman, 1982). When she first began to lack sexual desire, she denied that their was a problem. Specifically, Cynthia failed to understand how her own sexual rejection of Ricky and criticism of him contributed to the ISD and promoted the belief that Ricky was insatiable. Shortly thereafter, she became depressed and consulted her gynecologist.

Ricky also used projective identification and incorrectly interpreted her behavior. He thought that he was not good enough for Cynthia; otherwise, he would be able to take care of her by knowing what she needed. He had a history of feeling shame, inadequacy, and powerlessness when he was with women and interpreted Cynthia's lack of desire to mean that he was unlovable. This had most recently been demonstrated by his recent development of guilt and premature ejaculation while engaging in sex. In this instance, we have an example of the projection of power onto her. Ricky split his self-definition and projected his power outward onto Cynthia and retained the weak, "victim" aspect of his self-definition (cf. Feldman, 1982).

Interactional System

Cynthia and Ricky regularly used attack-defend, and reactive instead of responsive, communication patterns. Whenever they attempted to discuss an issue, it became lost in a series of rationalizations and attributions to justify each of their own behaviors. The following is an example of the attack and defend communication style and the vilification/blaming in this couple: (Husband states to wife:) "*You never want to make love*"; (Wife counters:) "*If you did not grab at me, then perhaps I would be more in the mood.*" An example of their reactive, instead of responsive, communication patterns and their rationalization process is as follows: (Wife states:) "*Why do you pressure me?*"; (Husband states:) "*I don't pressure you*"; (Wife states:) "*I need more space at home*"; (Husband states:) "*We never see each other.*" In both of these exchanges each partner took little or no responsibility to listen and respond, without rationalizing or emotionally responding, to the message of the sender, which impeded their ability to resolve conflict.

Intergenerational System

Cynthia was the youngest of two daughters born to an English/Jewish-German family. Her sister was two years older than she, married with two children, and described as being passive and unable to manage stress. Cynthia had assumed the role of protecting her from family problems, achieving this by minimizing her parents' fights and by forming an exclusive alliance with her mother, which distanced her sister from the conflict.

Cynthia's mother had died 12 years ago, from alcohol-related illnesses. When Cynthia's mother drank, she would become intrusive and clinging. Oftentimes, her mother would awake Cynthia from a sound sleep and proceed to hold or "sit on" her while discussing her distressing marriage. Cynthia's father also drank, but went into a process of recovery after the death of his wife. He disregarded Cynthia while she was a child, and she knew that he had extramarital affairs. All of this impacted upon Cynthia's development of a sense that she had to be in control of what happened in relationships and that men could not be trusted. She believed that people used each other unless you set rigid limits on their behavior.

Cynthia reported that her parents' addiction kept them from providing her with much parental guidance. She became sexually active at age 13, and was attracted to older men. There was a history of date rape by several of those older men, which she reported to her parents. They reportedly did nothing to protect her from those men, which led her to believe that people always took from her and that she had little control. In spite of the lack of parental guidance, Cynthia had an enmeshed relationship with her mother. She was privy to her parents' marital problems and became her mother's confidant. Although she described this as burdensome, she felt protective of her mother as well as close to her. Thus, she became the key figure in family triangles. For example, Cynthia reported that she would often fight with her father after her mother shared painful marital problems with her. Communication flowed through her, as she became the family mediator.

Cynthia received conflicting messages about sex from her family. Her mother said that sex was an obligation women had to their husbands and women should not enjoy it. Yet, she knew that her father was sexually active with many women and had overheard fights between her parents where her father bragged about his girlfriends' enjoyment of sex. Additionally, Cynthia was confused about why her parents did not intervene when she was being sexually abused by men.

Ricky was the youngest of two children born to a German-Jewish family, his sister being four years older. She was described as critical and unsupportive. Ricky's mother had died of cancer 10 years prior to his marriage. She was described as distant, passive, depressed, and overinvolved in her work. Consequently, she was generally unavailable to the family. This was thought to be because of Ricky's father, who was described as critical and demanding. Ricky wished that his mother were more assertive with his father and would have interceded when his father was being critical.

Ricky's disengaged family had little positive emotional expressiveness and few opportunities for intimacy. He often felt excluded from what he described as "the family conflict," which was viewed as the primary means of relating. He became the outsider and the family scapegoat, a shy and sensitive young man who resolved at an early age to have a loving and caring family. He would often find himself in relationships in which he would try to please others in order to receive love. Although he saw himself as having a lot to offer, he was uncertain as to how it would be received, which made him feel powerless and insecure about his competence.

Because of the emotional distance in Ricky's family, he had no memories of how affection was expressed and could not remember anyone ever discussing sex. He, therefore, had fantasies of what a perfect marriage would be like, which included a husband and wife being loving and expressing that love by desiring one another sexually.

The couples' family-of-origin material shaped their initial relationship contract. Cynthia was the parental child and family caregiver, while Ricky came from an emotionally disengaged family. Ricky's unconscious contract with Cynthia was to find someone to fulfill his needs and validate his self-worth. Cynthia's was to find someone who was not needy or demanding, but would "be there for her."

Their contract illustrates the level of mutual dependence the couple had, although Ricky was more outwardly dependent on Cynthia and would often try to change to fulfill her needs. The couple's contract also highlights two critical interactional concepts: since Ricky was looking for someone to validate his self-worth, Cynthia's lack of sexual desire was interpreted as an indication that he was not good enough as a husband; Cynthia, for her part, interpreted Ricky's request for sex and closeness as intrusive, demanding, and selfish. By the relationship definitions, they had each violated the initial relationship contract in that Ricky was perceived as needy and Cynthia was perceived as disapproving.

This interaction set up a rejection/intrusion pattern which served as a distance regulator in the relationship (Napier, 1976). Ricky became anxious when Cynthia would set personal boundaries and minimize his needs, while Cynthia became anxious when Ricky would request reassurance despite her stated need for emotional space.

Gender-Determined Behaviors

Cynthia believed that men were incompetent, passive, and not to be trusted. This developed from her experience with her father, who failed to protect her from her mother's intrusiveness, and failed to protect her from the men who violated her body. She developed an aggressive style of relating to men, demonstrated by her quickness to attack Ricky. She believed that in order to be heard she needed to have a strong presence and be somewhat demanding. Yet, somewhat paradoxically, she also believed that a good wife must always be sexually receptive to her husband, even when she was not interested.

Ricky believed that women were uncaring and cold. This developed primarily from his experience with his mother's preoccupation with work and his critical sister. He avoided conflict in an effort to not recreate his family environment. Thus, he became passive and withdrawn with Cynthia, feeling emasculated by her behavior and by the way Cynthia related to him. He believed a "real" man would have Cynthia's respect, and a "good husband" would also be able to sexually "turn his wife on."

Hypotheses Regarding The Clients

Each partner was acting out early introjects and family-of-origin relationship patterns that led them to recreate similar dynamics in the marriage. Ricky had become intrusive and demanding, like Cynthia's mother. Conversely, when Ricky felt rejected, he became abandoning like Cynthia's father. Cynthia had become cold and distant, like Ricky's mother. However, when Ricky asserted his needs, Cynthia appeared critical, like his father. They had a high level of narcissistic vulnerability which had led to projective identification and avoidant behavior (Feldman, 1982). For example, Ricky was perceived to be selfish and Cynthia was viewed as critical. The ISD was hypothesized as a means for Cynthia to modulate control over her space and body, which began to feel threatened when she moved in with Ricky. The immediate cause was Ricky's pressure for sex, which was rooted in his need to be loved. Cynthia was afraid of losing herself if she committed herself to Ricky, because of her earlier experience of not being able to set boundaries. Distance had become a primary means of protection, but also recreated the "abandonment" they both had experienced in their families of origin.

Treatment Goals

The treatment goals were created with the couple and planned sequentially in order to create a safe and trusting therapeutic environment for the addressing of the relationship issues. By successfully working on some of their misconceptions and attitudes, their belief system and communication problems, we believed that hope would be instilled, their commitment would be reaffirmed, and, therefore, a firm base would be established for the treatment of the ISD.

The specific treatment goals for the couple were as follows: (1) normalize the current problem and dispel the belief that they were sexually "abnormal"; (2) improve communication skills by decreasing their reactivity and increasing their responsivity; (3) improve conflict resolution skills; (4) increase "separateness" but decrease their emotional "distance"; (5) increase understanding of intrapsychic and family-of-origin issues that promoted the need to "create distance" (Cynthia) and "demand closeness" (Ricky); (6) reduce anxiety associated with sexual activity and intimacy; (7) help each of them differentiate from family of origin and enable the couple to create their own family identity, particularly with regards to sexual loyalties; (8) alter myths about sexual roles and behaviors; (9) confront cognitive distortions and irrational thinking about sex and attributions made regarding each others behaviors; (10) improve and enhance sexual pleasure; and (11) enable them to mutually agree to resume sexual intercourse.

Change Strategies

As with the treatment goals, the change strategies were conceptualized in a sequential fashion. The first order of business was to address the interpersonal and behavioral aspects of their relationship. Secondly, the intrapsychic and family-of-origin issues which inhibited their ability to change needed to be resolved. Lastly, the ISD needed to be addressed in a direct fashion.

The change strategies were outlined as follows: (1) the use of in-session communication-behavioral exercises, and insight-oriented techniques to decrease reactivity and increase responsivity (Weeks & Treat, 1992); (2) the use of the Fair Fighting Model, problem solving, and insight-oriented techniques to improve conflict resolution (Weeks & Treat, 1992); (3) the use of insight-oriented, object relations techniques (Scharff & Scharff, 1991) to address their projective identification and narcissistic vulnerability; (4) the use of cognitive therapy techniques to address distortions and irrational thinking (Dattilo & Padesky, 1990); (5) the use of the genogram as a tool to facilitate their understanding of how the family of origin impacted upon both and why they related as they did (McGoldrick & Gerson, 1985); (6) the use of Sensate Focus exercises (Masters & Johnson, 1970) to slowly reintroduce sexuality into their relationship, as a means of facilitating "non-demand pleasuring," and to create a forum for improving sexual expressiveness; (7) the use of bibliotherapy (e.g., Barbach, 1975, 1982; Zilbergeld, 1978) to increase their sexual education.

TREATMENT

Cynthia and Ricky were in treatment for a year and two months. Cynthia came to the first session alone because she thought there was something deficient about her because of her sexual problem. Cynthia was a petite woman who showed incredible emotional restraint as she reported her difficulties in the marriage and her very painful family/relationship history. Prior to seeking therapy, she had consulted several friends about her dilemma, as well as her gynecologist.

Her gynecologist found nothing physically wrong, which further added to her distress. She also found no answers from friends, but took their advice and entered therapy. Cynthia was relieved to hear that her sexual problem was not unusual (i.e., a normalization of the problem) and that therapy might prove to be helpful (i.e., the problem redefined as "solvable"). The latter part of the initial session was spent on discussing the importance of inviting her husband to join us, as he was feeling angry and alienated. The therapist communicated that Ricky's presence would be critical because a significant portion of the ISD was perceived to be related to the couples interaction (i.e., problem reframed from an individual issue to a couple problem).

Ricky eagerly accepted our invitation to become involved in conjoint sessions. At this point in the process, the therapist had four goals she wished to accomplish: (1) to provide Ricky and Cynthia with the opportunity to express directly their feelings and their thoughts; (2) to observe how the couple coped with the ISD; (3) to assess the marital relationship; (4) to test the initial hypothesis that couple's therapy was the most appropriate treatment modality.

A good deal of time was spent on eliciting Ricky's story and trying to ease his obvious anxiety. He presented as a nervous young man, and expressed helplessness and a sense of hopelessness. Ricky thought he was causing the problem, since their sex life was apparently problem-free before Cynthia moved to Philadelphia. He angrily stated that he needed to have sex and wanted to know how Cynthia could expect him to function without regular intercourse. He further reported the recent development of premature ejaculation, which added to his feelings of inadequacy and, he thought, demonstrated his lack of control.

The couple was very easily engaged in treatment and showed a high degree of motivation to change. During this first conjoint session, Cynthia attempted to exonerate Ricky from all blame, and attempted to take on the responsibility for the sexual problems. Those attempts were generally met with resistance in the form of supportive statements from Ricky, or with frustration that he could not make things better. As they described the reciprocal patterns that preceded sex, they too often became derailed by the all too familiar particulars of an old argument.

Two of the behaviors were reframed in order to shift their emotional meaning. Ricky's premature ejaculation was presented as a loving effort to make sex more bearable for his wife, and Cynthia's effort to take on the responsibility of the problem was framed as a loving act to change for him. They were also told that it made sense that they were having some problems, given the number of changes that had occurred in the last year. This effectively normalized part of their problems. Lastly, it was recommended that they avoid sexual relationships until a deeper understanding of the depth, scope, and meaning of their sexual interaction was achieved, offering a protective, therapist-assigned hiatus for both of them.

Ricky voiced protest against the sexual prohibition. He felt that he had already suffered enough from Cynthia's lack of desire. His feelings of deprivation were validated and it was pointed out that it appeared that they had tried a number of solutions without success, and that it might be to their long-term benefit to abstain from sex, which had obviously been very painful for both of them. It was further explained that removing the pressure of having to perform sexually might decrease their anxiety and allow them to have a successful experience. Reluctantly, they agreed. This approach was suggested because one of the positive advantages of non-demand, pleasure-oriented exercises is that they can relieve the anxiety of having to perform, which inhibits sexual enjoyment. Therefore, the exercises can help delay or prevent mobilization of the anxiety response/defense.

The couple wanted to begin working on the sexual problems immediately, which made it difficult for them to accept the total proposed treatment plan. They were informed that three additional sessions were needed to further assess the problems. The first of these three sessions was an individual meeting with Ricky to gather individual history and to balance the therapy, because Cynthia had been seen once individually. The latter two sessions were to further evaluate the presenting problems and to observe the couple's marital interaction.

At session five, specific treatment recommendations were discussed. The first order of business was to create a safe environment for the couple and help them experience a sense of success. The least toxic place to begin a sharply focused intervention seemed to be with their communication and problem-solving difficulties. Here they could strengthen the relationship and pave the way for sex therapy.

The couple were told that in order to address their conflict about sex they needed to learn how to talk and listen without attacking, blaming, and emotionally "running away." The therapist also noted that both partners were sensitive to approving and rejecting behaviors; therefore, they were prone to projecting the "bad and weak" self onto the spouse. It was thought to be critical to spend some time understanding why and how each of them was emotionally devastated when the partner was unable, or perceived to be unable, to fulfill a need. Since sex had a different meaning for each partner, it was recommended that this area be explored further, perhaps with a sexual genogram (Hof & Berman, 1986). After a clearer understanding of how each of them felt about sex was achieved, and after the meaning of sex in the relationship was explored, the behavioral technique of sensate focus (Masters & Johnson, 1970) was employed to slowly reintroduce sexual intimacy into their relationship.

The couple expressed an urgency to begin with the sensate focus exercises, against the advice of the therapist. Since the couple was grappling with such a strong need to have some control, it was decided that joining with the resistance and becoming more congruent with them and their expressed wants would be more useful than forcing them into the prescribed treatment plan. The couple's desire for sexuality was shared and congruent, which was an important step in defining the nature of their relationship. Therefore, the sensate focus exercises were assigned, but not before the following caveats were made to facilitate further congruence between the clients and the therapist: (1) if they did not experience success, they would agree to proceed with the original treatment plan; and (2) they were requested to agree not to terminate treatment prematurely, because the work could raise their fears and anxiety, which might lead them to want to stop treatment.

Because the couple tended to argue with each other and resist overt moves toward controlling the structure of treatment, the therapist had difficulties orchestrating the next three sessions. While preparing for sensate focus, each presented a list of excuses as to why he or she would not be able to find time to do the exercises. The therapist continued to push hard for a mutually agreed upon time, and the partners finally agreed. There were, however, two countertherapeutic outcomes, which stemmed from the therapist's interventions. First, the therapist, having allowed herself to become inducted into their belief system, failed to see the couple's signals that they were becoming frightened by the forthcoming closeness. As a result, the therapist colluded with the couple to keep their physical distance by agreeing to the doing of the exercises only once a week. In retrospect, the therapist believed that this negotiation mirrored how they made decisions about intimacy.

The couple reported that the only time they would be able to do the exercises was on the weekend. The therapist had initially prescribed that they be done three times a week, but gave up this plan in an effort to accommodate the couple. After the first week, the couple returned to treatment feeling angry at the therapist. They had attempted to do the exercises once and reported that it felt "mechanical." Since some couples report a degree of uneasiness when beginning sensate focus, the feeling was normalized, and the couple was directed to try again during the upcoming week. This was an affirmation paradox in that the therapist gave a directive designed to facilitate desired behavioral change. When directed to proceed with the exercise, they were told they would need to commit to making change happen in their relationship.

The therapist further told them that if they experienced severe difficulties in the upcoming week, then perhaps they both were more anxious than they understood. Although anxiety provoking, this directive made sense to the couple, as they had communicated motivation to resolve the sexual problem. This intervention could, therefore, be effective in two ways. The couple might be able to break through their anxiety and work on the sexual problem. Or, if they "failed" at the exercise, the therapist could explore with them why it was that they were having difficulty accomplishing the very thing that they said they would like to experience.

The remaining portion of that session was spent processing how their plan to execute the exercises had become unraveled and how they would guard against those problems in the upcoming week. By exploring these issues with the couple, the therapist would be able to use the exercise diagnostically in assessing whether they were currently prepared to do sensate focus.

The next session provided a way to enter into the dynamics of the marital relationship. Again, the couple reported that they had been unsuccessful at completing the exercises. Ricky assertively stated that he wanted to talk about what had occurred over the weekend. Cynthia had a period of feeling very low about her employment and Ricky unsuccessfully attempted to lift her mood. The following excerpt illustrates their communication patterns and underlying dynamics:

Ricky: My opinion doesn't count because I am your husband. It's got to be someone outside of us. It makes me feel like I don't have much input to what is going on.

Cynthia: You have to be more specific.

Ricky: With Jackie (a friend of Cynthia's) and feeling bad about how she was treating you. I have brought things up about that. It took people from the outside to basically say the same thing I was saying for you to see that it is valid.

Cynthia: Not necessarily. I told you that it's more difficult for me to absorb what you tell me about myself.

Ricky: I know.

Therapist: Is that what you are saying? (looking at Ricky)

Ricky: No. I don't think so.

Therapist: Try again.

Ricky: I just remember a comment a while ago when you felt down on yourself. You begin to say how worthless you feel, that you don't make anyone happy, and how horrible you feel about yourself. Whenever you get at opposite poles it will be like what I say isn't ...I don't know how to say it (silence). It doesn't count. What I say doesn't count. That is how it comes out.

Cynthia: But how? I do listen to you.

Ricky: Oh. I know you do. I feel like you.... You said one time that I was biased, because I loved you (looking confused and hurt). Oh, I said it is real nice that you know that I love you.

Cynthia: You know when I talk with you about these things, I am usually at the bottom. What you are saying helps, but....

Ricky: It makes me feel inadequate.

Cynthia: It is also that what you are saying helps bring me up out of it. But you can't expect me to say that it is all right, Ricky.... Thanks. (sarcastically, looking at him) Now that you have told me that I am a good person, I am going to be perfectly okay again.

Ricky: Is that what you think I am saying?

This pattern exposed Ricky's feelings of inadequacy and helplessness and Cynthia's sense of being controlled, which mirrored their sexual conflict. They were asked how they thought this pattern impacted on their relationships and how they related to one another. It became clear that Ricky pursued Cynthia when she became depressed or when he perceived she was avoiding her angry feelings at him. Cynthia's reaction was to physically and emotionally withdraw from Ricky, for fear that she would lose herself and her sense of control. Conversely, when Ricky reacted to her unavailability by becoming angry or depressed, Cynthia pursued him by trying to please, out of fear of criticism.

This was a very clear example of how interpretations and predications were used in their relationship. For example, when Cynthia became angry or depressed, Ricky's pursuit of her was interpreted as intrusive. She would predict his desire for closeness and withdraw in an effort to protect herself. Ricky interpreted her distance from him as related to something he did and, therefore, he would predict her avoidance and try to establish intimacy. A honeymoon period usually followed these interactions when both generally described their guilt and expressed desire to change their patterns of relating.

The therapist stated that it might be important for them to first understand where the reactions came from in order to change their behavior. They each were asked when they first remembered having those kinds of reactions; the inquiry was met with silence. They were then asked to think back to earlier experiences in their families of origin. Cynthia talked about her experiences with her mother, when she often felt she had no control over what happened to her, and that if she rebelled against her mother she was being a "bad girl." When her mother was drunk, she would sit or lie in silence next to Cynthia, feeling helpless and angry.

Ricky talked about feeling that he never measured up to the family's standard. Often he felt like a little kid excluded from family discussions and scapegoated. He did not feel as though he had a voice and that he would be heard. He wanted to please everyone, but his opinion was refuted and his arguments were often rebuffed.

This material clearly provided an understanding of the origins of a number of attributions they ascribed to one another. Ricky was able to see how and why he attributed Cynthia as rejecting and critical. Cynthia was able to see how and why she felt invaded and experienced extreme guilt. It further helped to define each partner's behavior as it related to the ISD. Specifically, Ricky interpreted his partner's lack of willingness to be sexual with him, after he offered supportive comments, as being rejecting and, therefore, concluded she believed he was not "good enough." In turn, Cynthia interpreted his behavior as pressure to give of herself and, therefore, believed he wanted to "use her." Thus, he pursued and she withdrew.

The therapist stated that it made sense why they responded to one another as they now do and suggested that it might have less to do with one another and more to do with the past, in that their earlier experiences had influenced and maintained the ISD. She further suggested that they postpone the sensate focus exercises and address some of the issues they had raised during the session. It became clear to both the couple and the therapist that they would need to resolve some of their intrapsychic and family-of-origin issues before they would be able to directly address the ISD. In other words, the etiology of the ISD was rooted in events that predated the marriage for Cynthia; for Ricky, his response to her behavior also predated their relationship. This intervention enabled the couple to accept a systemic framework in that they began to shift from linear to circular attribution. By broadening the context of the ISD and normalizing some of the barriers that inhibited change, the couple was able to join together, establishing congruence, instead of blaming and vilifying each other.

The following week the therapist began the session by stating that they needed to set some rules on how they were going to handle sex in their relationship. They both agreed that abstaining from sex was the safest method. This restraint from change is a negation paradox that helped to reduce some of the anxiety associated with sexual performance (Weeks & L'Abate, 1982). Ricky made it clear that he was not willing to completely abstain from sex for an undetermined period of time, so it was agreed that the decision would be reassessed in one month. In the meantime, we would continue to discuss how the past impacted on their relationship.

The next four sessions were spent on deepening their understanding of how early experiences had shaped their behaviors and how these behaviors were being reenacted in their relationship. The couple began to identify how they often had strong reactions to what appeared to be small conflicts, and how this stemmed from attributions to each other. For example, Cynthia perceived that Ricky was being demanding, and Ricky often perceived Cynthia as being withholding. Those reactions were exacerbated early in the marriage because of the narcissistic vulnerability each of them experienced in their rejection-intrusion pattern. They each continued to share their experiences in their families with one another, which seemed to neutralize some of their angry feelings at one another and enabled them to become more empathic and understanding of each partner's pain. The family-of-origin work served to broaden their understanding and definition of the problem in that they no longer believed it to be volitional, but saw it as deeply rooted in their early family experiences.

Additionally, the family-of-origin work helped to improve their communication and conflict-resolution skills, as well as reduce the degree of narcissistic vulnerability they each presented with at the beginning of treatment. The couple grew to understand that Cynthia's tendency to distance and Ricky's pursuing behaviors were outcomes from their experiences in their families of origin. Furthermore, they saw that their sensitivity to rejection and engulfment helped to polarize them and maintain the ISD. As they began to understand their behaviors within the context of their families, they demonstrated more ability to communicate without attacking and becoming defensive.

They simply stated that they felt safe to talk about their real feelings and fears. Now, they were ready to move on to the sexual material, which still evoked anxiety for the two of them. The family-of-origin work had enabled them to avoid blaming one another, which, in turn, reduced the perceived threat of being close to one another. They had stood by their contract to abstain from sex and Ricky was able to experience that Cynthia's lack of sexual desire did not mean that he was unlovable. This was an attributional shift, because Ricky had previously believed that he was unlovable because his wife lacked desire for him. It further allowed him to see and credit her with the other ways that she expressed her love for him.

Cynthia was able to feel relieved about not having any interest in sex and had to confront her belief that Ricky was "insatiable." This was a redefinition of Ricky's behavior which forced Cynthia to see him differently without ascribing her former beliefs. We agreed that the sensate focus exercises would probably not work for them and perhaps we should tailor a special plan that would utilize their creativity as well as their spontaneity. It was important for the couple to begin to develop shared beliefs about their relationship, particularly in the area of sexuality. The therapist hoped that by actively involving them in the specifics of the treatment planning process she would enable them to achieve more congruence in the relationship and therefore reduce resistance to change.

The couple decided to participate in mutual masturbation twice a week. This was suggested by Cynthia, after the therapist had recommended nonsexual activities to begin their journey of pleasuring. The couple thought the therapist was being overprotective and they humorously assured her that they could handle that activity. Although the therapist was hopeful that they would experience success, she predicted that they would both be very anxious and eager to please one another. The therapist thought that the anxiety and eagerness might inhibit their own ability to relax and experience pleasure, as well as evoking fear and inhibiting them from participating in the entire activity. However, the couple became playful with the therapist and assured her that they would be fine. The therapist continued to talk about what the worse case scenario might be, but agreed that they would probably be fine. She picked up on this playfulness and asked the couple to discuss how their plan could fall apart and how they might react if things did not work out as planned.

This is an example of a defiance-based intervention (Weeks & L'Abate, 1982), an intervention based upon the therapist challenging the clients' ability to perform the behavior. It is important to remember that both had failed to carry out most previous assignments, even those prescribed by themselves. This is also an example of restraint from change, another paradoxical intervention, chosen in an effort to maintain the progress they had already made in their relationship while predicting that change could potentially destabilize the system (Weeks & L'Abate, 1982).

Concurrently, the therapist made mention of the use of a sexual genogram (Hof & Berman, 1986) as a vehicle to help understand their beliefs and behavior about sexuality. Genograms had been constructed during their individual sessions, which the therapist updated during the treatment process, specifically focusing on the messages in their families about sex: which people in their families were intimate and how; what the secrets were regarding sexuality or intimacy; and, how they wanted their own family/relationship to be different. This intervention made the sexual messages they received from their families of origin explicit, and further normalized their unrealistic and incongruent expectations from sex. It enabled them to develop their own sexual script which was one of the central organizing principles that guided their sexual behavior (Gagnon, 1977).

During these sessions, Cynthia disclosed that when she was a preadolescent, her mother told her that sex was horrible and that you only "do it" out of obligation to your husband. She also had learned that men were unfaithful and could not be trusted, which was validated by her father's affairs. Cynthia felt violated and emotionally disengaged whenever she felt out of control of her body or when Ricky wanted more closeness than she desired. This example provided another attribution about men, in that she defined herself as a sex object for them.

Ricky's family did not show affection and did not discuss sex. He grew up feeling that sex was something you do when you love someone, but never dreamed that it may have occurred in his original family, secondary to the continuous conflict. His sexual education came secondhand, by way of his peers. Ricky was unable to differentiate between affection and sex. Consequently, whenever he desired affection, love, or nurturance from Cynthia, he would initiate intercourse. Since Ricky lacked models to learn about sex and intimacy, he interpreted sex and affection as being synonymous.

The many sexual and nonsexual ways they defined their roles and interpreted each other's behaviors were discussed, along with how they were enacted in their relationship. Concurrently, they continued to successfully use mutual masturbation for sexual pleasure. During a subsequent session, Cynthia and Ricky began to discuss having children. This was an area that had been briefly glossed over during the assessment period. Ricky wanted to have children relatively soon, which was another reason he was distressed by his wife's lack of desire. Cynthia was not sure if she wanted children. She was concerned about whether she would be a good parent, if she had time to parent, and did not want to find herself in a situation where she had to decide to abort because of bad timing. This was another area of incongruence for the couple that had contributed to the ISD.

After further exploration of this with Cynthia, it became apparent that she was afraid to have sex for fear of becoming pregnant. This was a sensitive area for both Ricky and Cynthia. The couple had had an abortion almost a year prior to their marriage. They had unresolved mourning about the abortion, they did not want to blame each other for making the decision to abort, and it also appeared that they both would have liked to have had the child. The therapist encouraged them to share their pain with each other along with the feelings and beliefs about where children fit into their relationship, both of which they were able to do.

The couple began to discuss their feelings about abandonment, needs, and unspoken desires during and between sessions with considerably more depth and understanding. It was also noted that some of the initial fears of rejection and engulfment were replaced with a longing to please self and partner. During sessions, they would plan a romantic activity where each one would share the responsibility for its execution. The Caring Days exercise (Stuart, 1980) was also used to enhance their intimacy and relationship enhancement skills. To do the Caring Days exercise, Ricky and Cynthia were asked to make a list of behaviors which, if done, would be accepted as showing that each partner cared about the other. The behaviors were to be small acts and stated constructively, such as asking about how their day went.

When their lists were completed, each partner shared his or hers and negotiated with the other which items on the list the partner was comfortable doing. After agreement, the couple then placed the written list in a visible place at home. Each partner then did three of the behaviors daily, and each kept a visible record of the caring experiences he or she did and the caring experiences received from the other. This exercise helped them "catch each other doing good," and to objectively assess the positive behaviors in their relationship. It also helped them to assess and demonstrate their commitment to each other, and their willingness to meet each other's needs. This, in turn, enabled them to further develop and enhance their communication and negotiation skills.

Despite Ricky's earlier feelings about the "need" to have sex, he reported a sense of being desired by Cynthia and desiring her that was more "complete." The Caring Days intervention prescribed was an affirmation paradox which facilitated their internal desires to be pleased and please one another. He enjoyed their intimacy and found that he wanted to do more caring things for her, which became more important than sex. Cynthia began to believe that the relationship was feeling more like it felt in the beginning. She was better able to relax when she was at home and particularly when Ricky expressed affection or concern. She attributed this to not feeling the pressure to perform and nurture. Cynthia began to have "sexy thoughts" about herself and Ricky, and found herself doing more things for Ricky, which she perceived as a measure of how much she really cared about him.

The couple began to express the wish to have intercourse. Although they were feeling good about the relationship and their ability to nurture one another, they were still afraid of failure. This is an example of spontaneous compliance change. Because Ricky and Cynthia were both satisfied with their relationship, and felt different about themselves, they "spontaneously" were ready to have intercourse. The therapist had enabled them to create a safe environment in which each was able to risk change in the relationship.

The couple began to have intercourse, and Cynthia's desire returned to premarital levels. She began to initiate affection with Ricky and was verbal about when she wanted to have intercourse. She was also more direct with Ricky when she was not feeling in the mood to be close or sexual. Ricky felt less vulnerable about how lovable he was and needed less approval from Cynthia. He enjoyed their mutual expression of affection and "love games," and became more comfortable when Cynthia declined to be sexually involved.

There were two remaining issues to be addressed in treatment. The first was to help them set realistic expectations for the frequency of intercourse. This couple had very demanding schedules, which afforded them limited time. However, they each had sexual beliefs that "normal" couples wanted intercourse three to four times a week. A psychoeducational approach helped them to see that they could establish flexible guidelines for their own frequency. Both were assigned *Male Sexuality* (Zilbergeld, 1978) and *For Yourself* (Barbach, 1975) to enhance their sexual information, and the readings proved extremely helpful to both of them.

The next issue was to revisit their parenting concerns. Specifically, they had identified fears about parenting and when they would decide to become parents. In the past, they were unable to talk about these issues without fighting or engaging in avoidant behaviors. Having successfully resolved the sexual issues noted above, they were able to have a meaningful exchange about becoming parents. What they uncovered was that both had fears that they might become like their own parents, who were considered failures at parenting. Again, the couple had made decisions based on their family-of-origin models and which they believed defined their abilities for the future. The treatment once again became family-of-origin focused, and provided them with the opportunities to discuss what they liked and did not like about their parents' skills. It also gave them the opportunity to discuss what kind of parents they wanted to be, how that was different from their families of origin, and why. This was another area where the couple was able to experience increasing congruence in their relationship.

CONCLUSION

When treating ISD, the Intersystem Model provided a treatment framework with flexible boundaries, which allowed the therapist to choose interventions to address the many of issues facing this couple. Dialectic metatheory, the foundation upon which the Intersystem Model is developed, requires the therapist to simultaneously think about the couple in a multilevel, inclusive framework. The therapist was able to achieve systematic integration through assessment and treatment of the individual, interactional, and intergenerational perspectives, and further fit the theory to the couple system.

In cases where couple problems contribute to the ISD, the therapist can work systematically, utilizing a wide range of psychotherapy theories. The treatment phase of this chapter began with the couple wanting to begin sensate focus. As treatment progressed, the therapist primarily used principles and constructs from the interactional and intergenerational aspects of the Intersystem Model. This couple used predictions and interpretations, but had a number of deeply ingrained definitions that inhibited and slowed the process.

Both affirmation and negation paradoxes were used to resolve the ISD. The negation paradox involved restraint from change, which was particularly helpful due to the resistance present in the couple. This work clarified for the couple what they needed to change if they were to achieve their self-defined successful outcome. The therapist created an environment for spontaneous compliance by helping them to understand the impact of the family-of-origin and intrapsychic issues they brought to the relationship and were projecting onto one another. This provided them with an alternative "lens" through which they could look at the relationship, and enabled them to develop strategies for accomplishing their goal.

CHAPTER 8

Beauty and the Beast: Object Relations Theory and the Intersystem Model

William Silver

INTRODUCTION

This chapter will discuss the Intersystem Model with an emphasis on object relations theory as it is applied to Harry and Rose Goodwill, a couple in marital therapy. The Intersystem Model provides a framework for viewing a couple in three dimensions: the individual, the interpersonal, and the intergenerational. Object relations theory primarily emphasizes interpersonal process, specifically focusing on how partners merge boundaries and differentiate as part of the marital dialogue. The process of incorporating aspects of the significant other, internalizing those aspects, and making them part of one's self is a process beginning in early development, setting the pattern for attachment, separation, and individuation for the rest of one's life. The tale of Beauty and the Beast (Mayer, 1978) serves as a superb metaphor for how two very different people struggle to understand each other's world and are permanently altered by that discovery.

Though a myriad of therapeutic techniques are incorporated into the process of therapy, the major ones focused on in this chapter will be framing and reframing of the individual, interpersonal, and intergenerational contexts for the couples conflicts, as well as paradox as an implicit aspect of therapy.

CASE FORMULATION

Harry and Rose Goodwill were referred by Rose's individual therapist, who felt that Rose used her time to complain about her husband and did not attend to her own issues. The goal of the couple's therapy was to help both of these needy, frightened, and enmeshed people learn how not to pin unrealistic hopes, fantasies, and aspirations of self-fulfillment onto the partner, and to help them develop themselves as whole entities, able to stand on their own merits and simultaneously be able to generate genuine empathy with their mate. A comment by Rainer Maria Rilke (Bly, 1981) sums up this focus:

> Once the realization is accepted that even between the closest human beings infinite distance continues to exist, a wonderful living side by side can grow up if they succeed in loving the distance between them which makes it possible for each to see the other whole against the sky (p. 87).

Initial Impressions and Presenting Problem

Harry, age 35, was an ambitious, energetic, intense, "wired" man, who inevitably wore a scowl when he entered the room. He was not particularly conscious of this scowl, and it seemed unrelated to his present surroundings. When this was brought to his attention, he seemed surprised, not having any idea of where that affect came from. Once he made personal contact, he could become congenial, funny, and at times interpersonally generous. He appeared to be a man caught up with some internal agenda that made him move purposefully and seem continually charged. A major part of his time and attention was invested in his work as a banker, at which he spent very long days and weekend hours. Work was his passion, and he channelled his productivity and creativity into investing other people's money to realize profits for them, and through commission, for himself.

Money was a particularly driving force in Harry's life. He was preoccupied by it, not only in terms of his productivity, but in terms of evaluating his "net worth," and he spent hours organizing columns of figures on his computer screen. A sense of great satisfaction, at times a kind of "high," overcame him when the numbers worked out, and a deep sense of fear and frustration occurred when they did not.

Rose was a girlish looking 31-year-old who prided herself on looking 10 years younger. She was hesitatingly soft-spoken, shy, even coquettish. She rarely finished a statement without making eye contact with her husband, checking her thoughts with him. When he gave his typically disapproving sign or gesture, she would stop mid-sentence and involve herself with her perception of his judgment of her, her original thought remaining unfinished, fragmented. Her energies were then gathered to defend herself against his attack. These energies were bold and intense, in contrast to her typical hesitancy when it came to self-initiated thoughts or actions. Rose would feel a sense of energy and purpose in reacting to Harry, a purpose she lacked when acting independently.

Rose was a full-time homemaker, raising two boys, seven and three years old, an occupation that she often found burdensome and unrewarding. She declared that, like her mother, she did not like to cook, so she relied on frozen foods, hastily prepared meals, and eating out as adjustments to this dilemma. In fact, Rose did not like domestic work at all, and even with the assistance of regular hired help, the home, according to Harry, was chaotic and unwelcoming. Harry's tirades were primarily focused on the state of the kitchen, with its profusion of unwashed dishes and continually empty refrigerator. After his long working hours, this became cause for biting attacks which either enraged Rose or rendered her tearful and speechless.

Another source of marital tension was Harry's perception of Rose as a compulsive spender. Despite their six-figure income, the Goodwills always appeared to be on the verge of financial collapse. Harry blamed this on Rose's extravagance on clothing for herself and the children, frivolous lunching out with her friends, and dinners out to compensate for her distaste for cooking. Rose readily acknowledged that eating out with friends was her only source of solace and comfort, something Harry could not give her. It was the only time she felt nurtured and it became an escape from the demands of home and marriage. After numerous tirades on Rose's spending, Harry was asked to bring his ledger of income and spending. This revealed that Rose's spending accounted for a very small fraction of his expenses; even so, she remained the target for Harry's financial concerns.

Another arena for conflict was Rose's avoidance of sexual intimacy. She complained of headaches, fatigue, and a general lack of interest in sex despite the fact that during those rare times when the conditions were right for her, she could engage in enthusiastic sex, which she blushingly admitted. But, even on those occasions, she would require persistent coaxing.

Rose interpreted Harry's behavior as aggressive, emotionally unavailable, and far from her fantasied erotic object of a muscular, youthful man, with warm eyes and a firm but tender touch. In addition, Rose was intensely jealous of Harry's relationship with his brother, on whom he bestowed warmth, care, and an intensity of involvement which he denied her.

Changes Sought by the Couple and Past Solutions

The timing of the initiation of treatment is always a crucial element for the therapist to consider in terms of who wants what to change in whom, and why now. Rose's initial involvement in individual treatment was sporadic and motivated by the crisis of the moment. She would seek support, but rarely follow through with treatment in any consistent fashion and rarely consider aspects of her own personality that would need changing. What finally mobilized her to seek marital therapy was not only her chronic discontent with her marriage, but her becoming aware of her eldest son's increasing oppositionalism, which at times became physical. She was extremely concerned about his future development and about her ability to control his attacks on her. It is not unusual for a couple embroiled in mutual projections to be motivated to get help when they see it affecting their children.

Harry, not an introspective man by nature, was initially skeptical of therapy, and like many husbands in marital therapy came to the first session to appease his wife. His monetary concerns at the time were heightened by his discontent with his job, his feeling undervalued by his boss, and his ambivalence about making a job change. Harry discharged his work frustrations at home in his attacks on Rose and his confrontations with his son. It was the acknowledgment of the impact of their troubled marriage on their son's development, particularly the boy's timidity outside the home and his clinginess and aggressiveness with his mother, that motivated this child-focused couple to seek help for themselves.

Intersystem Assessment

The art of organizing and formulating complex data on marital systems is a personal and technical challenge for the marital therapist. There are times when metaphor seems to capture the intricacies of that complexity better than technical description. "Beauty and the Beast" seems to be an apt image to portray the developmental journey of this couple. Beauty represents a woman's development from being "daddy's little girl" to a complex and mature personality. She must be able to see through the superficial patina of her own narcissism to empathy and love, which enables her to comprehend her partner's pain and his struggle alongside her own. Beast represents a man's struggle within the confines of his own limited self-definition as he learns to value and trust his own vulnerabilities as part of his self-definition of a man. He learns to incorporate aspects of what Beauty represents rather than vicariously owning and controlling her. Truly incorporating another's reality can be very difficult, even traumatic, for it challenges one's cherished views of the world and of the other person. Indeed, it challenges cherished concepts of ourselves. Yet, following this inquiry can serve to expand the soul and teach the seeker to become interpersonally aware and generous.

Beauty and the Beast, on another level, may be seen as dual aspects of the self. The vulnerable, interpersonally sensitive part, Beauty, merges with the goal- and task-oriented part, Beast, into an integration of the self, a complete person. Their marriage represents the integration inherent in the nascent psychological awareness of becoming a whole person. This awareness represents considerable personal introspection, which cannot be achieved when partners are involved in projection. When blame starts, dialogue ends.

To describe this couple from the perspective of the Intersystem framework, Harry and Rose need to be analyzed along the three parameters: the individual, the interpersonal, and the intergenerational. Object relations concepts will then be introduced to show how the author integrates them into an Intersystem approach.

The individual

Rose may be defined as a dependent personality with narcissistic features by virtue of her ambivalence, her eagerness to yield control to others, and her difficulty projecting an independent view of herself, including taking decisive action in crucial areas of her life. Hers was a hostile dependence in which she engaged in a dependent relationship, but then resisted the control implicit in that dependence. Indeed, her reasons for choosing Harry as a mate included her perception of his self-confidence and his sense of direction and hard work, characteristics she denied in herself. When they met, he was in graduate school and holding down a full-time job. During the course of their relationship, Rose gave up her employment and allowed Harry to help support her, though she herself completed her education.

Harry's obsessive/compulsive personality style manifested itself in his perfectionism and extreme preoccupation with detail. His focus on work and productivity to the exclusion of leisure was evidenced by his persistent fantasy of owning a piano, which he had loved to play as a youth, but which he felt he could not now afford, despite having gotten a $25,000 bonus that year. Rose was in agreement, feeling that a piano would clutter the living room; therefore, she joined in discouraging that fantasy. For Rose, attention to artistic pursuits was not considered manly. Her father had denied himself for the family's sake; therefore, she, through projection, tended to discourage qualities in Harry she deemed unmanly. In that sense, Harry's tendency to be frugal with his own pleasures and Rose's tendency to discourage them in him permitted an unconscious collusion that, in perpetuating historical patterns, served to limit their growth as a couple.

Harry's early attraction to Rose was to her expressiveness, her attention to him, and her ability to emotionally draw him out. Their relationship was one of his first with a woman, and they became attached shortly after he separated from his brother to attend graduate school. Like Beast, Harry relied on Rose to make him "feel." Rather than incorporating those emotional qualities into his own personality structure, he sought her to complete himself, thus remaining a partial self. It therefore required Rose's constant attention to make Harry feel human. Inattention on Rose's part would set him into a roaring rage. He would seek to control her for his own needs. When he failed, he would attack and belittle her.

The interpersonal

A person's search for a psychological "fit" in an intimate relationship remains one of the most fascinating areas of inquiry into marriage. Clearly, one can see the complementary nature of character traits as they emerged between Rose and Harry, each offering aspects of self that enhanced and complemented aspects of the other. From one perspective, one can frame these attributes in a positive light. Harry's intense drive was complemented by Rose's accommodating nature. Rose's intuitive style, her ability to reflect on Harry's emotions, enabled Harry to feel cared for and valued, freeing him to pursue his worldly goals.

As in many new couples, these were the kind of attributions they made early in their courtship. However, two years into their marriage, each focused on the negative attributions to these characteristics. Rose focused on Harry's drive as bullying and demeaning to her. She no longer saw the self-motivated, independent man she had married, but rather focused on his demandingness and his control. Harry had come to view Rose's emotionality as a form of whining and avoidance of responsibility. She no longer appeared to him as the sensitive and attentive girl of their courtship. He came to focus on her indecisiveness and her disorganization. Each of their perspectives, or frames of reference, shifted from mutual idealization to mutual devaluation.

This shift is a common process in couples. It may stem from the fact that mutual idealization and positive attribution are components of romantic attraction and may have their origins in the early symbiotic longings described by object relations theorists. As Von Franz (1981) wrote:

> At first you think you know the other person...you have the strong feeling of intimate knowledge. At the first meeting there is no need to talk; you know everything about each other...the wonderful feeling of being one and having known each other for many ages. Then suddenly the other behaves in unexpected ways and there is disappointment (p. 204).

Inevitably, in a marriage, these "narcissistic" projections are challenged, leading to a sense of betrayal, disappointment, and fear. These are the narcissistic wounds that couples incur following the idealized stages of their relationship. In response, the couple proceeds to coax, cajole, threaten, and manipulate each partner to conform to those idealized qualities, as a way of avoiding the painful work of mourning the loss of narcissistic visions and seeing the partner for who she/he really is. It was only when Beauty could accept the Beast for who he was that she found in him a prince. In Bar-Levav's (1988) words:

> Being in love is essentially a passive state; the goal of lovers, like that of children, is to be loved. By contrast, real love is active. When emotionally mature people love, they extend themselves to others. This is how sane parents love their child, for itself and not what if offers them in return (p. 148).

The intergenerational

Pragmatically, the marital therapist moves from noting the particular concerns, affects, and behaviors of each of his clients (linear level) to seeing them within a context of interpersonal patterns of transaction within the marriage (circular level). For example, though Harry defined himself as the initiator in the couple, his initiative was highly affected by Rose's feedback. A raise of her eyebrow could evoke a sense of anger and frustration in him. Similarly, though Rose defined herself as uncertain and directionless, her reaction to Harry provided her with deep-felt feelings, which became a poor substitute for personal conviction. She further attributed her lack of purpose in life to Harry's negative influence. When asked about her experience, she would rarely refer to herself, but prefaced her comments with a focus on Harry's annoying behaviors.

These patterns are imbedded in the history of the marriage. By the time the couple enters therapy, the origin of these patterns (family of origin) is forgotten or repressed. What remains in consciousness is the intensity of affect that is generated when similar (isomorphic) events are reevoked in the present. It is often surprising to a partner when the spouse exhibits a strong reaction to what is perceived as a trivial transgression. Rose, for example, would be taken aback by Harry's explosive reaction to a messy sink or an unplanned meal. She would then discount him as being childish. This discounting, for Harry, was reminiscent of being discounted in the past, when he was more vulnerable and his defenses less developed. These reminiscences were, however, unconscious, and his struggle remained in the present, with Rose. Similarly, Harry would have little idea of the importance of his attention to Rose at family gatherings. Rose's melancholy or her rage was baffling to Harry, and he would berate her for being petty and irrational.

Old templates, established early in life, are repeated and transferred, often unconsciously, in intimate relationships. The couple can be seen as attempting to reenact familiar patterns and/or attempting to resolve early conflicts. For example, as we shall see later in the chapter, Harry's ambivalence about his emotionally withholding mother played itself out not only in his choice of a partner, whom he initially saw as nurturing and later perceived as selfish, but also in his unwillingness to acknowledge aspects of Rose that disconfirmed those negative attributes. For example, when Rose bought Harry a gift, he would belittle it as too little, too late. Or, when Rose initiated affectionate overtures, Harry would criticize the control implicit in her selfishly choosing to initiate affection at her convenience. In this way, Harry maintained a rigid view of an uncaring, self-involved women.

Similarly, Rose's rejection by her parents in favor of her elder brother became a pattern repetitively reenacted in her marriage. Ensuring rejection from Harry by forgetting to shop for food or prepare meals, or by bouncing checks because of not balancing her bank account, Rose could again be martyred and abandoned by a rejecting authority figure, eliciting sympathy from others, including her children. However, one may also interpret such passive manipulation as a sort of triumph, in that now Rose could control the process of rejection. She could affect the source of power through her passive aggressiveness.

Her rejection was also reenacted in her often accurate perception of Harry's preference for his brother's company at family gatherings. Her enraged responses ensured an alliance of her husband and brother-in-law, defining her as childlike and petulant, just as she was in her family of origin. Rose's unconscious reenactment of early patterns was her way of reliving the past. One might assume that the unconscious repetition of early patterns can be viewed not only as a link to the past, but presenting the possibility of redoing the past. However, this often requires the self awareness implicit in the therapeutic process. This becomes the work of couples therapy.

One of the tasks of the therapist is to search for contexts for the couple's interpersonal patterns, templates learned from the past. Finding past patterns internalized from the individual's family of origin expands the couple's frame of reference. The intensity of affect is diverted from the current context and understood in terms of past experiences and introjects. This helps partners to understand why certain actions on a spouse's part evoke such strong reactions, "pushes their buttons." It furthers the process of reframing, which is so crucial to the work of therapy, by redefining what is perceived as negative intent on a partner's part as one's own vulnerability to specific issues. In this way the therapist hopes to elicit compassion from the spouse as opposed to anger.

Rose was the youngest of three siblings and, in many ways, the "baby" of a child-focused family. Her eldest brother had given up a career in medicine to enter the family business, which involved him and his wife in continual contact with his parents. The option to join the family business was not offered to Rose, probably because of her gender. At times she became intensely despairing of being left out of the family's intricacies and intensely envious of her sister-in-law's position in the family. The times that she could evoke the courage to ask her father to be included inevitably led Rose to experience feelings of being slighted by being offered what she felt was a demeaning role, particularly when compared to her sister-in-law, who was integrally involved in family business matters, and was a very organized and self-motivated woman.

Rose's father was a benign, non-expressive, conflict-avoidant, simple man who had inherited his business from his father and had generously provided for the comforts of his family. Rose characterized her relationship with her mother as conflicted. Depicted as narcissistic, her mother insisted on being the center of attention at any gathering, often jokingly comparing her waistline with her daughter's. In a competitive context, Rose would either withdraw or would get attention through self-defacing humor or by becoming helpless and requiring assistance. For example, at a family dinner, a slight cough or headache would become the focus for everyone's concern, and Harry's careful attention to her at those times could make the difference to Rose between a sense of being valued and a sense of personal desolation.

Harry, in contrast, had a financially strapped upbringing. His father, a tender but anxious and overprotective son of immigrants, eked out a meager living as a salesman, much to the dismay of his critical and fastidious wife. Harry's mother had enjoyed a more affluent upbringing and came to resent her husband's lack of financial success, feeling that she had married down. Harry described his parents' marriage as lacking in affection. His father invested his energies and affections in being accepted by friends and neighbors, while his mother invested hers in the rearing of her three children. His mother's efforts, coupled with her frustrations, were channeled into keeping an orderly, if not hospitable, home. The brothers provided warmth for each other, while their younger sister was excluded from the sibling relationship.

To satisfy his mother's ambitions for financial success, Harry became very competitive both in play and at work. During therapy he recounted an incident in early adolescence in which he had shared a paper route with a friend and was encouraged by his mother to take ownership of that route, keeping the profits for himself and thereby losing a friend. Another pivotal memory, which became a theme in therapy, involved basketball. Emotionally wounded by being passed over for the varsity team, Harry personalized it as an issue with his coach, determining never to be in a position of having to depend on anyone again.

Rose learned in early life that she could not compete with her eldest brother for her mother's affections. Her unacknowledged and unexpressed rage took the form of underachievement, passivity, and hypochondria. It was only through being needy that Rose got recognition and assistance from her father. Even when she was an adult, Rose's complaints about financial inequities were met by a cash gift, a kind of allowance, as a means of appeasement, defining her again as needy and demanding. Harry, in contrast, was encouraged to be fiercely competitive and to define his sense of self-esteem solely in terms of his ability to be a financial success. Vulnerable feelings, characteristic of his father, were suppressed and denied. It seems ironic, then, that Harry's choice of a spouse would give voice to those repressed and feared needs. However, as will be described later in the chapter, it is through the mechanisms of projection and projective identification that disowned parts of the self are denied and recovered through someone who fits the bill.

TREATMENT: PLAN AND ACTION

In formulating a plan of treatment that integrates the three levels of assessment, the individual, the interpersonal, and the intergenerational, the therapist uses a variety of theoretical perspectives to develop a hypothesis. Object relations theory can be extremely useful as a link for integrating the individual and the interpersonal theories. This section begins with some basic tenets of object relations theory, proceeds to a discussion of how those tenets were applied to the treatment of the Goodwills, and ends with a discussion of how object relations theory can readily be integrated into the Intersystem Model.

Object Relations Theory

Margaret Mahler (1975), in her book *The Psychological Birth of the Human Infant*, described a process by which the child emerges from a symbiotic fusion with the mothering person, its first intimate relationship, to the beginnings of a psychological entity able to think, feel, and act independently of the powerful and nurturant "other." This model of attachment and separation serves as a powerful template for individuation at each juncture of the child's, and later the adult's, life.

As the child becomes increasingly aware of its separateness from the mother, aggressive feelings become delineated from affectionate feelings in a "splitting" between the rewarding part object and the aggressive or withholding part object. The "good" mother is distinguished from the "bad" mother. The child, as yet unable to integrate the possibility of rejection from someone it is so dependent on, psychologically splits its view of that person, as if there were two distinct people. In that way, the attachment to this powerful parent is not disturbed.

Most fairy tales, including Beauty and the Beast, begin with a time of perfect symbiosis, when the protagonist had a kind and beautiful mother, or had a magical golden ball. This bliss is threatened by some calamitous event, the loss of the good queen mother and the ascendence of the evil stepmother, or the loss of the golden ball to the hands of a monster. In Beauty and the Beast, it was the father's gift of the perfect rose to his beloved daughter that put in motion the subsequent trials, for the daughter needed to separate from the father. She needed to learn to understand and care for a man different than the father, and her willingness to struggle with the strange Beast was part of her emotional development.

The subsequent ability to integrate both parts of the mother within the same person becomes the hallmark of functional individuation, thus enabling the child, and later the adult, to tolerate increasing degrees of frustration, anxiety, and depression when his or her needs go unmet. To do this without unduly impinging on the person's developing abilities to master the environment, and without having to cling to or abandon the object of his or her attachment, is the hallmark of true individuation.

Applied to adult development, adequate integration of good and bad objects, that is, the ability to perceive the other as having both strengths and weaknesses simultaneously, allows a person to maintain an attachment even when the partner is not satisfying a need. It further encourages each partner to perceive the other as having characteristics and needs independent of, and at times conflicting with, his or her own. This ability to recognize a partner's "difference" without maligning or vilifying those characteristics constitutes the basis for true empathy, a foundation of mature love.

Romantic love, in contrast, is based on a pattern of mutually reinforced idealization of the self and of the other. The "agreement" is that each spouse will see only the positive or enhancing aspects of the other, those aspects that conform with the spouse's need to be cherished or admired, and will ignore contradictory characteristics. In that sense, perfect fusion or codependence is maintained at the cost of true individuation. Beauty's fantasied prince—handsome, gallant, protective, and sensitive—represented an idealized (mirror) image of herself. In a dream, this magical prince spurned an old hag who came begging at the palace gate: "I showed her no pity, she was so ugly. The sight of her did not move me and I sent her away without food or money." The hag warned that the prince would spend his life wandering in his fine palace without a friend until someone could find beauty in him.

In Harry's ability to compete in the world, Rose found a source for her own personal security, something afforded to her by her father, but at the expense of her own independence. She managed to ignore aspects of Harry's controlling nature, aspects she later came to resent. Harry similarly interpreted Rose's attentiveness and expressiveness as filling a void left from an emotionally withholding mother, but later came to devalue those qualities as weak, manipulative, and self-serving. The fantasy of romantic fusion is a universal one. It is the wish to have all of one's needs met in a relationship hallowed by perfection. It is tied to the belief that somewhere in the world is a person capable of fulfilling those needs, thus making us whole. The wish is to be cared for so completely and unconditionally that no demand be made on the subject of that fantasy.

That fantasy of perfect fusion touches on the deepest issues of one's life. Indeed, one can come to perceive that one's very survival may depend on the preservation of that fantasy. Beauty, at the point of experiencing feelings for Beast, becomes ambivalent and visits her ailing father. She finds it difficult to give up the protective image of an all-giving, beneficent protector, and escapes into that fantasy as a means of fleeing adult intimacy.

Harry, following the gender determinants of most men, suppressed his more vulnerable and dependent feelings early in his development. In the interest of developing the capacity to compete in the world, Harry learned quite well how to become task- and production-oriented. His sense of personal value was primarily determined by what he could produce, acquire, and amass. He had few close friends and, driven by his father's financial failure—or more precisely, by his mother's dissatisfaction with his father's financial failures— Harry invested enormous energies "never to feel dependent on anyone again." Those unmet dependency needs then went "underground" and were suppressed, later finding their focus, through projection, in his future mate, Rose.

This process typically involves psychological mechanisms of splitting and projective identification. Splitting entails the keeping apart of contradictory experiences of the self and of significant others. Men are encouraged to "split off" dependent components of their personality and identify with those aspects most related to competition, strength, endurance, and the will to control. More tender components of the personality conducive to attachment and nurturance are repressed and become the focus of interest in a female partner.

Harry, then, split off those aspects of himself, projected them onto a "suitable" partner, Rose, and vicariously identified with vulnerability and nurturance through her, not defining them as his own. Similarly, Rose, was trained to define herself in terms of her attachment to significant others. In that sense, qualities such as attentiveness and identifying and anticipating others' needs were highlighted, while the more "masculine" components of her personality, such as the drive to compete, master, and control, were relegated to levels of unconsciousness and emerged in her choice of partner, projected onto someone who might play out those fantasies for her.

The processes of splitting and projective identification are in fact built into our concepts of gender and gender-based role assignments. Like Rose and Harry, many couples begin their relationships as "part objects," seeking to be more whole through identification with aspects of the significant other. There is a Hebrew myth that depicts the soul at birth as splitting in two and spending a lifetime searching for the other half. However, as with Rose and Harry, most discover that projective identification cannot adequately sustain the sense of completion or wholeness over time. We see those split-off and projected aspects of self in terms of our own needs and fantasies, and not in terms of what they mean for and about our partner.

This distinguishes mature from immature forms of loving. In that sense, projections are narcissistic in origin. To the degree that the partner adequately reflects those needs, we feel secure, important. To the degree they do not, we feel anxious and devalued. Our defense against this sense of devaluation is often to try to force or cajole our partner to respond in ways that will sustain our sense of security or "pseudo-wholeness." For example, Rose needed Harry to be a reliable provider in order to feel safe herself, just as Harry needed Rose's attention to feel valued. To the degree that we fail, we are met with a sense of helplessness, worthlessness, anger, and depression. Linking our spouse's lack of fulfilling our projected expectations as causal to our sense of devaluation (vilification), we resort to trying to control and/or devalue our spouse. This becomes the source of bitter struggles between partners, which often underlies the apparently superficial content of the quarrel and explains the intensity of the affect. Thus, Harry's stinging attacks over a depleted cupboard may be better understood as an expression of Harry's sense of personal depletion, and his desperate though distorted calls for nurturance. Rose's compulsive need to shop itself symbolized an attempt to fill an internal void.

Object relations concepts are compatible with the Intersystem Model of treatment in identifying the developmental roots of the concepts of impression management and attribution. How a partner presents him/herself to the other and how that impression is framed by the recipient is, according to object relations, highly determined by early developmental sequences. Further, the defenses of projection and projective identification add a particular frame of reference to why, at one point in a marriage, certain characteristics may be valued, and at another point those same characteristics are devalued. The systemic nature of the mutual attributional process is deeply imbedded in object relations theory in the definition of the boundary between the self and other. A partner's perception, thought, or action deeply affects the thought, affect, and behavior of the other, continually redefining cause and effect in relationships.

A clear example of projective identification was afforded by the Goodwills following Harry's elaborate anniversary gift to Rose of an expensive fur coat. Though Harry spends little on himself, and despite the fact that he appeared constantly anxious about having enough money, the therapist surmised that having his wife draped in fur not only appealed to his split-off and projected need to be cared for, but at the same time signaled to others his financial success. He simultaneously would demean his wife, describing her as unworthy of such generosity, given that she did not adequately care for the home or stock the cupboards. Harry could unconsciously identify with his need for indulgence while consciously putting down the excesses inherent in that indulgence, through projection onto Rose.

Harry and Rose would attack each other (linear attributions), and these attacks would further reinforce each other's sense of worthlessness. For Rose, rather than focus her energies on her own introspection and attending to issues related to her own self-esteem, she would focus her rage at Harry's attacks and try to enlist the therapist in siding with and protecting her from those assaults. Attempts to interpret Rose's lack of interest in home care or her forgetting to clean the kitchen as a passive form of resistance toward her husband were met with denial and a sense of betrayal on the therapist's part. In that sense, the therapist did not live up to the fantasy of the kind, protective father who would help ward off this "beast" of a husband.

The therapist attempted to reframe each partner's linear attributional system in an attempt to shift the focus of the problem from an individual level (his control/her passivity) to an interactional level (their process of mutual devaluation or vilification). The goal was to move Harry and Rose away from seeing each other as the enemy and the source of pain toward seeing each other as struggling with personal issues, and toward attempting collaborative solutions. This collaboration is preceded by a deep sense of loss of the fantasy of fusion. It is in the working through of that grief that couples achieve empathy for each other, which facilitates the laboring together (collaboration).

Indeed, Disney's recent adaptation of *Beauty and the Beast* did a psychological disservice to the original version, in which Beauty needed to choose between her father and the Beast. Giving up the narcissistic fantasy of being daddy's cherished little girl, working to see through the brittle veneer of her mate, and learning to understand and value what she finds, even though it does not mirror her own fantasy, is indeed the beginning of mature love. There is a price to be paid, and that price is grieving the loss of that fantasy. Disney made an unfortunate accommodation to his audience by diluting that loss and allowing Beauty to have it all.

Object Relations and the Intersystem Model

As Chapter 1 indicated, therapy is itself paradoxical in that clients look to the "expert" therapist to offer directives or solutions when it is they who must do the changing. The therapist must convey to the clients that they control their own destinies. Much like the protagonists in the *Wizard of Oz*, who gain courage, wisdom, and love, not through some magical bestowal from a powerful force, but with trust and careful guidance, these characteristics come to the clients in the old fashioned way—they earn them. It is, indeed, in the belief system established between the clients and the therapist (the transference) that encouragement for this process of change occurs—permitting the client to use the powers they intrinsically have, but may not recognize, to effect their desired goals. A skilled clinician might adequately diagnose and chart a course of change for a client or a couple in a comparatively brief period of time. However, the artistry and hard work of therapy is in dealing with client resistance to the novel ideas. The repertoire of techniques incorporated in the Intersystem Model provides a theoretical framework for dealing with the paradox of therapy—the injunction to change, but to do it spontaneously.

Therapy with the Goodwills extended over a period of 26 months. In the initial phase of treatment, characterized by mutual blame (e.g., justification, rationalization, debilitation, and vilification), the role of the therapist was (1) to provide a safe container for the expression of deep-felt wounds; (2) to join with, identify, and reflect the affect experienced by each partner without taking a position on them, avoiding at all costs attempts to align with one member against another; and (3) to begin to introduce the possibility that the hurts experienced by each may not be an intentional act of aggression by the other. In that sense, a process of "reframing" of causality can emerge by which each partner may begin to view the other's actions as defensive in nature, and not malicious.

This reframing is central to the therapy in that as one perceives a deep-felt wound of rejection or attack as emanating from the partner, that partner becomes "the enemy." Defenses are erected to either ward off further rejections or attacks or to attack in kind. This process inevitably ends in defeat for both partners, not only in not having those wounds (which often predate the marriage) redressed or needs met, but in not being "heard." Each partner perceives his or her needs as not being mirrored by the other. Reframing is typically the first major intervention in attempting to shift the linear thinking of each partner, to finding the complementarity of responses that maintains the dysfunctional set. This reframing allows each spouse to reinterpret the partner's reaction as stemming from his or her own conflicts, past or present, rather than as an attempt to degrade or vilify the other.

When Harry returned home exhausted and depleted, the image of an empty refrigerator would evoke feelings of personal negation, which he acted out by demeaning and negating Rose. Rose, herself barely coping through the day, would oscillate between rage at her needs not being recognized and passive aggressiveness, acting out through forgetting food preparation and indulging herself in personal shopping, or through psychosomatic withdrawal. The nature of her acting out became humorously evident when she talked of preparing and enjoying an elaborate meal with her housekeeper, whom she found good company.

The therapist's first and foremost function is to mirror and recognize those needs for each partner, serving both to diminish the intensity of affect stirred by the lack of external validation and, potentially, to introduce the recognition (reframing) in each spouse that his/her partner is suffering as well—that both are victims. The resistance to this phase of intervention is profound, as it was with the Goodwills. One may define the source of resistance on the three levels suggested earlier—the intergenerational, the interpersonal, and the intrapsychic.

The intergenerational

The patterns established in early life are often transferred, and repeated in intimate relationships. Harry's ambivalence about his withholding mother may have played itself out not only in his choice of partner, but in his unwillingness to acknowledge aspects of Rose that disconfirmed that perspective. Rose's rejection by her parents, in favor of her brother, became reenacted by her ensuring rejection from her husband, but was disconfirmed by her passive manipulation of that rejection.

The interpersonal

The struggles of approach/avoidance in couples can be seen as a form of pseudointimacy. By vacillating roles between pursuer and distancer, each partner avoided genuine intimacy, which each may have feared and been unprepared to experience. Both Harry and Rose attached to each other out of mutual need. Rose had no direction for herself after schooling, and Harry needed to fill the void of the separation from his brother. Neither had a period of experimentation with the opposite sex, and therefore their fights often covered their fear and awkwardness regarding intimacy, enabling each to see himself or herself as emotionally available to the spouse, but victimized by an unavailable partner.

The individual

The fear of not having one's deepest longings realized and, therefore, the possibility of having to relinquish them or make some adaptation usher in a deep sense of loss and of mourning. Indeed, couples able to work through their mutual projections will often go through a period of loss prior to establishing a new sense of interpersonal identity.

The Goodwills both resisted the interventions that challenged their fantasies of narcissistic gratification by the other. Some of their fights and mutual recriminations sustained their fantasies of fusion and also intensified their continued enmeshment. The more Harry criticized Rose for her inattention to the kitchen, the more Rose became despondent of ever getting the support she needed. Her despondency led to passive resignation, passive aggressive resistance, or an aggressive assault on Harry's character, in hopes of getting the support she longed for. Those reactions would trigger a symmetrical response from her husband, including biting attacks on her character, her mothering, and her worth as a person. Each hoped to get something from the spouse while behaving in ways that would ensure disappointment. Beast would either go into tirades when he could not buy or control Beauty's attention or withdraw into his solitary tower, tending to his pain alone, lest anyone discover his vulnerability. Those defenses tended to distance Beauty, making each more desperate.

Reframing Rose's need for external nurturance as a way of enhancing her sense of personal worth was met by Harry with attacks on her selfishness, her emotional and physical stinginess, and her inadequacy as a person. Similarly, reframing of Harry's assaults on Rose's homemaking skills as Harry's awkward way of asking for nurturance was dismissed by Rose's belief in her husband's brutality and sadistic intent. Attempts at reframing continually failed because of both partners' unwillingness to let go of the idealized image of each other they felt in need of and entitled to. Therefore, they were unable to see themselves as impeding the progress they consciously desired.

The impasse created by their mutual projections and projective identification reached its peak after about 16 weeks of struggle. Movement by one spouse was counteracted by acting out by the other. The therapist gave them a paradoxical directive. He suggested a trial separation whereby the couple would maintain separate residences and would have contact only when mutually agreeable. A bold intervention like this goes against the couple's inherent expectation that the therapist would serve to magically keep them together and have their needs met without their having to do the hard work of restraint and genuine self-reflection and introspection. In essence, it confronted Harry and Rose with the reality that if change were to occur, they would have to work for it themselves or risk the stability of the family. This work required both to view the spouse as not simplistically all-giving or all-withholding, but as a person with frailties like their own, struggling to feel connected and empowered, and fearing each. It capitalized on the months of encouragement, support, and education previously ignored or rejected. But, with the consequences of separation facing them, the couple chose the strain of letting go of their assumptions to the pain of losing the relationship.

The specter of separation and the fears inherent in that served to jolt the couple's frame of reference. Curiously enough, Rose, who was perceived as the more dependent of the two, showed initial signs of being intrigued about the possibility for greater autonomy. This independence was something she was denied and denied herself in her own development. Harry, who saw himself as carrying the major burdens of the family, was confronted with the depth of his emotional dependence on his wife. From the standpoint of projective identification, Rose was able to take back some projection of power coming from outside herself and consider the potentially positive aspects of autonomy. She played with the idea of part-time work and even experimental dating, something she had not allowed herself to do in her transition to adult life.

Harry, jolted by the enormity of his dependency needs, was both worried and intrigued by seeing aspects of his wife he had not seen before, and he started to become more conciliatory. Initially, this change was provoked by fear, but as therapy progressed conciliation turned to respect for their individual differences.

Though this was the turning point in the therapy, there were still periodic regressions to old patterns. But, the impact of those regressions was buffered by an emerging ego of each person, which helped change their self-definitions. At first, Rose very anxiously took on part-time work outside the family. Her struggles to define herself in a competitive, hierarchical world served not only to bolster her own confidence in her ability to fight for herself, but to help her gain a greater appreciation for Harry's world. It also helped her more effectively manage her oppositional son.

Similarly, Harry began to recognize not only the warmth and support Rose brought to the household, but also his own pent-up need for them that he had never confronted. With great difficulty, workaholic Harry allowed himself occasional weekends to play. To the degree he could integrate some of his own dependency needs, he became less caustic, less critical. In seeing his more nurturant side, Rose was more able to warm up to him, cook his meals, and take greater pride in herself and her household.

CONCLUSION

Not all of their problems had been resolved, but in integrating projected and split-off aspects of themselves, the Goodwills were beginning to see themselves as whole beings, having the capacity for true empathy and love for the other. Beauty/Rose found her strength in her ability to work through her own narcissism and confront the Beast as a peer. She saw his aggressive behavior as a front for deep fears and longings. Rose began to take real pleasure in her home and pride in her ability to nurture her family. Harry/Beast confronted his narcissism by recognizing his dependency and seeing it not as a threat to his autonomy but as a part of his humanity. He bought himself an electric keyboard—but projected a time when he could enjoy playing his baby grand. Both were moving towards that place and time when personal and relational wholeness and integration would make the dichotomous split between Beauty and Beast no longer necessary.

CHAPTER 9

Sexual Inhibitions from an Intersystem Approach

Kate Sexton-Small

INTRODUCTION

The goal of this chapter is to present the reader with a specific case that represents the Intersystem Model. The case of Anne and Steve was selected because of the therapist's thorough assessment of the couple's needs, as well as the consistent use of reframe and prescriptions. Furthermore, the solid client/therapist relationship was significant in providing a context in which spontaneous compliance could occur as well as other changes generated through the work of insight, family-of-origin work, and some traditional behavioral exercises.

CASE FORMULATION

Identifying Information

Anne, age 44, and her husband of five and one-half years, Steve, age 45, sought therapy after a brief discussion of their marital difficulties with their family physician. Both partners were Caucasian and of Protestant descent. Steve was employed full-time as a consulting engineer in a relatively large engineering firm. The projects he was involved with did not involve any creative initiative on his part. He described himself as basically "doing what the others told me to do." Anne worked part-time as a hairdresser in a local salon and spent the remainder of her time involved in her crafts and art work. This couple was referred for therapy by their family physician because of Anne's dissatisfaction with the couple's sexual relationship.

Initial Impressions and Reactions

In the initial visit, Anne reported that she was the partner who insisted that the couple seek therapy. Both partners seemed very tense and anxious in the initial session and clearly felt that their marriage was dependant on the success or failure of the therapy. Anne more clearly verbalized this, stating that if the couple did not work out their problems in treatment, then she would start a divorce process. She also expressed fear that the marriage might not survive the therapy. She even went on to say that seeking therapy meant a probable divorce in her mind. She had already predicted the outcome of the therapy.

Immediately upon meeting this couple, the therapist was struck by the differences in their presentations. Anne seemed much more verbally active and expressive and at an entirely different point in her level of awareness of the "problem" in the marriage. Steve, on the other hand, was not as reserved as he appeared, but was withdrawn and perhaps even depressed. His whole temperament seemed more tentative, more hesitant, and simply slower to act. Anne presented as having much more drive and energy.

Care was taken not to label their differences as either positive or negative in the therapist's own thinking or out loud to the couple. The point was to see the differences and to understand the impact on their relationship, to realize that each partner had very different expectations of their marriage and of their sexual relationship. Steve would have been satisfied with the status quo, and Anne clearly wanted more. The primary motivation for entering therapy for Steve was the fear that Anne would leave the marriage. Each partner had been married and divorced twice in the past. Thus, for each of them, the stakes were very high around the marriage and the therapy.

Presenting Problem

Anne spoke initially, reporting that the primary problem was that the couple's "sex life had gone to nothing." Each partner reported that it had been two years since they had either sexual intercourse or any sexual contact. The week prior to their initial visit, Anne had found a pornographic tape of Steve's. Finding this tape had raised her level of hurt and anxiety about the couple's sexual relationship. When confronted about the tape, Steve reported that he had used the tape as stimulation for masturbation. Anne reported that she was not "upset" about the tape per se, but was "annoyed" that Steve was masturbating and not having sexual intercourse with her. Although Anne denied any feelings of anger, she was visibly hurt and shaken by the experience of finding the tape, and feelings of intense rejection were highly evident and verbalized. She reported feeling rejected "once again."

Steve expressed feeling "badly" that he had upset Anne. He felt extremely responsible for her hurt and pain and very quickly went on to say that he felt he had little to no sexual desire in the relationship. Later in treatment, he clarified that the problem was not so much that he had *no* desire as it was a certain slowness in the awakening of his desire as well as his hesitancy in claiming his own sexual needs. He would refer to this in the therapy as his need to get a "jump start" from Anne to initiate sexual activity. He reported that he was not an aggressive person and that outside (as well as inside) the bedroom he did everything possible to avoid a confrontation. Abstinence from sexual activity with a partner had always been easier for him. In fact, he had never felt sexual or comfortable with sex, before or during any of his three marriages. While Steve felt more comfortable and somewhat more at ease with self-pleasuring, Anne reported that she had masturbated perhaps "once or twice" in her life. She reported intense distaste for self-pleasuring, primarily because of the lack of contact with another person, and expressed no desire in attempting to become more comfortable with masturbation.

Anne clearly saw the problem as primarily a problem with her, namely, that she was not attractive enough to arouse Steve's sexual desire. Likewise, Steve felt that the problem was related primarily to him, in that he had an ongoing history of no sexual desire. He saw himself as completely inadequate in being able to please a partner sexually.

History of the Problem and Solutions Attempted

The differences in this couple's level of desire and their very different sexual needs had always been a problem in their relationship. This was not a couple in which a highly charged sexual attraction had drawn them together. Anne reported that she had made attempts to work on their sexual relationship over the course of their marriage, but that Steve showed little or no interest in her attempts. Most of her attempts centered around buying sexy lingerie, initiating massages, and so forth.

While the couple were dating, it seemed as if they attempted to use alcohol as an aphrodisiac, which apparently worked for a brief period of time. Each reported that while they were living in their home state of Wisconsin, they had a close circle of friends with whom they spent a significant amount of time socializing in a bar. The alcohol appeared to have quelled their sexual inhibitions enough to give Steve the "jump start" he felt he needed. Anne reported that Steve initiated sex more often during this period of their relationship.

The couple had scheduled an appointment with their family physician in an attempt to address their physical and emotional concerns. Steve suffered from high blood pressure as well as from consistent and annoying indigestion and stomach pain. Anne complained of chronic dissatisfaction with her weight and general unhappiness with her body image. She had also stopped smoking within the month of starting therapy, and both reported some increased irritability on Anne's part. The family physician listened attentively to their concerns, and placed Steve on medication for his blood pressure. He also recommended the use of an over-the-counter antacid for Steve's indigestion, as well as some dietary changes. According to the couple, the physician gently asked them about their feelings regarding their marriage, which opened up a discussion about Anne's dissatisfaction with the couple's sexual relationship. The physician then suggested that the couple consider entering couple's therapy, framing their medical concerns as possibly linked to their marital and sexual relationship.

The couple had never sought therapy together during their relationship. Steve had a couple of individual sessions with a psychiatrist in 1979, during his second divorce, which he described as an "I'm OK, You're OK" type of treatment which he did not find helpful. Anne also had some brief individual therapy which was beneficial to her in understanding her difficulty separating from her emotionally abusive first husband.

Changes Sought by Clients

This couple's goals were stated very simply within the first session of their therapy. Steve wanted "to have more of a sex drive" and to "have Anne recognize that I am not just appeasing her by coming to therapy or by altering my behavior." Anne's goal was simply to "create a good sex life before it affects the other parts of our relationship."

Individual and Intergenerational System: Steve

An essential part of understanding a client's behavior is understanding how he or she interprets events. The concept of interpretation was discussed in the first chapter and it was referred to as the fact that the behavior of another is not some objective reality. Furthermore, a person's psychological history and experiences play a major role in how social events are interpreted. Therefore, a client's individual history is critical in understanding how that client interprets events.

Steve was raised in a working-class family in Wisconsin. He was the middle child in a family of three children—having both an older and younger sister. Steve's father was a double amputee, having lost both his legs during World War II, before Steve's birth. His mother worked full-time outside of the house as it became more and more difficult for Steve's father to find work. She apparently was quite successful as the head of a large department in a national chain store. Steve had a rather sketchy memory of his early life. There appeared to be emotional voids of depression which corresponded to his sketchy memory. In the work with Steve, it became clear that his primary defense mechanism was denial, which was the primary defense mechanism for the entire family as well.

There appears to have been a great deal of emotional deprivation in Steve's early life. He described his father as a very proud man who spent a lot of time outside of the family at the local Veterans club. He also described periods of time during which his father drank very heavily, and reported that his father refused medication for pain after the loss of his legs and that he believed his father drank to cope with the physical and emotional pain in his life. Steve denied that any strong sense of anger or loss affected the family as a result of his father's injury. He did have some recollections of going with his father at various times to bars and clubs in order to spend time with him. Steve's father died of a heart attack in 1963, when Steve was 14.

As the therapist listened to Steve telling his story, it seemed that part of what he struggled with individually was the family secrets surrounding his father. One would think that there had to have been a tremendous sense of pain and loss with his father's disability; yet, according to Steve, the disability was rarely mentioned. Clearly, his father never was able to make the painful but necessary adjustments to his disability. The father's alcoholism was also consistently denied. The consistency of the family pattern had taught Steve to deny his own affective experience (pain, loss, anger, pleasure), which most notably was impacting his role in his sexual relationship. It was terribly confusing for him to have a partner who showed signs of distress about his lack of pleasure when he had been raised in such an emotionally numb family. It appeared that Steve's powerlessness and lack of initiative were indications of his loyalty to and introjections of his father.

Underneath what Steve described and was conscious of, the clinician was left with a sense of Steve's internal shame. Early in his life he felt shameful of his own body, and had memories of hiding his body from fellow students in high school locker rooms out of fear of being ridiculed and humiliated. He had been overweight since childhood and had never been happy with his appearance, but felt too "lazy" to do anything about it. He also reported always feeling that his genitals were an "inadequate" size.

Sexuality was never mentioned during Steve's childhood and adolescence. There was a sense of the forbidden which hung over the subject in the family. Predictably, both of Steve's sisters became pregnant as teens before marriage. His older sister reportedly believed she had no other option but to marry; to have done otherwise would have brought shame to Steve's mother. She has since had two divorces and is an active alcoholic. Steve's younger sister raised her child alone without marrying, but with considerable dissonance in her relationship with her mother. Steve reported that these experiences, somewhere in his semiconscious mind, taught him that sex and sexuality were dangerous and that there would be very considerable negative consequences to enjoying his sexuality. He never learned that sex was for pleasure, and reported that masturbation was always an "easier" sexual activity for him, in part because it did not carry the same potential negative consequences of pregnancy and in part because it was done in isolation and did not involve intimacy with another person.

Therefore, what is learned from Steve's individual and intergenerational history is that he interpreted all feelings as a threat, as something that needed to be self-medicated away or "numbed" in some fashion. He also learned to interpret his own body and his sexuality as shameful and inadequate. He predicted that sex and sexuality were dangerous to him as they were to his two sisters, who clearly suffered negative consequences in enjoying their sexuality. Finally, he learned to predict that masturbation was always easier than intercourse with a partner, because it did not involve meeting someone else's needs and possibly leading to disappointment in him. He clearly had learned to predict Anne's dissatisfaction in their mutual sexual activity.

Individual and Intergenerational System: Anne

Anne also was raised in a working-class family in Wisconsin. She had an older sister and an older brother who were in their early 20's when Anne was born. Anne's "story" is a very poignant one and underscores the power of certain "stories" in a family and how the messages that are communicated with the stories get internalized. When Anne's mother was pregnant with her, she reportedly never went outside of the house during the day, thus avoiding being seen. Anne attributed this to her mother's reported sense of shame about being pregnant at the age of 40. She very quickly went on to say that her mother had a very painful history of her own, which certainly had left a legacy for Anne. Anne's maternal grandmother had died during childbirth and her mother was reportedly raised by an "elderly woman." Anne's maternal grandfather rejected his daughter at birth, and her mother had many stories of having been neglected and abused by her foster mother. Anne's mother clearly never felt accepted and loved as a child and greatly feared that her own daughter would face a similar rejection. It seemed that the best way her mother knew to protect Anne from this anticipated rejection was to consistently warn her of the "evils" of men—abuse, neglect, and ultimate rejection. Anne grew up very conscious of her mother's fears and her feelings of being unwanted and unloved.

Anne reported that her father physically and emotionally abused her mother during the early years of Anne's parents' marriage. Her siblings have discussed with her the nature and extent of the abuse as they had witnessed it. She denied ever having experienced or witnessed the abuse and reported that her parents had a very different marriage when she was born. Anne attributed this difference primarily to her father having aged by the time she was born and having simply "burned out" his anger. However, she did report one incident of sexual abuse during her latency age, a traumatic evening when both of her parents had gone out to dinner with friends and Anne was supposed to stay with her sister and brother-in-law. She was about age 11, and her sister and brother-in-law were about 34. Apparently, Anne's sister was called into work at the last moment and Anne was left alone with her sister's husband. He forced her into their bedroom, made her take her clothes off, and then proceeded to rub her vaginal area with oil. She somehow managed to get away before there was any penetration and ran home in fear.

Anne recalled telling her parents as soon as they arrived home, and her father reportedly confronted her sister and brother-in-law. However, Anne did not know what came of the confrontation. All other details of this traumatic evening were repressed by Anne when she told the story. There was some slight fear and anxiety evident, but most of the affect associated with the horror seemed to be very distant to Anne. Her sister remained married to the man and Anne reported that he never again attempted to touch her. She still sees him at family functions and reports a tremendous mixture of anxiety and rage before these gatherings. There has never been another word spoken in the family about the sexual abuse.

Anne learned to interpret all of Steve's behavior as a personal rejection of her. It was difficult for her to view his feelings of sexual inadequacy and his masturbation as anything other than a rejection of her. She also learned to swallow her rage and depression about her experiences of sexual abuse. In summary, she had learned to predict rejection, that men would neglect and abuse her in one way or another, and that she should not talk about her sadness and rage about her own history.

Interactional System: Steve and Anne

One of the most evident emotional contracts (Sager, 1976) unconsciously built into their marital agreement was that Anne would take the lead in almost all matters of this couple's life. It was she who was motivated to seek therapy and seek a more pleasurable and active sexual relationship. Steve very consciously stated that he felt more comfortable with someone taking the lead and, in fact, had searched out this type of individual in his professional and personal life. He certainly would have felt fine with their relationship as it was before they entered treatment when they had not had intercourse for two years. Steve has always maintained a high level of unconscious loyalty to his family of origin by maintaining an asexual relationship. This allowed him to continue to believe his family's myth that sex and sexuality were dangerous and, therefore, brought negative consequences. Furthermore, he learned to predict that masturbation was always easier than intercourse with a partner, because it did not involve meeting someone else's needs and arousing their possible disappointment in him. He never had to risk any of this as long as the relationship was asexual. That part of his expectation of a partner just so happened to "fit like a glove" with a different part of Anne's unconscious expectations of a partner—Anne's belief that her role was to protect Steve (and any husband) from dealing directly with his own anxieties and feelings of inadequacy. She learned very early on, in part from the legacy of her mother's adoptive experience, to both anticipate rejection and take responsibility for those rejections. She came into therapy not only protecting Steve from his own sexual anxieties and inhibitions, but convinced that she was responsible for them because she was not attractive enough, or sexual enough. Almost all of her attempts to solve the problem were focused on "solving" some aspect of "her." She assumed all responsibility for discussing the conflict and all responsibility for virtually every aspect of the conflict.

Another clear emotional pull between this couple was the extent of past pain and emotional deprivation in each of their lives. They were both highly conflicted about their own sexuality and felt a tremendous amount of shame, not only about their sexuality but also about who they were as people. But they seemed to have found in each other the ability to work on some of those internal issues as they never had before. Although their shame united them, there was a sense of hope in them because of their ability to be more aware of it, to project it less onto each other and take more individual responsibility for it, and to begin to work it through.

Interestingly enough, his lack of desire protected her from dealing more directly with the sexual abuse she experienced as a child. It was not until after the couple was consistently maintaining a more pleasurable sexual relationship that Anne requested some individual therapy to deal with her affect and memories of the sexual trauma. The relationship protected Steve from his feelings of shame and deprivation by maintaining his asexual nature. Steve never had to confront his feelings of sexual inadequacy and shame as long as the relationship was asexual. The relationship allowed him to continue to believe the family's myth that sex and sexuality were dangerous and therefore brought negative consequences. Each had a part in the collusion around confronting their feelings of inadequacy and rejection by avoiding intimacy for a two-year period.

This couple's style of communication was mainly one of avoidance. Just as they had avoided sexual contact for two years before entering treatment, they also had avoided true verbal communication for many years. Therefore, they had very poor conflict-resolution skills and the only strategy they had learned was to avoid the issues between them.

TREATMENT

A discussion of the treatment initially involves the process of defining problems and then defining pathways to change. It also involves a reflection on the outcome of the treatment itself. These can be very difficult issues to evaluate since, in fact, "one man's ceiling is another man's floor." What may constitute clinical success to the therapist may be very different from the individual's or the couple's perspective regarding successful outcome. Chances are that even the two members of the couple will have very different ideas of whether or not their therapy was successful. Another significant component of evaluating problems, goals, and outcome is the time period during which the evaluation occurred. This chapter discusses a couple who, at the time of this writing, had been in treatment for the prior six months. If the same criteria were examined two years down the road, there is little doubt that the outcome would be very different. With that in mind, we proceed to a discussion of the treatment process and the outcome of the case in question.

Treatment Plan and Strategies

In the beginning of the treatment process, a strong reliance is placed upon the clients' stated goals. By establishing a treatment relationship in which the clients participate in setting the agenda of the therapy via his/her/their goals, the therapist is working with the therapeutic paradox of taking control by giving it back to the clients. It is the clients, not simply the therapist, who establish the goals. Also, this sets the stage for the use of the symptom as the point of departure in the therapeutic process. The clients understand the message that change occurs from naming, accepting, and working with the symptom, and not, as pointed out in the introductory chapter, by fleeing from it. Their goals are also a reflection of how they view the problem.

This couple's goals were stated very simply within the first session of their therapy. Steve wanted "to have more of a sex drive" and to "have Anne recognize that I am not just appeasing her by coming to therapy or altering my behavior." Anne's goal was simply "to create a good sex life before it affects the other parts of their life." In many ways, these two statements defined the problem as each partner viewed it when the couple entered therapy. The statements also defined the pathways to changing what had felt very burdensome to the couple over the past two years. The statement of their goals was the core of the treatment agenda; if those stated goals were not met, one could say that the therapy had failed.

Over the course of the therapy, the goals were continually reevaluated and updated. Each partner, over time, added other individual problems and goals to be worked on during the course of the therapy.

Anne identified unresolved depression and grief from her family of origin, and established the goal of opening up and talking more about that part of herself to alleviate the sadness. To address old messages of anticipated rejection, she established the goal of separating out the attribution from the reality, so that she could see the ways Steve was not rejecting her currently.

Steve identified depression and grief from his unresolved family-of-origin issues, and established goals related to the psychiatric evaluation of his depression, with a possible view towards medication, along with increased expression of the affective side of his personality. The learned messages that sexual pleasure brings negative consequences were to be addressed through the goal of separating out prediction from reality, so that sex could be pleasurable without negative outcomes.

The couple also established some couple goals, namely to improve their communication via the expression of their grief, anger, fears, rejection, and their sexual inhibitions as well the context of the therapy. They continually reported that the single most important strategy that they found helpful was talking to each other. They also made a commitment to work on their sexual relationship via sexual exercises at home.

From an intergenerational perspective, the goal of the therapist was to help the couple to see the larger pattern established by their experiences within their families of origin. That goal was facilitated by the use of consistent reframing and highlighting where each partner was repeating within the marriage interpretations and predictions from the learned experiences from the families of origin. Furthermore, the Bowenian task of "sending the client home" was utilized to increase insight into the various definitions, interpretations, and predictions utilized by the couple.

Hypothesis Regarding the Client

Once grounded in the couple's perspective on their problems, and having discussed their individual and couple goals, the therapist added her own clinical judgement and experience about those issues. From very early on, it was felt that Steve's Inhibited Sexual Desire (ISD) was related to an unresolved depression. He had a complete physical examination which suggested none of the physical factors that may be associated with inhibited sexual desire. His testosterone level was well within the normal range, his thyroid function was fine, and he was not on any medication that would inhibit his desire. He had been evaluated by a physician well known to the therapist, whose examination could be accepted as highly competent. Moreover, when his history was explored, there certainly was more than enough evidence to support psychogenic hypotheses regarding why Steve was experiencing ISD. Also, on an interactional or couple level, there was a great deal of unresolved anger, resentment, and fear on each of their parts; this played a large contributing role in the ISD within the couple.

Anne likewise had a history that one could say would inevitably lead to sexual difficulties as an adult. Her history of sexual abuse as a child, and then later strong verbal abuse by her first husband, could clearly be seen as contributing factors to the couple's ISD. Also, her mother's legacy of anticipated rejection was an affective legacy which defined the core of Anne's self and, therefore, in part, defined her sexuality.

Once a perspective has been gained on the client's goals and views of the problem, then the way of achieving these goals can be an outgrowth of this information and the therapist's own clinical judgment. Therefore, the initial individual goal for both Steve and Anne was to come to understand how their individual histories contributed to their sexual issues within the marriage, and more broadly, to their general roles in the marriage. When this was done, basically by separating out the interpretations and definitions which were projected onto each other, the stage would be set for the couple to begin to work together on their marital and, more specifically, sexual relationship.

Prognosis and Expected Length of Treatment

The expectation was that the couple would remain in therapy for approximately one year, and that they would gain some initial relief from the symptom with which they presented. This was based on the assumption that the preliminary, required family-of-origin work could not be accomplished in a shorter period of time. Having achieved that, the therapist sensed that they would also choose to reenter therapy at another point in time and would then work on some of the deeper, underlying issues that faced each of them. Their prognosis was excellent for symptom relief and for gaining some insight into the deeper issues.

Process of Treatment

A description of the process of therapy must essentially begin with a description of the treatment relationship between the couple and the therapist, for, in part, it is the corrective and reparative experience of the treatment relationship that can facilitate and promote client change and growth. The nature of that relationship is somewhat paradoxical. Within the first chapter, it was noted that the therapist provides the techniques and the relational context in which clients learn to change symptoms. In the case of Steve and Anne, the techniques (i.e., reframe, prescriptions, sexual exercises, etc.) as well as the relational context (a highly congruent client/therapist relationship) were utilized to alleviate the presenting problem of lack of sexual desire within the couple.

It was also essential that the therapist accept the presenting problem or symptom. The clients needed to learn to see the symptom positively; Steven and Anne needed to see the protective function of their inhibited sexual desire. After all, the inhibitions had protected Steve from examining some very painful feelings of inadequacy and depression. His avoidance of sexual contact with Anne was, in essence, his form of "medicating" the feelings. The inhibitions also protected him from suffering any negative consequences to his sexuality. For Anne, the inhibited sexual desire on their part, as a couple, allowed her to protect herself from her own rage and depression about her sexual history. As long as she was focused on Steve's lack of sexual desire, her own history of pain was pushed into the background.

Each of these clients entered therapy with a very fragile sense of self as individuals and as a couple, and anticipated that the therapist would disapprove of their symptomatic behavior. Forming a good relationship with this couple (highly congruent) and accepting their inhibitions (and labeling them as protective and, therefore, useful) went a long way in establishing a working relationship.

When the couple entered therapy, they defined the relationship in a particular way and, in turn, their relationship defined each of the partners. It quickly became apparent that Anne assumed a tremendous amount of emotional responsibility for Steve. She had learned within her family of origin that it was her role to protect everyone else from what she was feeling. She carried all of the anger within their marriage. Her anger clearly served a function of protecting her partner from dealing with his own sexual desires. As long as she was angry, the focus was never on Steve's feelings.

One of the most consistent strategies used throughout the work with this couple was that of reframing. In fact, the entire therapy can in some ways be thought of as a reframe. The purpose of reframing is to alter the client's current belief system about the "problem" and about each partner's role in the problem. During the initial phase of the therapy, the clients were attributing negative and linear meanings to their partner's behavior. This was helping to keep them stuck in their sexual dilemma—in fact, maintaining the problem.

Anne was attributing Steve's lack of desire purely as an intent on his part to reject her as others had clearly rejected her in the past. She initially saw no other way of viewing his masturbation and lack of sexual desire other than as a rejection of herself. Her own introjection of her mother's legacy (namely one of rejection) kept her from seeing the problem in a larger context that would have freed her. Therapeutic interventions consistently pointed out to Anne that Steve's ISD was in part connected to his own feelings of sexual inadequacy and shame. The couple was reminded that Steve had not had a satisfactory sexual relationship at any point in his life. Obviously, the scope of the problem went beyond Anne's relationship with Steve. Consider the following excerpt from one of the sessions:

Anne: I just feel hopeless. He certainly has no interest in me sexually. All he is interested in is masturbating or avoiding me. It must be that I'm not good enough for him. No matter what I do, I can't arouse him.

Therapist: You seem to feel the problem is all your "fault" or Steve's "fault." It's not clear to me that Steve is consciously rejecting you, as much as he is having difficulty dealing with his own sexual feelings of inadequacy. You both seem to have come from families with a lot of sexual inhibitions. I think that's at play here. Maybe you're both maintaining some loyalty to old messages. What do you think? Does what I'm saying make sense to you?

Anne: My mother never wanted to touch me or kiss me goodnight. She felt she was preparing me for what was to come in the future. She always felt rejected and wanted me to prepare myself for rejection as well. I guess I have. I see it everywhere.

Steve: I've always felt inadequate. I was ashamed of my body as a kid and hid in the locker rooms when it came time to undress. I was constantly humiliated about my body and I always felt ashamed of my father's disability.

There were moments in the therapy when the reframe clearly "fit" for them and the shift within them could be "felt." It was a relief to them to be given a different meaning for the problem, namely, that the sexual inhibitions of each had allowed this couple to join together at their psychological cores in order to work through their inhibitions and fears of rejection and to become more whole as individuals and as a couple. The relationship between them and with the therapist was "safe enough" to expose those inhibitions and desires and work them through. Without the inhibitions, they would have been even more alienated and alone in the relationship. It was the inhibitions and fears of rejections that, in fact, initially joined the couple.

This reframe was successful in altering the linear and negative attributional processes within the couple. It allowed all members of the system to accept some responsibility for the problem. It probably would not have been successful without a congruent client/therapist relationship. The clients were congruent in the sense that each desired a more positive sexual relationship with their partner. They also were in congruence in that they anticipated abandonment and rejection if they desired a sexual relationship.

Altering this linear and negative attributional process in the couple was a very powerful experience for each of them. Part of what made this so powerful was the shift away from the responsibility for the problem being all Steve's or Anne's to the more circular definition of the problem as one which existed between the two of them as well as within their experience in their families of origin. Basically, the shift away from blaming and negative thinking to a deeper understanding of how their individual histories contributed to their sexual concerns within the marriage freed them up. The reframe highlighted and then separated out for the couple the negative projective process that had been occurring between them. It also set the stage for the couple to begin to work together on their relationship in a more congruent way.

As noted in Chapter 1, reframing is an essential part of therapy; however, alone it is rarely enough to affect change. The second ingredient most consistently utilized throughout the therapy with Steve and Anne consisted of prescriptions. These grew out of the goals the clients had established in the first session and continued to modify throughout the therapy. A choice was made to work with affirmation prescriptions based on the sense that the couple was only moderately resistant and that they had the ability to reflect. In general, these clients appeared to have symptoms over which they believed they had no control, but they did not seem resistant to change.

One of the prescriptions used was a series of sexual exercises designed to enhance the couple's sense of sexual pleasure. The talking within the therapy hour was focused around freeing up some of the inhibitions to enable them to utilize the exercises in a beneficial way. The exercises were the tried and true components of traditional sex therapy (e.g., Kaplan, 1974). Along with the behavioral exercises, a series of instructional reading was assigned to serve as support for the ongoing work. The couple read *ISD* (Knopf & Seiler, 1990) and *For Each Other* (Barbach, 1983). Steve also read *Male Sexuality* (Zilbergeld, 1978) and Anne read *For Yourself* (Barbach, 1975) as well as *The Courage to Heal* (Bass & Davis, 1988). They learned to utilize the exercises and reading successfully and reported that this was helpful in reestablishing their sexual relationship.

One of the things that struck the therapist immediately about this couple was that despite not having intercourse for two years, they started having intercourse immediately after their first session. Generally, when working with couples where there is an issue of lack of desire that has been ongoing for a year or more (especially where there is literally no sexual contact), it can take quite a long period of time before that begins to be resolved. Shock was the feeling experienced when they came back after their initial session and reported having had intercourse twice in the previous week. Initially, the possibility was considered that this was simply a "flight into health" and that the therapy had given them permission to be sexual with each other and to talk about their secret feelings of inadequacy and inhibition. Yet, by allowing her room to talk about her anger, Anne was freed up to assume her normative role in their sexual relationship, which was to initiate or take charge. After she did this, the couple enjoyed having sex with each other and showed no difficulty at any other point in the sexual response cycle. Of course, a deeper issue would be Steve feeling freed up to initiate sexually. The couple continued to have intercourse at least once weekly throughout the treatment.

This could also be explained/framed as an example of spontaneous compliance, as described in Chapter 1. The use of permission, positive reframes, and the forming of the highly congruent client/therapist relationship established almost immediately the prerequisites necessary for this couple to change rapidly.

Another prescription utilized throughout the therapy was essentially a Bowenian technique (Bowen, 1978). I encouraged both Steve and Anne to meet with various family members to simply ask questions about their past. The hope was that this process would provide some insight for each of them about how their family-of-origin experiences were impacting their current sexual relationship.

Steve linked his relationship with his mother to his relationship with Anne and with women in general. He discussed how his own mother had been the "aggressive" and "dominant" parent and partner and that as a child he had felt embarrassed and ashamed of her assertiveness/aggression. He acknowledged that he had learned very early on to feel comfortable with someone taking the lead and that in fact he had looked for that throughout most of his life. He connected this with his pattern of wanting Anne to assume responsibility for initiating sex with him.

It was during this family-of-origin focused phase of the therapy that Steve began to gain some understanding of how he had coped with his own feelings throughout much of his life. He came to describe himself as "naturally avoidant," always being able to focus inwardly and avoid confrontation with anyone else. He talked about feeling frustrated with Anne's expectation, but denied that he was angry with her. He went on to say that he "never" gets angry with Anne, which, of course, was linked to his experience in his own family where so much of his own affective world had been denied.

At the same time, Steve was working on deepening his understanding of his connection with his father, whom he had lost as a teenager. He began to explore in more depth his difficulty with anger, his identification with his father, and his fears around confronting his mother. He spent a lot of time in the therapy focused on the deprivation of affect within his family and recounting experiences with the recognition that he had learned to cut off his feelings around those experiences at the time. Slowly, he began to connect some affect, primarily loss, to those events. Most of the events centered around stories of his father's alcoholism and the painful denial of that in the family. He began to see how well he had learned to deny all feelings, including sexual ones, and how much he was repeating that process within the marriage.

It was during that phase of the therapeutic process that Anne disclosed her experience of childhood sexual abuse, a fact that she had repressed for many years. She began to understand how that trauma had contributed to her own sexual inhibitions and conflicts about desire. Her own sexual history was closely linked with the taboo of the abuse, which strongly contributed to her ambivalence about feeling good about sexual desire. She had learned from the experience that men are abusive toward women and with girls and "use" them to meet their own needs. This was also coupled with her mother's experiences as an "illegitimate" child and the legacy that left for Anne. That issue, as well as the inevitable pain and loss that surrounded it, was the core aspect of the issues which emerged for Anne in that part of therapy. She was able to make connections between those past issues and her feeling of being sexually unwanted by Steve and her discomfort at being the more aggressive sexual partner in the marriage.

CONCLUSION

Anne and Steve made considerable progress during the year they were in couples therapy. Despite not having had intercourse for two years prior to entering therapy, they were able to maintain at least weekly sexual contact during the time that they were in therapy. They attributed this change primarily to their increased awareness and understanding of themselves as individuals and as a couple. Also, they attributed the change to their increased ability to effectively communicate with each other. The treatment relationship appears to have been "safe enough" for each of them to discuss and learn more about their sexual inhibitions as well as their experiences within their families of origin. This was facilitated by a complete "team" assessment of the couple's needs, the establishment of a congruent client/therapist relationship, and the consistent use of reframe and prescriptions. Furthermore, the solid relational context went a long way in supporting the clients' own growth and change, in providing a context in which spontaneous compliance could occur along side of changes which occurred through the hard work of personal insight, family-of-origin work, and skill-based training to effect behavioral change.

CHAPTER 10

Chronic Illness and Couple Conflict

Joellyn L. Ross

INTRODUCTION

The following case is especially illustrative of the value of the multidimensional Intersystem Model. The couple's problems were the result of the interaction of many systems and factors—intergenerational and individual systems, with issues around chronic illness, gender roles, and life cycle development. The challenge for the therapist was to orchestrate and balance working with all of these systems and issues, as they all were important to the couple's learning to interact in a more productive fashion.

The presenting problem for the couple was the husband's chronic illness. The illness had upset the balance of the couple's relationship and had become the focus of marital arguments as the couple struggled to cope with periodic life-threatening hospitalizations. Chronic illness can develop a presence in the couple and family system such that it functions as a member of the system. Attention to the illness and its impact on the system, therefore, was an important part of therapy.

CASE FORMULATION

Initial Impressions

The Landons were an attractive couple in their late thirties, married for 15 years with three children, ages 14 to 10. Susan, sounding somewhat panicked, did all of the talking. Brad had been in a diabetic crisis three weeks ago and she said, "Something has to change. I can't live with his ups and downs anymore. I'm tired of worrying about him." Brad, looking relaxed, said he really was okay, but he came to therapy because Susan wanted him to: "Susan's been reading too many psychology books, and she's always trying to analyze me. She should just calm down." Both acknowledged they were not "getting along," but were unable to be more specific, other than to say, "We fight over nothing."

The couple had been referred to the therapist by their physician because of the therapist's work with couples and families in which someone has a chronic and/or psychosomatic illness. During the inital phone contact, Susan had indicated it was important that whomever they saw understand Brad's diabetes, because she said it was causing conflict. After meeting with the couple, the therapist's impression was that, like most families in which someone has a chronic illness, the illness had become the focus, but was not necessarily the whole problem. Another impression was that each partner was setting the other up to behave in gender stereotypic ways that neither one liked nor wanted, but which served to maintain their bickering.

Presenting Problem

According to Susan, the presenting problem was Brad's lack of responsibility for controlling his diabetes: "He's not as careful as he should be and knows how to be." According to Brad, the problem was Susan's being overcontrolling of him, as well as her recent interest in psychology, which he felt she was using to analyze and criticize him.

When they were questioned further, it became clear that the couple's daily bickering about Brad's diabetes was the most visible manifestation of their ongoing conflict. Also at issue were the following: (1) the couple's individual and joint relationships with their families of origin; (2) Brad's career, currently in a slump, and his relationship with his family and their business; and (3) Susan's having gone back to school after being a full-time homemaker for 12 years, which resulted in her expecting that Brad help with the children and the household chores.

The therapist observed that the couple's focus on the diabetes served the purpose of preventing other issues from being discussed or resolved. Susan's reading of self-help psychology books had increased her awareness of how family issues can affect people, but her tendency to use her newfound information to analyze Brad and his diabetes (more so than herself, Brad said) had become another source of conflict. As with the diabetes, Susan's becoming an "expert" about what she saw as Brad's problem resulted in her overfunctioning, and his underfunctioning, in their relationship.

The couple's interactions were marked by their lack of listening to and responding to one another. Susan tended to lecture Brad, which he did not take seriously, as indicated by his bored expression and tendency to look away. When he did not take her complaints seriously, she would escalate into harangues. Like the classic "warm-sick wife" and "cold-sick husband"

(Martin, 1976), Susan's efforts to connect with Brad seemed to push him further away, while his distancing increased her frustration and her efforts to connect.

History of the Problem

Brad's diabetes had been diagnosed seven years previously after what the couple said were many frustrations trying to find out what was the matter with him. Unfortunately, he was not able to be maintained by oral medication and had to give himself insulin injections. Over the past seven years, he had had a number of crises and ended up in the hospital, "Near death," Susan said; "Not that serious," Brad countered. The couple had a seven-year history of Susan's trying to be in charge of Brad's medical care, and his being at times noncompliant. "She even makes my doctor nuts with all her questions," he said. "She doesn't trust that I can manage myself."

In conversation, Brad downplayed the significance of his illness and its impact on his life. Diabetes, however, alters one's existence irrevocably, which also causes changes in self-concept. It requires the person to live by the clock and to adhere to a strict schedule of diet, insulin, and exercise. Regardless of how carefully the person follows the medical regime, s/he still can go into insulin shock, and this often is unpredictable. Most people resent having diabetes and the self-attention and management it requires (Kerson, 1985). Life cycle stage can be a significant factor in the person's (and spouse's) ability to cope with chronic illness. Having a chronic illness as a young adult, as with Brad, puts one "out of sync" with one's peers, as few people in their mid-thirties suffer health problems or have to follow medical regimes. This can lead to feelings of isolation, particularly when the person is in the company of healthy peers (Glueckauf & Quittner, 1984). Most healthy younger people are loathe to discuss health concerns, so the person with the illness can feel bereft of support. The spouse can feel similarly isolated.

Another significant factor in Brad's life, also during the past seven years, was that he had left his position in his family's business in order to start his own business, which was not doing as well as expected. The couple mentioned that there had been many problems within Brad's family over the management of their business, which had been started by Brad's father. Conflict with his father had led to Brad's leaving. Although money was currently not a problem, Susan expressed concern about their long-term financial security, especially given the status of Brad's business. The ongoing issues with the business served as a backdrop problem to the diabetes.

The couple said their problems with each other had gradually developed over the last seven years, but had intensified once Susan went back to school full-time to earn her teaching certificate. "She's never around," Brad complained, while Susan said she had decided to finish her education "because you never know what's going to happen; I need to be able to work."

Solutions Attempted

The couple had not been in therapy previously. Susan's reading of self-help books and her trying to talk with Brad about what she saw as his part of their problems was the only solution attempted. Unfortunately, this "solution" served only to anger Brad and to escalate the couple's conflict.

Changes Sought by Clients

Both Susan and Brad said they were tired of their bickering. Susan said she wanted Brad to manage his diabetes responsibly, and Brad said he wanted Susan to "get off my back and quit getting hysterical about things."

Recent Significant Changes

Susan's going back to school full-time had made her less available, which had reverberated through the family. Brad complained that she was "constantly tense," and never had any time for him. He described the household as being in an uproar. Susan complained that Brad didn't help with the children or the house: "I can't do everything by myself." They agreed that their bickering had intensified with each semester Susan was in school.

Intersystem Assessment

Individual systems

After several conjoint sessions, the therapist had individual sessions with each partner in order to develop a connection with each of them, and also to ask about their family histories and experiences. Each related well and connected easily with the therapist. Brad kept himself more distant than Susan, but he relaxed once he realized he was not being judged.

Susan Landon looked the therapist straight in the eye as she began talking about herself. Her intensity changed the energy level of the room. She shifted in her chair, leaned forward, and smiled, saying she wanted this joint therapeutic project to work well. She wore attractive, comfortable clothing, and looked ready for action, but very appropriate.

Susan was the youngest of three children, and described her family as "crazy." Her father was an alcoholic, "very loving," but he also could be nasty and cruel. Her mother was an exceptionally attractive woman, but interpersonally judgmental and cold. Her parents divorced when she was six and Susan and her older brother and sister were left to rear themselves, as their mother worked full-time. "Our mother ignored us," Susan said, and "I was very self-reliant." She survived by being a good student and close with her sister, and by having many friends, whose families she adopted. She was very close with her high school boyfriend's family, whom she described as being very accepting. "I was never home," she said.

Susan met Brad when both were in college. "We had good chemistry," she said. She also was attracted to his family, which appeared to be closer and more solid than her own.

Susan reported that currently there was ongoing conflict between herself, her mother, and her sister. All three rarely got along at the same time, and numerous incidents were described in which two of the three women were angry with the third. Her mother was viewed as not being a very good mother or grandmother, as being "very self-involved," and as one who never praised Susan's skills as a mother. Although her sister and her mother lived at some distance, contact with them was rather frequent. Susan said she rarely saw her older brother, an alcoholic, "who has his own problems."

Finishing her education was very important to Susan, who was studying to be an occupational therapist. She thought she had had learning problems when in school (although she did very well) and that two of her three children had minor learning disabilities, all of which served to intensify her interest in what she was studying. She was very active in her children's school's parent-teacher association, which was a source of conflict for her and Brad. As she explained it, "He doesn't understand that my involvement helps *our* children. He just gets annoyed that I'm not at home."

Susan impressed the therapist as a bright, mildly anxious woman who assumed full reponsibility for her husband's and children's emotional welfare, despite the fact that her current schedule did not allow her to be as involved with them as she had been in the past. She complained about being overwhelmed by her responsibilities and undersupported by her husband and extended family. She was very committed to her husband and children, and repeatedly said, "There will be no divorce. This (therapy) isn't about divorce. This is about making our marriage work."

Brad was much quieter than Susan, and at first less forthcoming. He was tall and smoothly handsome, with a sardonic twist to his smile. His body posture was rigid, suggesting he was very uncomfortable, but he maintained good eye contact and an open expression. He looked like a man who might have been athletic in his youth, but had long since given up trying to be physically fit.

He also was the youngest of three children, with an older brother and sister. He described his relationship with his family as "terrible." "I haven't spoken with my brother in seven years, don't speak with my father much, and don't like to see the others," he said.

Most of Brad's distress about his family centered on the family business, which Brad had been a part of until seven years ago, when he and his father became locked in a power struggle. Brad got out of the struggle by leaving Father's business and starting his own. "I don't think my father's ever forgiven me," Brad said, "I think he was more upset about losing the battle than about losing me as an employee." Brad was diagnosed with diabetes at about the same time, something he still struggled to accept. He hated how it restricted his life and forced him to pay attention to his diet. His family also had difficulty with his being diabetic and, as a result, tended to deny the illness and see him as malingering, rather than as having a legitimate medical problem. "They thought Susan just wasn't feeding me right," he said, "even though they know better than that."

Brad admitted to the therapist that he did not always follow his diet and medication regime, which is what had led to some of his diabetic crises and hospitalizations. He said, however, that his recent hospitalization was not due to carelessness: "I don't know what happened. I woke up in the hospital." He reluctantly admitted that the recent crisis had frightened him, but that he had not told this to Susan. The illness had made him cautious about himself and his life, and he was afraid business associates would find out he was diabetic. "I don't want people to think they're dealing with a sick person," he said.

The therapist pressed Brad into discussing all of these issues, as well as others related to his having a chronic illness. He said that on the one hand, he had been relieved when the diabetes finally was diagnosed, but that he also felt his life had ended that day. "I just feel I'll never be able to relax ever again."

Brad's relationship with his father was, in some ways, similar to how Susan characterized her relationship with her mother, although the therapist's impression was that Brad's family was more a shame-based system than was Susan's. Brad's father was very domineering and self-centered, and criticized all his children. "My father was a maniac and my mother enabled him." Brad said that although he discussed business plans with his father, the older man tended to denigrate Brad's ideas. His mother, on the other hand, was "very sweet," but afraid of her husband so she did not question or challenge his actions with the children.

The therapist assessed Brad as a man who still was coping with the diagnosis and management of a chronic illness, as well as coping with the effects of growing up with an abusive father. He presented as bright, insightful, and mildly depressed. He said he wanted his marriage and family life to be more peaceful, but sadly noted, "Susan's never there for me anymore."

Interactional system

The couple's communication patterns swung back and forth between the two extremes of unproductive bickering and calm intelligent conversation. When they bickered, they were awful: defensive, accusing each other of not caring, diagnosing each other's personality flaws and their respective families' bad influence on them, and criticizing each other's child-rearing abilities. When they talked calmly, however, they were remarkably insightful about themselves and their families, and they were able to do productive problem-solving.

The shifts, especially their inability to remain calm, seemed to serve the function of keeping the couple from developing lasting emotional intimacy. As neither claimed to have enjoyed emotional fulfillment in their families of origin, their distance as a couple was consistent with their early emotional experiences, albeit very unsatisfactory. When both were calm, they were able to acknowledge that they each had difficulty accepting the possibility that they deserved the kind of relationship they wanted. Both admitted to feeling defective and unworthy of love.

The couple's knowledge of conflict resolution skills was better than their presentation might have suggested. When they were calm, they actually were quite good at negotiating decisions. The challenge for the therapist was to stop their most destructive behaviors, namely, negative attribution and vilification, manifested by their diagnosing each other and the influence of each other's family, accusing each other of bad intentions and destructive behavior, and criticizing each other's interactions with the children. The goal in therapy was to increase the amount of time the couple could interact calmly and respectfully.

Intergenerational system

Both Brad's and Susan's families of origin played a significant, ongoing role in the couple's conflict. Neither Susan nor Brad felt valued by their families, yet both were strongly tied to them, especially their respective same-sex parents. Susan looked to her mother and Brad looked to his father for validation, confirmation, and support. They did this despite the fact that both described these parents as self-centered and insensitive, and unlikely to satisfy their needs. Susan repeatedly tried to develop a close rapport with her mother, and Brad attempted to get his father's respect. Neither was successful in these efforts.

In addition to their frustrating relationships with their parents, both Brad and Susan had conflictual relationships with their siblings. They reported frequent disputes, usually over something relatively insignificant, which then mimicked other relationships in the family. In the end, distance was maintained.

Despite their terrible interactions with their families, the couple did have frequent contact with them. They received minimal emotional support from them, but did get some financial support. The limited emotional support was enough to keep them hoping for more, which never materialized. The two families seemed to come together relatively well around special occasions and holidays. The couple was disappointed, however, that their parents and siblings were not more supportive of their childrearing. Both of them took pride in their children and wished for more acknowledgement from their families.

Brad and Susan's children seemed to be relatively unaffected by their parents' bickering. All did satisfactorily in school and had many friends. The couple reported their house was the neighborhood meeting place for children, which they encouraged. Susan was active in school programs and scouting, while Brad was the one father most available to many of the neighborhood children. The family was highly regarded and popular in their neighborhood and community.

Gender-Determined Behaviors

Gender, along with gender-role expectations, was a major source of conflict for Brad and Susan. Brad had grown up in a traditional family where his father worked outside the home and his mother was a homemaker. According to Susan, Brad's mother did everything for her children, and Brad did not disagree with her. Division of chores in Brad's family was gender-based: the sons worked with the father at his business, while the daughter helped her mother at home. His father was very traditional and "macho," and he disdained men's being involved with anything he considered "women's work." Brad indicated that if his father knew he was helping out at home, he would view him as weak. Thus, changing gender roles was perceived by Brad as threatening to his identity as a man and to his relationship with his father.

Susan's parents, on the other hand, divorced when Susan and her siblings were young, and her mother then worked outside the home. Susan was "pretty much on her own" growing up, and she and her siblings did what was necessary to survive and to help their mother. Because her experiences were different from the traditional, Susan had an easier time adjusting to contemporary shifts in gender roles.

When Brad and Susan first married, they assumed traditional roles, although they did not discuss this decision. Like many couples, they assumed that they were doing what was expected and what the other wanted. Brad worked many hours in the family business, while Susan stayed at home and reared the children. In retrospect, both said they felt underappreciated during that time, and that the other did not understand how difficult it was for them. Susan felt all alone in rearing the children, while Brad felt isolated from the family by the extra hours he had to work in order to support them.

A significant shift in gender-role expectations—and in the family's dynamics—was effected when Susan decided to complete her education. Once she was in school, she was overwhelmed trying to maintain the household and children along with doing her schoolwork. She repeatedly pleaded with Brad to help, but he was, for the most part, unresponsive. "If you'd adjust your schedule and not try to do everything for everybody, you wouldn't 'spazz out'," he told her. Susan's wanting to share household and childcare responsibilities, and Brad's resistance, became major issues for the couple.

Another significant but unacknowledged gender role shift had occurred earlier, when Brad was diagnosed with diabetes. Discussing that time, Susan realized that at that point she had felt herself assume leadership for the family, although she never expressed this to Brad. She just took over. He was very aware of her becoming more authoritarian, but not of its origin. He recalled feeling numb and upset about the diagnosis and struggling to keep up at work. His reaction to Susan had been to rebel and to be uncooperative. This dysfunctional pattern already was in place when Susan went back to school. Her shifts then served to stress the system even more.

Treatment Plan

The predominant change strategy used with this couple was the use of affirmation paradox and reframing interventions designed towards helping Susan and Brad experience themselves, individually and as a couple, as positive and proactive people capable of behaving in ways more mature and constructive. The Treatment Plan consisted of the following specified problems and change strategies:

Problem 1: Brad's illness and its management. The change strategy focused on putting Brad in charge of his illness and decreasing Susan's involvement; exploring Brad's understanding of his illness and its management, and factors that contributed to his resistance to managing it better; and increasing collaboration with his physician.

Problem 2: Lack of trust, along with self-esteem problems of each partner. Here, the change strategy was to build a supportive, trusting, and positive therapeutic alliance, working throughout therapy to affirm each partner and enabling them to become more supportive of, and trusting and caring towards, each other and themselves.

Problem 3: Ineffective communication. In this area, the change strategy focused on modifying negative attributions and stopping vilification, while working with the couple to increase the length of non-defensive, calm interactions and to decrease behaviors that interfered with good communication, e.g., blaming, accusing, "diagnosing" each other, etc.

Problem 4: Household and child management. In these areas, change strategies included exploring gender issues that prevented a better division of labor plus the use of behavioral prescriptions to help them to shift the balance of responsibilities.

Problem 5: Family-of-origin issues. The change strategy involved exploring each partner's family-of-origin issues and working with each to help him/her to differentiate and individuate in a more proactive and responsible manner.

Problem 6: Brad's career. The change strategies planned and utilized here involved discussing with Brad his career plans, supporting his goals for developing his own business, and encouraging him to be more assertive with his father when he discussed business issues with him.

Problem 7: Lack of intimacy. In this core problem area, the change strategies involved using a negation paradox during the process of a crisis, then the use of reframing in order to encourage loving and caring behaviors.

TREATMENT

Treatment with this couple was ongoing at the time of writing. During the intensive phase of treatment, the couple was seen weekly for 24 sessions, then biweekly for 13 visits. They were then being seen about once every three weeks.

The therapist worked with the couple on all of their problems simultaneously, as all were interrelated. As with most therapy, issues have varied in their prominence, and attention to pressing issues has taken precedence. For example, family-of-origin issues were discussed within the context of working on communications skills, as the couple's worst communication often occurred when they were discussing their respective families. As noted above, the predominant change strategy was that of affirmation paradox and reframing interventions.

Brad's Illness: Self-Responsibility and Management

This therapist believes strongly in working with couples' presenting complaints, regardless of whether the most salient issue is behind the complaint. Therefore, Brad's illness management was tackled first and reframed as Brad's problem (rather than it being Susan's problem). In order to do this, the therapist met several times wth Brad to discuss his illness and its meaning to him, and his management of it. Exploration of the issues helped Brad to grieve the healthy life he had lost and to begin to cope with the life ahead of him. The therapist obtained Brad's permission to collaborate with his physician, and then spoke with the doctor about Brad's medical treatment. After meeting alone with Brad, the therapist met alone with Susan, in order to provide balance for the therapy and also to develop an individual rapport with her.

When the therapist met again with the couple, she told Susan that henceforth Brad would be in charge of his illness and that if he had problems, he was to contact his physician and then to discuss the problems with the therapist. The therapist underlined the importance of Susan and Brad *not* being doctor and patient with each other, as this was harmful to the marriage. Susan was able to accept this plan once she knew the therapist was working with the physician. She admitted, "I don't trust Brad on his own, but since you're involved, I'll keep quiet."

The spouse often is an unrecognized co-patient when the partner has a chronic illness, and can suffer serious stress-related problems (Rustad, 1984). Therefore, the therapist explored with the couple the effects of Brad's illness on Susan, an area they had not been able to acknowledge. Her having taken charge was reframed as her method for coping with how helpless she had felt when Brad was ill and they did not yet know what was wrong with him. The therapist encouraged Susan, with Brad's permission, to communicate occasionally with his physician, so that she could ask questions without Brad's believing that she was interfering.

Once this agreement was made, the therapist was able to shift the therapy so they could work on other issues. Throughout therapy, when Brad had problems with his diabetes, the therapist spoke with him privately, in order to enforce and maintain his having full responsibility for his body.

Developing Trust and Self-Esteem

During the first three months of therapy, the therapist felt more like a referee than a helping professional. It was very difficult to help the couple to discuss issues rationally, or even to focus on any one issue. Both Brad and Susan were very emotionally needy, and they competed for the therapist's support as they accused each other of various affronts. The therapist's notes from that period indicate the frustration *she* was feeling: "Trying to get them to talk with each other. She wants change...he acts a little silly. They set each other up to act in gender-stereotypic ways. She 'goes nuclear' and he teases and 'cuts.' They don't resolve anything." Behavioral tasks assigned at this time failed totally. In retrospect, the therapist realized there was insufficient trust—of each other and of the therapist—to make behavioral change possible.

The therapist coped with her own frustration in the early months of therapy by discussing the couple's children with them, e.g., the children's personalities, activities, and school progress, all the time emphasizing how well Susan and Brad collaborated in their parenting. This strategy led to the first real gain in therapy. It served to build trust with the couple, as they were desperately seeking support for themselves as parents, and they responded gratefully to the therapist's positive remarks about the children and about their parenting skills. The therapist's attribution of good parental traits to both Brad and Susan also helped to shift their perceptions of each other so they could see each other more positively.

The therapist also helped the couple to expand and reframe their understanding of their roles as parents by discussing with them how the lack of extended family emotional support impacted on them as parents. Susan and Brad were able to be somewhat less critical of themselves and each other once they realized they were rearing their children with less support than many other people.

Once assured of the therapist's understanding and support for them as parents, Susan and Brad were better able to hear and to respond to what the therapist said and suggested. As a result, the therapist was able to underline for the couple how the lack of emotional support from their extended families negatively affected their coping ability and caused friction between them. This connection helped them to see how their individual frustrations led to many of their arguments, and they were able to see the circularity in their patterns. This first recognition of the larger system in which they functioned helped them to have a little distance and improved their ability to be non-defensive. As a result, the level of bickering was somewhat reduced, and they began to trust each other a little more. "Things are better," Susan said, "Brad's been very considerate and good with the kids." "She's not on my back," was his assessment.

Developing Effective Communication Skills

Once a basis for trust was developed, the therapist was able to work with them on improving their communication skills. Specific problem behaviors were identified: accusing each other of not caring, diagnosing each other's personality and motives, vilifying and criticizing each other (sometimes in front of the children), and being disrepectful of each other. The therapist helped the couple to identify these bad habits, and then repeatedly had the couple practice more productive ways of talking with each other. During one session when they were bickering, in a moment of exasperation, the therapist ordered Brad and Susan to be quiet, and then commanded them to "Talk nicely" to each other. This "prescription" was surprisingly effective, as the couple was able to speak productively with each other for the rest of the session. Further, the couple remembered it and began to remind each other when they were not "talking nicely." This spontaneous, very negative reframe of their behavior as exceedingly childish seemed to "shock" them into spontaneously complying by behaving as adults. Apparently, reminding each other of the therapist's words made them less defensive than when they used their own words.

In addition to the focus on specific conversational behaviors, the therapist helped the couple to identify the stressors in their lives and then to figure out some ways to deal with them more effectively. For example, the couple had a tendency to become overfocused on the children, and so the therapist repeatedly encouraged the couple to go out together and to take time for themselves as a form of stress management. Doing enjoyable things together helped to remind them of their "chemistry" and their genuine liking for each other.

Household and Child Management: A Matter of Balance

Discussion with the therapist made it obvious that there was a large discrepancy between Susan's and Brad's handling of household and childcare responsibilities. They agreed, albeit not wholeheartedly, that things should be more equal—Brad, for example, was not willing to take on very much of what he saw as Susan's jobs. Not surprisingly, the couple's initial efforts to equalize the family and household responsibilities were relatively unsuccessful. Brad started doing a few things, but found that Susan tended to supervise him, so he gave up, pronouncing, "People don't take responsbility for that over which they have no control." When Brad did participate, Susan discovered it did not necessarily make things better: "He is helping more—so why am I not more grateful?" The therapist approached the problem with them academically, asking them about gender roles and expectations. This resulted in some lively discussions about what is and is not appropriate for men and women of this generation, but prompted little change in their behavior.

When she explored this issue, Susan was able to acknowledge that she was somewhat fearful of giving up her role in the family. She admitted that she enjoyed being central to the family's functioning and feared that if Brad were more involved, he would soon take over and she would have no role at all. As with many women, control over the household was all the control Susan believed she had.

Brad, on the other hand, realized he was afraid to participate more in the household because he feared his father's reaction. The therapist talked with him about what chores he could do without risking too much disapproval, which helped Brad to identify some areas over which he was willing to take some responsibility, e.g., the children's homework and outside activities, and running some errands.

What ultimately "turned the corner" for Brad's becoming more involved was the therapist's creating a new definition of his participation in the household as a method he could use to get more of what he wanted from Susan. "I can guarantee you that if you do more, Susan will be more loving towards you," the therapist told Brad, with Susan present. "I know you don't believe that, but I'm asking you to take a leap of faith—give it a try." Brad did, and Susan responded by being more attentive to him, most of the time. The change was intermittent, however, and both needed frequent reminders in order to maintain it.

Working on Family-of-Origin Issues

One pattern of Susan and Brad's was that their bickering was often related to one or the other's having problems with his/her family of origin. Once the therapist became aware of this, she was able to point it out to the couple and then to help them to identify the link when it happened. As a result, they sometimes were able to short circuit their bickering and talk about what was bothering each of them.

Both Susan and Brad wanted to redefine themselves as adults in relationship with their families. Their respective frustrations were discussed repeatedly in depth. The therapist's goal was for them to realize that their parents and siblings were not likely to change, so that both Susan and Brad needed to learn to deal more effectively with them as they are. Specifically, the therapist worked with them towards being more appropriately assertive and speaking from a strong "I" position.

Susan initially made more progress than Brad. She spoke more often to her family (and to his, as well), while he tended to avoid his. She also was less fearful about confronting her family and its "demons." Susan practiced being less defensive and offensive with both her mother and sister, with good results. At the time of writing, Susan was continuing to work on her own family issues, and the therapist was encouraging Brad to do so with his.

Building Brad's Career

Once most of the problems were being addressed in a relatively proactive manner, the therapist talked with Brad about himself and his career goals. Brad was a remarkably capable businessperson with good instincts, but he did not trust himself. He and his father had a long history during which the father denigrated Brad's abilities, rather than encouraging them. Like many aggressive entrepreneurs, Brad's father did not like sharing power or giving it up to the next generation.

During these sessions, the underlying strength of Brad and Susan's connection with each other was never more evident. Susan was obviously pleased that the therapist was interested in Brad's career and listened quietly as they discussed various issues. "I really want him to do well—it's so important for him," she said, "I'm behind him 100 percent, no matter what he does. I'm doing something for myself (going to school), and I want him to do the same." Susan's acknowledgement of the couple's interdependence indicated to the therapist that there had been growth in the couple's trust. At the time of this writing, Brad was expanding his business.

Developing Intimacy

As with many couples, the change process for Susan and Brad was not linear. Their pattern was that they would make signficant progress and do very well, then go backwards for awhile. The most dramatic demonstration of this was a session about a year into treatment when they came in and announced that they had separated. "She threw me out," Brad said. "I just can't take any more of the way he treats me," Susan said. The therapist herself was surprised at this announcement, as during recent sessions the couple had seemed to be doing quite well.

The therapist decided to take the separation very seriously, and to use a negation paradox in which the couple was affirmed in their decision not to change and not to live together. She proceeded to tell the couple that perhaps the separation was the best thing for them, as "perhaps the only way you each can grow and change is if you live on your own for awhile." This intervention also could be categorized as going with the resistance. The therapist discussed with the couple the logistics of separation, with a focus on how they would each be involved with the children. It was a sobering and frightening session for the couple as the therapist treated this "separation" with earnest seriousness.

Several days later, the therapist contacted Susan (rather than Brad, who the therapist did not know how to reach as she did not know where he was staying) to see how they were coping. Susan said that she had asked Brad to move back home and he had agreed to do so. "It's amazing how things have changed," Susan said.

At the next session, the couple seemed very different, much more in tune with each other, and significantly less defensive. The therapist inquired about what had changed between them. "Everything's really the same," Brad said, "but our attitudes are different." Indeed, the couple appeared to have changed their interpretive framework, which allowed them to accept the possibility that they could learn to fulfill each other's emotional needs. Susan said Brad was talking to her more than he ever had and that even the children had noticed he was nicer to her. The couple acknowledged they were in a "honeymoon" period, but that they could see that real change was possible.

The couple was unable to articulate what had prompted their shift other than to say that they both realized they wanted the marriage to work. What had happened within each of them which allowed such a significant change of attitude toward the partner? Was it that they teamed up against the therapist, who used a negation paradox when she said she was willing to help them to separate? Was it the net result of months of affirmation, when the therapist repeatedly indicated she believed both Susan and Brad could behave in mature and constructive ways? Perhaps the two treatment strategies interacted to create a synthesis that propelled change. Their reaching out to each other was a tremendous risk, which fortunately was eagerly and well received by each partner—spontaneous compliance at its best.

At the next session, the therapist opened a discussion of intimacy and talked with the couple about how they might work towards becoming closer emotionally. With some reluctance, they each were able to accept their respective contributions to the lack of intimacy, a circular definition of the problem. Susan's acknowledgement was most dramatic: "I look back and I realize that we were doing very well and feeling very close about a month ago, and then I picked a terrible fight with Brad. I guess I really am afraid of being too close to him."

The therapist was aware of the fragility of this couple's beginning efforts towards closer connection. Trust at this level of interaction still needs to be developed, and backsliding is expected (and predicted). At the time of writing this chapter, the couple has continued to work in a positive direction on these issues.

CONCLUSION

This couple illustrates the importance of viewing the systemic context in which couples live. Individually and as a couple they had many strengths, but they existed alone, without the emotional support of their extended families. This lack of support undermined them almost daily, as both Brad and Susan struggled to maintain the self confidence necessary to function autonomously. Most of their struggles with each other were the manifestation of their individual difficulties sustaining a consistently strong self-concept. Literally, they took out their self-frustrations on each other.

Additionally, they struggled to cope with Brad's diabetes, the effects of which they felt, but had not articulated. As a result, they worked at cross purposes, which undermined their coping and also Brad's health, because he was not fully compliant with his medical regime.

In retrospect, the therapist believes that the most effective therapeutic intervention was the combination of her acknowledgement of their individual struggles and strengths with her ability to communicate her genuine affection and support to them: the affirmation paradox. Rarely has this therapist worked with people who were so openly grateful for her affirmation, and who used this infusion of confidence in order to shift their perceptions of themselves and of each other.

Another strength of the therapy was the ongoing conversation the therapist and couple had about gender issues. The therapist saw this couple during the time she was writing on gender issues in couples' relationships. The therapist told the couple she was writing about gender issues and solicited their ideas. The result was an ongoing conversation about women and men and changing gender roles and dynamics. This conversation had several benefits. It helped the couple to see their gender-related struggles in the larger sociocultural context; by valuing their ideas, the therapist helped build the couple's esteem; and the couple was able to nurture the therapist (by encouraging her to keep writing), something they were unable to do with their own parents and which they obviously enjoyed since this, in part, served a reparative function for them.

This conversation also served as a metaphor for the couple's relational dialectics—the ongoing constituting of oneself and the relationship, transformed through interaction. Through this conversation, Susan and Brad were able to experience the process of positive, proactive change, negotiated with another person. They learned, by doing, that issues can be discussed without having to be resolved. Instead, they can be explored, then set aside and revisited repeatedly until a consensus emerges as part of the process.

Therapy with Susan and Brad is ongoing, although sessions are less frequent. The groundwork for a successful relationship has been laid. The task now is for the couple to continue to develop in the direction already set.

CHAPTER 11

Jim and Sandy: Rebalancing Relational Responsibility

Michael J. D'Antonio

INTRODUCTION

The case discussed in this chapter presents one version of the Intersystem Model. It thoroughtly integrates assessment and treatment as well as intergenerational, individual/intrapsychic, and interactional perspectives around the concept of relational rersponsibility. The intergenerational perspective identified how Sandy and Jim learned to feel and act overresponsible for others and underresponsible for themselves in their families of origin. The intrapsychic perspective targeted Jim's and Sandy's regulation of self-esteem by continuing the patterns of over/underresponsibility learned in childhood. The interactional perspective focused on day-to-day interactions between Jim and Sandy, as well as between each of them and others, which reinforced those patterns and which needed to change for the couple to enjoy a mutually satisfying and empowering relationship. Therapeutic interventions addressed all three perspectives to effect changes in the couple's construction of themselves and the relationship (e.g., predictions, definitions); their feelings about themselves, the relationship, and one another; and their behavior with one another and their children, families, and coworkers.

ASSESSMENT

This case began atypically for the therapist in that one partner came in alone for the first session, unsure of whether he even wanted to remain in the marriage. Thus, the composition of the first few sessions violated the usual pattern of conjoint first session, one individual session with each partner next, and conjoint thereafter. It took five sessions to assess the couple, engage them in *couples* work, and lay the groundwork for them to trust the therapist. Each of these assessment sessions is presented, followed by the formulation based upon them.

Assessment-Contracting Phase

First session

Jim came to the first session alone. He had been referred by a counselor at his place of employment because he had developed an emotional affair with a woman at work and was feeling neutral about his marriage of 12 years. (An emotional affair is similar to a sexual affair except that there is no genital involvement.) Jim explained that there "had been a decline in the marriage over the years, especially in the past year.... We don't spend much time talking to each other.... She sleeps more." Jim reported that his wife said he would not be happy regardless of what she does, but he believed that, while he had questioned himself whenever he felt dissatisfied in the past, he was making a conscious effort to think differently about their relationship now.

A family history revealed that Jim, then age 36, is the third of four children. He has two older brothers and a younger sister. His parents, of Eastern-European Catholic background, divorced when he was 16. Father, a physician, is an active alcoholic, drinking during Jim's youth mostly on weekend nights and "becoming quiet." When Jim was 10, father and brothers began a regular pattern of angry confrontations about brothers' behavior. Father began spending less and less time at home. The history disclosed that Jim always tried to be "a good kid." He did well in school and kept out of trouble. He served as mediator between (older) brothers and parents and worked at being a big brother for his younger sister whom he saw as neglected by the rest of the family.

Jim saw father as unhappy. He stayed home, rather than go to friends' houses, in order to help father with his projects (e.g., home repairs, woodworking, crafts). Jim reported that "Mom didn't need as much taking care of." He went on to say that he would clean the house for her because the condition of the house was a source of conflict between parents, that he kept sister out of mother's way, and that he didn't cause her any problems.

His past experience with psychotherapy consisted of three sessions with a previous therapist of his wife's. He reported that the therapist blamed him for making too many demands on his wife and that he "told the therapist what she wanted to hear."

As the first session was coming to a close, Jim restated his confusion, saying that he wanted to be alone, but "there are our two children to consider." The therapist underscored the position he had held all his life: feeling and acting overresponsible for others and underresponsible for himself. The therapist suggested he "try marriage [as a mutually satisfying and empowering relationship]; you haven't tried it yet." He said he could not picture himself in therapy with Sandy, his wife, because he would start "caving in" when he saw her hurt and then take back whatever he said. Then, he reported what he considered a pivotal incident a year before their marriage: Jim had gone to visit Sandy to break off the relationship but recanted because she did not want to end it and he "couldn't say 'no'." The therapist reassured him that he would help Jim hold his ground in the sessions if he came in with Sandy.

Second session

Jim returned the following week with Sandy. With couples therapy, the first joint session, usually the first session, is that in which each partner presents his or her view of the problem and some statement of goals for the therapy. This session began with Sandy voicing her anger over a conversation during the past week, in which she said that Jim had accused her of "not being a good person, a good wife, or a good mother." Apparently, he had tried to talk to her about his dissatisfactions in the marriage.

She stated that, until two months earlier, she saw the marriage as "perfect for [her] and the same for Jim." He countered that, in the past, he had talked himself out of complaints fearing that he would add to the troubles that already burdened Sandy in her career. She confirmed that she had been depressed in the past and had had career problems. (Like Jim, she is a professional with an advanced degree.) She concluded that she was "not going to change every time Jim changes his mind about what he wants. I'd like him to like me the way I am. I am a lot of [good] things." The discussion was rather diffuse. Apparently, Jim had not told Sandy about his emotional affair with a woman at work and Sandy was not clear about why he wanted them in conjoint therapy. The therapist then shifted the focus to get a history of their relationship, something he would normally do in the first joint session anyway.

Sandy and Jim met at age 17 and started dating as juniors in the Catholic high school they attended in New England. She was attracted to him because he was "quiet, intelligent, gentle." He was attracted to her because she was "intelligent, good looking, and had her priorities straight (liked school)." In high school, they spent a lot of time together, talking, doing homework, going to the movies, and "fooling around." They agreed that the major struggle during this time was her "clinginess and jealousy, to which [he] would accede." She "did not have many other people." They went to college in different cities, with Jim remaining at home and commuting to a local university. Because they were miserable apart, Jim transferred in his sophomore year to her university. There, they took the same major, spent a lot of time together, had satisfying sex on Fridays and Saturdays, and had no major struggles.

They married right after college with the blessing of both families, except for his sister who was jealous for a while. Marriage seemed a "natural evolution since [they] were together all the time." The early years of marriage were difficult for both because they attended graduate/professional schools at universities some distance apart. She hated professional school and dreaded being alone. She wanted to quit but feared disappointing Jim and her father. Jim was invested in her completing her studies and kept reminding her that she could complete them. They argued a lot. Their first child, a son who was eight when treatment began, was born the June after she completed her graduate degree. This first joint session ended with an appointment for Sandy to come in alone. (The therapist wanted to balance Jim's individual session and make some connection with Sandy around issues related to her family of origin.)

Third session

In Sandy's individual session, the therapist learned that she came from a working-class, Irish-Catholic family. She was the youngest of six children born over an 18-year period. Father was hardworking but aloof. His brother had died of alcohol-related problems; his sister was in and out of the hospital with manic-depressive illness. Mother, who died when Sandy was 13, was a "happy, caring homemaker who liked [being a homemaker]." Sandy believes her mother did too much for her grown children, enabling Sandy's oldest brother's alcoholism. (A second brother and a brother-in-law were also alcoholic.) Sandy remembers resenting her mother's involvement with her older siblings—for example, her mother not being home many evenings because she was baby-sitting grandchildren. Sandy had a vague sense that if she were "good," if she were somehow different, her parents would engage her more. (Being an A student was certainly not enough.)

After her mother's death, Sandy was even more neglected emotionally because her father withdrew even more. (Now, more than 30 years later, he tends to be very critical of her.) The sister with the alcoholic husband left him and moved back into their father's home with a toddler. Her alcoholic oldest brother also moved back into their father's house with his family and subsequently abandoned his children there after his wife died of cancer. Sandy did much of the housework and childcare for the siblings who returned home.

Sandy reported major bouts of depression for which she sought help in her sophomore year of high school, again at age 18, several times during her professional education, and twice after she and Jim settled in the Philadelphia area. She had been treated with antidepressant medication, including tricyclics and Prozac. When this therapy began, she was taking no psychotropic medication. She found her most recent course of treatment, ending about six months earlier, most significant for her. She learned that she cannot permit others to define her. She also became better able to define and ask for what she needed. The therapist pointed out that her therapy seemed to have addressed what he saw as the major impact of her family of origin: inducting her into a role of overresponsibility for others and underresponsibility for herself. The therapist suggested she read Bepko and Krestan's (1990) *Too Good for Her Own Good* as the session ended because he believed it would normalize her struggle to take more control of her life and help motivate her to put into action what he believed she had learned only intellectually in the latest therapy.

Fourth session

The second joint session began somewhat diffusely with the therapist posing de Shazer's (1985) miracle question to help Sandy and Jim define their goals for the therapy. Put simply, this intervention asks clients how they would know a miracle had occurred solving all the problems for which they came to therapy. The question was introduced to help Jim and Sandy be concrete about the positive changes they sought. Jim expressed a desire for more verbal, physical, and emotional contact and more joint activities, including social activities. Sandy expressed a desire to be able to decide what she wanted and "not have it seen as mean"—a wish that Jim not disapprove of what she wanted to do—and an interest in their doing more together, including socializing more with people other than Jim's coworkers. She also said that she wanted some changes in the sexual area, but she could not talk about sex at the time.

While the goals they outlined seemed to fit what they needed, Jim and Sandy seemed disconnected both from one another and from their own expressions of desire. As the session came to a close, the couple was asked to negotiate, during the week, several matters which had come up in the session, and they readily agreed. One task was, for example, for them to negotiate whether or not to go together to an upcoming party that Jim wanted to attend and, if they went together, how to make it more comfortable for Sandy. In closing, Jim was given a list of Adult Child of an Alcoholic (ACOA) readings which he was encouraged to read because the therapist believed that Jim needed to understand the impact of his role in his family of origin on his current behavior in the marriage and in other relationships.

Fifth session

The fifth session, their third conjoint, concluded the Assessment-Contracting Phase of the therapy and signaled the engagement of both Sandy and Jim in the therapeutic process. It also initiated the next phase of the therapy, the Honeymoon Phase. Jim came in and reported that he could not do the tasks he had agreed to the previous week because he felt he needed to be honest about his other relationship. He had to tell Sandy about Wendy, his confidante at work, and he reported that he was not simply telling her what she wanted to hear. She reported that she felt Jim was "back"—his conversation about Wendy and the marriage seemed truthful about himself and his needs. Jim reported that Sandy responded to his disclosures better than he could have imagined. She seemed to be listening more, seemed to give what he said more credibility, and was physically more responsive. He noted, "I had deprived her of the good feelings of doing something for me." Jim was almost euphoric over having been able to disclose his emotional infidelity to Sandy and over a less cataclysmic reaction from her than he had expected. This euphoria almost blinded him to Sandy's pain and anguish over the affair; it took her months to fully recognize and work through these feelings, along with her anger.

Sandy told how her brother-in-law had had an emotional affair and how she had warned Jim that if did that, she would end the relationship. She said that she did not want to end the relationship, but would not tolerate another affair. Then, she asked Jim to tell Wendy it was over. It took the following session for Jim to make a firm commitment to do this. Because Jim had such difficulty not giving others what they wanted from him, he countered that Wendy would figure it out after a while of his not associating with her. With support, Sandy persisted, and Jim negotiated a two-week grace period in which to tell Wendy explicitly that their relationship was over. During that time, he worked up his courage and finally told Wendy it was over.

Initial Case Formulation

Initial impressions and reactions

Both Sandy and Jim seemed like bright and articulate, but disempowered, people who were hypersensitive to one another's (and others') reactions to whatever they might say or do. Thus, the marriage felt precarious to both, as each lived in fear of imminent rejection and abandonment.

Presenting problem

Jim saw the problem originally as how to get out of a marriage he found unsatisfying but could not leave. (Without intervention, he might well have provoked Sandy to take some action to end the marriage.) In the Assessment-Contracting Phase, Jim's problem became that of making the marriage more rewarding. Sandy's original problem was meeting Jim's expectations in order to fend off a threat to the marriage. Her problem became that of making the marriage more mutual. The unrewarding and non-mutual quality of the marriage was maintained by each partner in the following ways: 1) making his or her sense of well-being contingent on the feelings and behavior of the other, and 2) sequestering from the relationship any thoughts, feelings, desires, or expectations that might threaten the other. This withholding of the self contributed to feelings of disconnection in each of them. These feelings, in turn, increased their insecurity, heightened their hypersensitivity to one another, and amplified their discounting of themselves.

History of the Problem

As was clear in both family histories, Jim and Sandy were each valued for meeting the needs of others. Neither was rewarded for individuality, initiative, self-definition, or self-articulation. Whatever security they had as children rested on their ability to discern and gratify the needs of others. They entered into a marriage in which each could maintain self-esteem by continuing this pattern. The untenableness of this arrangement was not dealt with openly. Instead, they receded from one another. Jim flirted with affairs. (Later, Sandy revealed that he had done this before.) Sandy confirmed the feelings of helplessness that fueled her depression. Since their life circumstances had not changed in years, there seemed to be no immediate precipitant to the current problematic nature of their relationship. Like other reciprocally reinforced patterns of interaction, Jim and Sandy's ratcheted toward crisis or shutdown.

Individual/Interactional/Intergenerational Assessment

Intergenerational system

Both Sandy and Jim were inducted into roles of feeling and acting overresponsible for others and underresponsible for self. Their value as children lay in their ability to gratify the emotional (especially for Jim) and material (especially for Sandy) needs of the adults in their lives. Both were also inducted into the belief that they were responsible for the relationship with their parents. They felt *they* had to engage their parents, and keep them engaged or lose them. The sense that they were responsible for the relationship with their parents reinforced their feeling overresponsible for parents (and others). It also undermined self-worth. Sandy and Jim were objectified in that whatever recognition they got from their parents seemed to be for services rendered, not for some inherent worth of their own. They were also implicitly blamed for whatever they failed to receive as children: inattention, unresponsiveness, and neglect must be their fault because they just weren't good enough.

Individual/intrapsychic system

Both Jim and Sandy maintained self-esteem on the basis of what each could be for others. Each defined self based on the other. Each valued self on the basis of how the other felt (Is he happy? How depressed is she?) and how the other behaved toward him or her (Is she distant? Is he angry?). When her withdrawal or depression thus defined him as bad, Jim could not contain this condemnation. It recapitulated the self-condemnation he experienced at failing to meet his parents' needs and at not getting his own needs met as a child. Unable to tolerate these feelings, he had to project them onto her: "She is wrong [i.e., 'bad']." Correspondingly, she experienced his unhappiness and anger as a failing on her part. She did contain her self-condemnation and it was a major contributor to her chronic depression. By thus giving over to the other person the power to define self, both Jim and Sandy set in motion powerful projective processes.

In the course of this treatment, Sandy was referred for a psychiatric consultation. She was diagnosed as having a bipolar disorder, which was successfully treated with Tegretol and Zoloft. Jim's emotions ranged from anxiety to guilt and depression. A psychiatric evaluation was recommended to Jim about a year into therapy during a period when his emotions were particularly volatile, but he deferred acting on it. He claimed that he was responding to transitory situational factors such as pressure from his family of origin during the Christmas holidays and his father's illness and that he did not see the value of an evaluation until these stresses had past.

Interactional system

Jim and Sandy played out their overresponsibility for others and underresponsibility for self. Women typically do this by working on themselves; men, by working on women, things, or other men. Thus, Sandy felt she needed to conform to Jim. She would back down after some conflict in order to regain Jim's good graces. She refrained from making emotional claims on him in order to protect him from parts of her that could frighten or overwhelm him. She accepted blame, for example, fearing that Jim could not handle confrontation or her anger. She tried to conceal her depression, fearing that Jim would feel overwhelmed by it.

Jim's overresponsibility for Sandy took the form of monitoring both her moods and behavior. He would try to alleviate her distress by doing the typical things men do when they cannot tolerate distress in women, such as talking her out of it or offering unsolicited solutions. Jim worked at fixing Sandy by trying to alleviate her depression, telling her how to remedy her work difficulties and instructing her on how to be a good mother and wife. He believed he had to give her life meaning and that he would lose her if he failed. Jim played out his underresponsibility for self by withholding from Sandy whatever thoughts, feelings, reactions, dreams, and aspirations he feared might distress, frighten, or overwhelm her. Thus, he could not broach the issue of his own feelings of helplessness in the face of her depression or his fear of losing her.

In the hope of feeling good (or, at least, not worse) about the self, each calculated his or her own behavior in anticipation of the other's response. The intrapsychic and interactional realms came together, in effect, when each manipulated herself or himself in order to influence the other and maintain self-esteem and then experienced it as control by the other. Jim and Sandy experienced the confusion of (internal) compulsion with (external) coercion, typical of the couple with the boundary problems evidenced here in their unbalanced over- and underresponsibility.

Treatment Plan

Both Jim and Sandy had been inducted into roles of feeling and acting overresponsible for others and underresponsible for self. The overarching goal of treatment was to help each give up behaving responsible for the other, assume total responsibility for self, and take on shared responsibility for the relationship and their joint life. Collaterally, the goal included giving up the over/underresponsible role with others in their lives (family members, colleagues, subordinates).

TREATMENT

Honeymoon Phase

Beyond the Assessment-Contracting Phase described above, Sandy and Jim's treatment can be considered to include four other phases, specific to them: the Honeymoon Phase, in which the simple fact that they were talking about issues gave both Jim and Sandy a sense of relief; the Regression Phase, in which Sandy went into a serious depression and both partners had to come to terms with her depression and their individual pasts; the Parallel-Therapy Phase, in which individual sessions with Sandy alternated with the conjoint sessions; and, finally, the Balanced-Resolution Phase, in which Sandy and Jim consolidated new patterns of self and other responsibility as relative equals. In the following pages, the focus will be on the Honeymoon and Regression phases. The Parallel-Therapy and Balanced-Resolution phases will simply be summarized since the therapeutic frame had been established and all of the major specific interventions had already been introduced earlier in the therapy.

The Honeymoon Phase consisted of 14 conjoint sessions conducted over a five-month period. Five major interventions characterized this phase: 1) explicating the repetitive patterns of over/underresponsibility that formed the texture of their lives with each other and others; 2) solution-focused interviewing; 3) assigning the between-session task for each to say "No" to someone daily; 4) the talking-listening exercise; and 5) assertiveness coaching to help each identify his or her wishes and express them clearly to one another and to others.

1) Patterns of over/underresponsibility

One example of Jim and Sandy's pattern of over/underresponsibility was their inability to talk about her depression, a recurrent fact in Sandy's life. Jim felt he had to fix her. So, he tried to talk her out of feeling depressed; he offered her solutions to what he thought were her problems; finally, he got irritable or angry when he felt overwhelmed. For her part, Sandy tried to conceal her depression. She believed she was stronger than Jim and wanted to protect him from it. She also feared the criticism contained in his irritation and anger. Neither could let the other be with his or her own feelings and connect empathetically with them. In the language of Intersystem theory, each interpreted the other's behavior as defining himself or herself as inadequate in the relationship and predicting blame from the other. Empowering interdependence could not be built on such projections.

Another example was a pattern of closeness and distance they described. Their discussion of one instance illustrated the underlying issues. One Monday, Jim came home from work annoyed. In our discussion, it became clear that he had wanted Sandy to figure out what was wrong because he could not talk about how he felt. He was afraid he would feel like an "inconvenience," and he dreaded "getting into feeling what it was like to be an inconvenience to my parents." His sense of failure at not winning over his parents was too strong to allow him to take responsibility for himself by letting Sandy know clearly and directly what he wanted from her. To fail to get what he needed from her as well would be devastating.

On her side, Sandy sensed that the stakes were high, that there was no room for error. She felt she was on the line. She could not tolerate being put to the test and withdrew in hurt, shame, and (concealed) anger. Sandy was unable to take responsibility for herself and state her needs with respect to the bind she experienced around Jim's distress. She was even less able to take responsibility for herself with respect to her own relational needs and desires, independent of Jim's turmoil.

A similar scenario played out the next night when Jim came home tense about going to a Cub Scout den leaders meeting for his older son. He did not want to go but felt guilty about it. He was angry at his son for putting him, he believed, in this bind. He could not talk to Sandy about any of this because he had a hard time disclosing "such selfish feelings." Once again, she became guarded. Her relational needs went on the proverbial back burner. He felt hurt and rejected.

In reviewing these and similar patterns, the therapist had to help Sandy and Jim identify these patterns and the ways of thinking that supported them. Then, he helped them articulate more self-empowering ways of thinking. Finally, he helped them verbalize and mentally rehearse alternative ways of responding. In the example of Jim coming home distressed but not saying anything about what was bothering him, each identified how she/he had experienced the event. Both were reminded that Jim's distress was his, not Sandy's, responsibility. He was encouraged to identify how he would have wanted to deal with it, what he might have wanted from Sandy, how he would have asked her, and so forth. Sandy was encouraged to identify how she could have stayed connected with Jim without taking responsibility for his feelings; how she might have responded, whether acceding or declining, to whatever request he might have made; and how she could have taken seriously her own needs, both with respect to Jim's dilemma and otherwise.

2) Solution-focused interviewing

The techniques of solution-focused interviewing attempt to change self-definition. They are well documented (de Shazer, 1985; O'Hanlon & Weiner-Davis, 1989; Berg & Miller, 1992) and need not be detailed here. They include cognitive-behavioral interventions to encourage hopefulness, feelings of accomplishment, willingness to attempt new behaviors, and self-reinforcement of positive changes. Generally, the therapist uses these from the very beginning of treatment to build on any changes that might occur, even those predating the first session. Since Sandy and Jim required several sessions just to define the therapeutic contract, however, there was little opportunity to reinforce successive approximations of their therapeutic goals until we got beyond the Assessment-Contracting Phase. Then, the therapist took every opportunity to have them identify positive changes, claim ownership of them, and see them as a springboard for moving forward, much in a manner described by White and Epston (1990).

3) The "No" exercise

The "No" exercise is one the therapist developed several years back. Like the "talking-listening" exercise below, it is one of several he uses frequently with couples to facilitate differentiation and help them relinquish the over/underresponsible role. It also affords him concrete opportunities to reinforce changes in the positive direction.

The standard instructions are: "I want you to make a point of saying `No' to somebody each day for the next week. Do so totally capriciously, without justification and, if possible, without explanation. You do not have to have a good reason to say 'No.' Select different people. You may feel uncomfortable, tense, anxious, or guilty. You may feel selfish. If you don't, you are probably not doing the task." If clients agree, the therapist asks them to keep a daily log of their "Nos," including the persons to whom they say "No" and about what.

Clients typically agree to the task, the frame for which is the inducted patterns of over/underresponsibility around which they have already identified some sense of feeling burdened. (One notable exception was a man of 50, owner of his own consulting firm, who broke into tears when the therapist presented the task. He said he could not do it because "Then, who would I be?" Several months later, he agreed to do the task and accomplished it for several week-long periods, with positive results.)

By declining spoken, implied, or inferred requests from others, each partner rapidly realizes how much he or she controls self on the basis of the anticipated response of another. Each actively engages the (possibly, only anticipatory) feelings of anxiety, guilt, or shame that accompany the prospect of not giving another what he or she perceives that person wants from himself or herself. Thus, each begins to break a self-reinforcing cycle of avoiding or terminating strong self-condemnatory affect by acceding to the needs of others. Experiencing and correcting these patterns with others, as well as with the partner, also helps each take back the powerful projections directed at the partner. The task constitutes a paradox that helps mobilize changes in clients' predictions about themselves and others, as well as in their definition of themselves.

It should be noted that for clients like Jim and Sandy to begin declining others' requests represents a major reorientation of their lives and reorganization of their esteem-maintaining systems. Both in suggesting and reviewing the task, the therapist must recognize the full import of what the clients are taking on. Thus, each session after this assignment was given, the therapist reviewed with Jim and Sandy each experience in detail, using a combined solution-focused (O'Hanlon & Weiner-Davis, 1989) and constructivist (White & Epston, 1990) method of inquiry.

In the first week they did the "No" exercise, Jim reported that he declined the request of a friend of Wendy's (his confidant) to borrow Jim's video-camera for Wendy's birthday party. He told of feeling guilty about saying "No" to the man and afraid of disappointing Wendy. He also reported, among other events, that he had missed opportunities to deny requests of people at work who imposed on his time. He recounted that, a year before, he would not have even thought of the possibility of saying "No." (In the course of therapy, Jim made major changes at work by protecting his own time, holding subordinates accountable for their assigned projects, and not simply telling his superiors what they wanted to hear.)

Sandy reported that she had not gone to her mother-in-law's suite to make the bed for the relatives who were visiting for a holiday. While it was difficult for her to withhold this (unsolicited) service, she realized that, if she had performed it, she would have felt unappreciated and resentful. One other example of Sandy's, during that week, resembled all of her attempts to assert herself or decline others: saying "No" to a subordinate at work took an extraordinary amount of psychic effort but did not mobilize a lot of feeling. She was pleased with herself afterwards.

4) The talking-listening exercise

In its standard form (Scarf, 1987), the talking-listening exercise is a form of affirmation paradox that requires each partner to talk to the other for a predetermined length of time about something he or she wants the other to know or understand about self. The other is to listen closely, without comment or verbal response. When the time has passed, the couple is to go on to some other activity, separately or together. Sometimes, to help clients identify feelings of overresponsibility, the listener is asked to make a mental note of when he or she felt the impulse to respond.

This exercise gave Sandy and Jim experience tolerating the stressful feeling that arose from relating to one another differently. Early on, Jim had difficulty not getting immediate feedback from Sandy. When Jim was the speaker, he reported missing her "reassurance and guidance." She "felt guilty not saying anything" —i.e., not giving him what he wanted. She found that it was not difficult to be the speaker; she enjoyed having Jim be quiet and not interrupt. He found it very "frustrating" not to respond. He reported feeling angry and afraid whenever he felt the impulse to jump in: "afraid that we will come apart if I can't fix things." Sometimes, the exercise had a specific focus (e.g., her depression, his caretaking role). By doing something under their voluntary control (withholding feedback) and tolerating any subsequent negative affect, Jim and Sandy changed the framework of their relationship and gave up their over/underresponsible roles.

5) Assertiveness coaching

In this and every phase of the therapy, Sandy and Jim were encouraged to identify their thoughts, feelings, desires, and expectations and to communicate them compellingly to whomever these concerned. One such opportunity presented itself several weeks into the Honeymoon Phase. Sandy and Jim announced that they would be going on vacation in a couple of weeks. The therapist encouraged them to think about what each needed of the other to help make it a successful trip. In the session before the vacation, each was asked to communicate these to the other. Their requests were surprisingly simple but powerful in defining themselves and their relationship.

Sandy asked Jim to do the things he wanted *without her* if she didn't want to do them or *if* he preferred to do them alone. Jim asked Sandy to state clearly what she wanted to do even if it included taking a nap. (Her naps had provoked anxiety in him as a sign of either her depression or withdrawal.) They returned from vacation claiming it was their best ever.

In anticipation of a visit to both their fathers in Florida on a trip with the kids to Disneyworld, they discussed how they wanted to be treated and how they would deal with potential problems. Her father was likely to badger them to stay and they agreed that they would keep to their schedule. Her father was also likely to comment disparagingly on some aspect of her appearance; she would remind him firmly that her weight, hair color, or whatever was not up for discussion. Jim would be firm about his father keeping his German shepherd away from their four-year-old son who was afraid of the dog. He would also act to protect himself and the family from any verbally abusive behavior on his father's part. Jim's resolve was challenged when his father launched into a sudden, unprovoked attack on Jim's brother, who now lives with his father, for turning down the thermostat. Jim unceremoniously gathered his family together and left, but not before experiencing a welling of panic and fear similar to that which he felt as a child when father and brothers fought. They commented afterwords that they had had the least upsetting visit to their fathers ever and that these visits in no way detracted from their family vacation at Disneyworld.

As a final example of the results of assertiveness coaching, Sandy wanted to make a temporary change in her work hours. While she did not exactly present her point of view in an entitled way, she was clear with Jim that she did not want him to give her a hard time about it.

Regression Phase

Toward the end of the Honeymoon Phase of therapy, Sandy began to feel depressed again. Her primary symptoms were, as in the past, extreme lethargy, fatigue, and loss of interest in things. Sandy's depression was a regression in Sandy's emotional state and in Jim's feelings of responsibility for Sandy, but it allowed the couple to revisit a major issue and deal with it in a new way for both of them. When Sandy first became depressed again, she went back on Prozac, prescribed by the psychiatrist who had treated her most recently. After several weeks, Sandy reported that Prozac no longer alleviated the depression. An evaluation by another psychiatrist led to a diagnosis of bipolar disorder. Sandy's mood and energy level responded well to lithium before she started having serious side effects. It took several months of trials on various medications to relieve her depression with Tegretol and Zoloft. Until she found relief, Sandy experienced several bouts of rather severe depression.

This phase, comprising 10 sessions over a period of two and one-half months, provided the couple with an opportunity to deal with Sandy's depression and both Jim's and Sandy's deep-seated negative emotions in a new way. (While Sandy's depression had a biological substrate, the fact that Jim acted out his overresponsibility for her by trying to control her behavior, feelings, and perceptions only fed her feelings of helplessness and hopelessness and reinforced her depression. Of course, it then intensified his feelings of responsibility.)

The bipolar diagnosis had very different impacts on Sandy and Jim. She felt relieved. Somehow, her past made more sense to her. She had experienced changes in mood from early childhood. She had found them confusing and isolating. She had blamed herself. Now, the bipolar diagnosis gave Sandy a *medical* frame for her problems. In effect, the diagnosis constituted a reframe that enabled her to understand her behavior better. In turn, the reframe freed her up to make other changes by alleviating self-blame for her depression. (Her father's sister was bipolar. He took care of her and had said in the past, when he brushed aside Sandy's depression, that he did not want Sandy to turn out like his sister.) She had a new interpretation of her past and a new definition of herself. These, in turn, allowed her to define her relationship with Jim differently.

Jim was very disturbed by the diagnosis, fearing that a biological basis for Sandy's depression put her beyond the reach of his putative help. She told him she wanted him to stay out of it unless she asked for his help. Thus, Jim was faced with another challenge to give up the overresponsible role. Interestingly, in one session, when Sandy asked for reassurance from Jim, he became panicky with fear that he could not provide what she asked. When Sandy was asked to repeat her request in video-language (O'Hanlon & Weiner-Davis, 1989) (i.e., in observable, behavioral terms), she said she wanted Jim to hug her more and to talk to her more. He said he could and would do that.

"Feel bad"

To the five major interventions used earlier in the therapy was added the suggestion, a negation paradox, that Jim let himself feel bad. In this phase of therapy, Jim reported for the first time that he had begun to feel somewhat depressed. Several factors contributed to this. He had been giving up the overresponsible role in various ways since the beginning of treatment. He was grieving the loss of a role he had from early childhood. Also, as he continued to take back his projections from Sandy, the children, and others, he became more aware of the *self*-blame, the *self*-condemnation he leveled as anger at others. In effect, anger and criticism toward others were framed or constructed as self-blame engendered by his belief that he had failed to meet his parents' emotional needs and that he was responsible for what he failed to get from his parents while growing up.

In one session, Jim talked about how he identified with a character in the movie, *Defending Your Life*. In an effort to detoxify the bad feelings, the therapist encouraged him to let himself feel bad and, at another time, to let his bad feelings wash over him. The assumption was that these were the feelings that he had been fleeing all his life, that his caretaking behavior was meant to assuage, and against which his anger was supposed to defend him. Prescribing the symptom would remove its sting. Jim subsequently reported strong feelings of sadness and loss over the relationship he and his father *could* have had. He recounted fleeting experiences of anger at his father that he could not sustain. He talked about how he cannot let himself enjoy the things he likes because his father likes them. As he went through this process, Jim appeared less anxious. Sandy was gratified to see Jim become aware of his feelings and express them.

During this phase of treatment, Sandy allowed herself to acknowledge her anger toward several key people in her life: her father, for discounting her distress ("What do you have to be so unhappy about? You have the perfect life"); her sister, whose problems could make anyone else's pale ("Nothing could be wrong with you"); a seventh-grade teacher, with whom she had maintained contact and developed an adult relationship, who made it clear that she did not want to know how bad Sandy had felt; and Jim, who told her, in effect, that, if she acted happy, she would be happy. Such attributions made to her had confirmed Sandy in her over/underresponsible role.

When Sandy was asked how she wanted to deal with the people in her life about her anger, she said she did not want to deal with her father about her anger toward him; that she might, with her sister; that she would, with the teacher; that she could not, with Jim, because: "It would be the end of the relationship. Being in a relationship with me does not matter enough [to him] to make it worth his going out of his comfort zone." This prediction of minimal response was, of course, made in Jim's presence.

Toward the end of this phase, Sandy asked for a referral for individual therapy. When the therapist suggested several people, she asked if she could see him. He declined, stating that he was *their* therapist and did not want to run the risk of unbalancing the couples therapy. At the following session, the therapist told her that he had changed his mind and, if she still wanted to see him and if Jim had no objection, he would see her in individual sessions alternating with the conjoint sessions. It would be on an experimental basis; its impact on the couples work would have to be tracked. The therapist had rarely combined individual and conjoint couple sessions before. He reasoned now that he knew Sandy very well and another therapist might not focus so clearly on the issues as they had been defined. The same point could be made, however, in all the instances where the therapist had previously refused to combine sessions (except, of course, one individual session with each partner during the assessment). Inexplicably, it made sense to try.

Parallel-Therapy Phase

The defining characteristic of this four-month period was the fact that nine individual sessions with Sandy were conducted along with the eight conjoint sessions. The pattern of the sessions was fairly consistent. Sandy discussed her negative feelings toward, and about, Jim in the individual sessions. These ranged anywhere from intense anger at him for not taking her seriously (i.e., considering her less "smart, complicated" than he; not giving her credit for what she does around the house; not letting her opinions be) to anxiety about how to deal with him when he is needy (not voicing what he wants but evidencing some requirement that she do something to "make him feel better").

The main point to be made about these sessions is Sandy's consistent use of them to marshall her resources to confront Jim about whatever issues she had raised in the individual sessions. She did this either before or during the next conjoint session. (The fact that the individual sessions fed directly into the couples work indicated that they did not compromise the couples therapy.) Sandy seemed to need the individual sessions to organize, articulate, and give herself permission to express directly diffuse thoughts and feelings she had concerning Jim. With Sandy, the therapist reinforced the view that rebalancing over/underresponsibility meant taking herself seriously in her relationship with Jim, meant self-responsible assertive behavior, not vilification or blaming.

It was striking to note how powerless Sandy, a professional woman with openly held feminist views, must have felt holding back feelings that spanned the years of their relationship. She had genuinely believed that open expression of her feelings would signal "the end of the relationship." These negative feelings had accumulated over the years to the point that Sandy was not even sure she liked, let alone loved, Jim. As Sandy learned to behave more entitled with Jim, he showed he could handle her anger, her holding her ground with him, and her demands that he treat her as an adult.

In the joint sessions, as Sandy became more assertive, both partners were encouraged to hold on to their point of view and hold their ground. An example of this was a sequence of interactions reported in one of the conjoint sessions. Jim returned from a business trip on Thursday, telling Sandy that he had made plans to go out Friday night with a friend he had not seen for several months. Sandy was annoyed that he was not staying home after being away for the week. On Friday, Jim left in a huff after a brief exchange. On Saturday morning, their anniversary, they went about their household chores in anticipation of leaving that afternoon for a hotel where they had planned to have dinner and spend the night as part of their anniversary celebration. Missing from the scenario was Sandy's apologizing for getting angry at Jim, and Jim's "conniving to get her to take it [her anger] back" or apologizing for going out. While their way of dealing with this difference did not constitute a model of couple interaction, it was a real advance for them. Each took responsibility for self. They went on to celebrate their anniversary in a manner they described as "relaxed and uncluttered"—they "talked, had fun, enjoyed sex," and even allowed themselves to have breakfast in bed, a pleasure they both enjoy but seldom experience, because they "don't deserve it."

During this phase of the therapy, rigid patterns of the past were broken down. Both Sandy and Jim became aware of their circular attribution strategy and made significant progress in changing it. As each gave up the over/ underresponsible role, they became more real to one another, they became more genuinely responsive to each other. This phase of the therapy ended when Sandy said that she no longer needed the individual sessions because "I feel that what I have to say is important and that Jim will listen." Her predictions of herself and the relationship had changed.

The Balanced-Resolution Phase

This phase is characterized by relative equality between Sandy and Jim in terms of both dependency and power. Only two conjoint sessions, a month apart, had been held since Sandy's last individual session. It was the Christmas holiday season. The sessions focused on the pressure Jim was getting from his family of origin to conform to old patters of interaction (e.g., drink too much, be the spokesperson for mother and siblings with father, go along with whatever holiday arrangements mother wants). While he experienced some anguish over holding his ground with the family, he did not project any of it onto Sandy. He was able to find support in talking about his feelings with Sandy; she was able to listen without feeling or acting responsible for his feelings. Once the holidays were over, the therapy began to focus on consolidating the gains made to date and defining what the couple wanted and needed to do in order to make their relationship even more mutually gratifying. The therapy continues in progress at this writing.

SUMMARY

Sandy and Jim presented a case example of one version of the Intersystem Model: the integration of intergenerational, intrapsychic, and interactional components within the framework of over/underresponsibility. The intergenerational system identified the matrix in which Jim and Sandy had learned to feel and act overresponsible for others and underresponsible for self—i.e., to define self, the partner, and the relationship simply in terms of what one is for others and to attribute to others the power to define one's worth as a person. The intrapsychic system comprised the esteem-regulating cognitive/affective self system that motivated each to maintain these definitions, attributions, and predictions and to interact in ways that continued the patterns learned in childhood. The interactional system consisted of the myriad exchanges, short or extended, that embodied the reciprocating, interdigitating patterns of over/underresponsibility. Therapeutic intervention focused on all three components of the Intersystem Model by using prescriptions, paradoxes, reframes, and solution-focused interviewing to shift the couple's linear attributions and definitions of themselves and the relationship and to rebalance relational responsibility.

References

Abroms, M. (1981). Family therapy in a biomedical context. *Journal of Marital and Family therapy*, 7, 385–390.

American Psychiatric Association. (1987). *Diagnostic and statistical manual of mental disorders* (Third edition, Revised). Washington, DC: American Psychiatric Association.

Amundson, J., Stewart, K., & Valentine, L. (1993). Temptations of power and certainty. *Journal of Marital and Family Therapy*, *19*(2), 111–123.

APA (American Psychological Association). (1992). Ethical principles of psychologists and code of conduct. *American Psychologist, 47*, 1612–1623.

Ascher, M., Bowers, M., & Schotte, D. (1985). A review of data from controlled case studies and experiments evaluating the clinical efficacy of paradoxical intention. In G. Weeks (Ed.), *Promoting change through Paradoxical Therapy* (pp. 216–251). Homewood, IL: Dow Jones Irwin.

Baldwin, M., & Satir, V. (Eds.). (1987). *The use of self in therapy*. New York: Haworth.

Bandura, A., & Walters, R. H. (1963). *Social learning and personality development*. New York: Holt, Rinehart & Winston.

Barbach, L. (1975). *For yourself: The fulfillment of female sexuality*. New York: Doubleday.

Barbach, L. (1976). *For yourself: The fulfillment of female sexuality*. Garden City, NY: Anchor Books.

Barbach, L. (1982). *For each other*. Garden City, NY: Anchor Books/ Doubleday.

Barbach, L. (1983). *For each other: Sharing sexual intimacy*. Garden City, NY: Anchor Books.

Bar-Levav, R. (1988). *Thinking in the shadow of feelings*. New York: Simon & Schuster.

Bass, E., & Davis, L. (1988). *The courage to heal: A guide for women survivors of child abuse*. New York: Harper & Row.

Bassaches, M. (1980). Dialectical Schemata: A framework for the empirical study of the development of dialectical thinking. *Human Development, 23*, 400–421.

Beck, A. (1976). *Cognitive therapy and the emotional disorder*. New York: International Universities.

Bepko, C., & Krestan, J. (1990). *Too good for her own good*. New York: Harper & Row.

Berg, I. K., & Jaya, A. (1993). Different and same: Family therapy with Asian-

American families. *Journal of Marital and Family Therapy, 19(1)*, 31–38.

Berg, I. K., & Miller, S. D. (1992). *Working with the problem drinker*. New York: Norton.

Berman, E., Lief, H., & Williams, A. (1981). A model of marital interaction. In M. Scholevar (Ed.), *The handbook of marriage and marital therapy* (pp. 3–34). New York: S. P. Medical and Scientific Books.

Berne, E. (1961). *Transactional analysis in psychotherapy*. New York: Grove Press.

Bly, R. (Ed.). (1981). *Selected poems of Rainer Maria Rilke*. New York: Harper & Row.

Bopp, M., & Weeks, G. (1984). Dialectic metatheory in family therapy. *Family Process, 23*, 49–61.

Boszormenyi–Nagy, I., & Spark, G. (1973). *Invisible loyalties*. New York: Harper & Row.

Bowen, M. (1978). *Family therapy in clinical practice*. New York: Jason Aronson.

Brehm, J. (1966). *A theory of psychological reactance*. New York: Academic Press.

Brehm, J. (1972). *Responses of loss of freedom: A theory of psychological reactance*. Morristown, NJ: General Learning Press.

Brehm, S. (1976). *The application of social psychology in clinical practice*. Washington, DC: Hemisphere.

Breunlin, D., Schwartz, R., & Karrer, B. (1982). *Metaframeworks: Transcending the models of family therapy*. San Francisco: Jossey-Bass.

Burns, D. B. (1986). *Feeling good*. New York: William Morrow.

Carter, E. A., & McGoldrick, M. (1980). *The family life cycle: A framework for family therapy*. New York: Gardner.

Carter, E. A., & McGoldrick, M. (1989). *The changing family life cycle* (Second edition). New York: Guilford.

Case, E., & Robinson, N. (1990). Toward integration: The changing world of family therapy. *American Journal of Family Therapy, 18*, 153–160.

Cottone, R., & Greenwald, R.(1992).Beyond linearity and circularity: Deconstructing social systems of therapy. *Journal of Marital & Family Therapy, 18*, 167–178.

Courtois, C. (1988). *Healing the incest wound*. New York: Norton.

Dattilo, F. M., & Padesky, C. A. (1990). *Cognitive therapy with couples*. Sarasota, FL: Professional Resource Exchange.

Deissler, K. (1985). Beyond paradox and counterparadox. In G. Weeks (Ed.), *Promoting change through paradoxical therapy* (pp. 60–99). Homewood, IL: Dow-Jones.

de Shazer, S. (1985). *Keys to solution in brief therapy*. New York: Norton.

Dolan, Y. M. (1991). *Resolving sexual abuse.* New York: Norton.

Duhl, B., & Duhl, F. (1981). Integrative family therapy. In A. Gurman and D. Kniskern (Eds.), *Handbook of family therapy* (pp. 483–516). New York: Brunner/Mazel.

Duhl, F. J. (1981). The use of the chronological chart in general systems family therapy. *Journal of Marital and Family Therapy, 7(3),* 361–373.

Duncan, B., & Parks, M. (1988). Integrating individual and systems approaches: Strategic behavioral therapy. *Journal of Marital and Family Therapy, 14,* 151–162.

Feldman, L. (1982). Dysfunctional marital conflict: An integrative interpersonal–intrapersonal model. *Journal of Marital and Family Therapy, 8,* 417–428.

Feldman, L. (1985). Integrative multi–level therapy: A comprehensive interpersonal and intrapsychic approach. *Journal of Marital and Family Therapy, 11,* 357–372.

Fisher, L., Anderson, A., & Jones, J. (1981). Types of paradoxical intervention and indication/contraindications in clinical practice. *Family Process, 20,* 25–35.

Fowler, J. W. (1981). *Stages of faith.* San Francisco: Harper & Row.

Framo, J. (1970). Symptoms from a family transactional viewpoint. In N. Ackerman, J. Lieb, & J. Pearce (Eds.), *Family therapy in transition.* Boston: Little, Brown.

Framo, J. (1976). Family of origin as a therapeutic resource for adults in marital therapy: You can and should go home again. *Family Process, 15,* 193–210.

Frank, J. D., & Frank, J. B. (1991). *Persuasion and healing.* Baltimore, MD: Johns Hopkins.

Friday, N. (1972). *My secret garden: Women's sexual fantasies.* New York: Crown.

Friedman, E. H. (1985). *Generation to generation.* New York: Guilford.

Friedman, E. H. (1991). Bowen theory and therapy. In A. S. Gurman & D. Kniskern (Eds.), *Handbook of family therapy: Volume II* (pp. 134–170). New York: Brunner/Mazel.

Gagnon, J. (1977). *Human sexualities.* Glenview: Scott, Foresman.

Glueckauf, R. L., & Quittner, A. L. (1984). Facing physical disability as a young adult: Psychological issues and approaches. In M. G. Eisenberg, L. C. Sutkin, & M. A. Jansen (Eds.), *Chronic illness and disability through the life span* (pp. 167–183). New York: Springer.

Gould, R. (1978). *Transformations: Growth and change in adult life.* New York: Simon & Schuster.

Gravitz, H. L., & Bowden, J. D. (1985). *Recovery: A guide for adult children of alcoholics.* New York: Simon & Schuster.

Guerin, P. J., & Pendagast, M. A. (1976). Evaluation of family system and genogram. In P. J. Guerin, Jr. (Ed.), *Family therapy: Theory and practice* (pp. 450–464). New York: Gardner.

Gurman, A., & Kniskern, D. (Eds.). (1981). *Handbook of family therapy.* New York: Brunner/Mazel.

Haley, J. (1976). *Problem solving therapy.* San Francisco: Jossey-Bass.

Hatcher, C. (1978). Intrapersonal and interpersonal models: Blending Gestalt and family therapies. *Journal of Marriage and Family Counseling, 4,* 63–68.

Hochschild, A., & Machung, A. (1989). *The second shift.* New York: Avon.

Hof, L. (1987). Evaluating the marital relationship of clients with sexual complaints. In G. R. Weeks & L. Hof (Eds.), *Integrating sex and marital therapy: A clinical guide* (pp. 5–22). New York: Brunner/Mazel.

Hof, L. (1993). The elusive elixir of hope. *The Family Journal,* 1(3), 220–227.

Hof, L., & Berman, E. (1986). The sexual genogram. *Journal of Marital and Family Therapy, 12(1),* 39–47.

Hof, L., & Miller, W. R. (1981). *Marriage enrichment: Philosophy, process, and program.* Bowie, MD: Brady.

Hof, L., & Treat, S. R. (1989). Marital assessment: Providing a framework for dyadic therapy. In G. R. Weeks (Ed.), *Treating couples* (pp. 3–21). New York: Brunner/Mazel.

James, M., & Jongeward, D. (1971). *Born to win.* Reading, MA: Addison-Wesley.

James, W. (1907). *Pragmatism.* New York: World Publishing.

Jones, W. (1986). Frame Cultivation: Helping new meaning take root in families. *American Journal of Family Therapy, 14,* 57–68.

Jourard, S. M. (1971). *The transparent self.* New York: Van Nostrand.

Kaplan, H. S. (1974). *The new sex therapy.* New York: Brunner/Mazel.

Kaplan, H. S. (1979). *Disorders of sexual desire.* New York: Brunner/Mazel.

Kaplan, H. S. (1983). *The evaluation of sexual disorders.* New York: Brunner/Mazel.

Kaslow, F. (1981). A dialectic approach to family therapy and practice: Selectivity and synthesis. *Journal of Marital and Family Therapy, 7,* 345–351.

Kerson, T. S. (1985). *Understanding chronic illness.* New York: The Free Press.

Kim, R., Poling, J., & Ascher, M. (1991). An introduction and research on the clinical efficacy of paradoxical intention. In G. Weeks (Ed.), *Promoting change through paradoxical therapy* (Revised Edition, pp. 216–251). New York: Brunner/Mazel.

Knopf, J., & Seiler, M. (1990). *Inhibited sexual desire.* New York: William Morrow.

Kolb, D. A. (1979). Disciplinary inquiry norms and student learning styles: Diverse pathways to growth. In A. Chickering (Ed.), *The future American college*. San Francisco: Jossey-Bass.

L'Abate, L. (1976). *Understanding and helping the individual in the family*. New York: Grune & Stratton.

L'Abate, L., & McHenry, S. (1983). *Handbook of marital intervention*. New York: Grune & Stratton.

Lankton, S., & Lankton, C. (1991). Ericksonian styles of paradoxical treatment. In G. Weeks (Ed.), *Promoting change through paradoxical therapy* (Revised edition, pp. 134–186). New York: Brunner/Mazel.

Lazarus, A. A. (1988). A multimodal perspective on problems of sexual desire. In S. Leiblum & R.C. Rosen (Eds.), *Sexual desire disorders* (pp. 145–167). New York: Guilford.

Lebow, J. (1984). On the nature of integrating approaches of family therapy. *Journal of Marital and Family Therapy*, 10, 127–138.

Leiblum, S. R., Pervin, L. A., & Campbell, E. H. (1989). The treatment of vaginismus: Success and failure. In S. R. Leiblum & R. C. Rosen (Eds.), *Principles and practice of sex therapy* (Second edition, pp. 113–138). New York: Guilford.

Leiblum, S., & Rosen, R. C. (1988). *Sexual desire disorders*. New York: Guilford.

Lew, M. (1990). *Victims no longer: Men recovering from incest and other sexual child abuse*. New York: HarperCollins.

LoPiccolo, L., & Heiman, J. (1976). *Becoming orgasmic: A sexual growth program for women* (3 films). New York: Focus International.

Lovinger, R. J. (1984). *Working with religious issues in therapy*. Northvale, NJ: Jason Aronson.

Mahler, M. (1975). *The psychological birth of the human infant*. New York: Basic Books.

Maltz, W. (1991). *The sexual healing journey*. New York: HarperCollins.

Marlatt, G. A., & Gordon, J. R. (1985). *Relapse prevention: Maintainance strategies in the treatment of addictive behaviors*. New York: Guilford.

Martin, P.A. (1976). *A marital therapy manual*. New York: Brunner/Mazel.

Masters, W., & Johnson, V. (1970). *Human sexual inadequacy*. Boston: Little, Brown.

Mayer, M. (Ed.). (1978). *Beauty and the beast*. New York: Four Winds Press.

McCarthy, B. (1984). Strategies and techniques for the treatment of inhibited sexual desire. *Journal of Sex and Marital Therapy*, *10*, 97–104.

McGoldrick, M., & Gerson, R. (1985). *Genograms in family assessment*. New York: Norton.

McGoldrick, M., Pearce, J. K., & Giordano, J. (Eds.). (1982). *Ethnicity and family therapy.* New York: Guilford.

Med–Pro Productions. (1976). *Sensate focus I–IV* (4 videotapes). Palisades Park, NJ: Med–Pro Productions.

Millon, T. (1969). *Modern psychopathology.* Philadelphia: Saunders.

Minuchin, S. (1974). *Family and family therapy.* Cambridge, MA: Harvard University.

Monte, E. (1989). The relationship life-cycle. In G. R. Weeks (Ed.), *Treating couples* (pp. 287–316). New York: Brunner/Mazel.

Nadelson, C. C. (1978). Marital therapy from a psychoanalytic perspective. In T.J. Paolino and B.S. McCrady (Eds.), *Marriage and marital therapy* (pp. 89–164). New York: Brunner/Mazel.

Napier, A. (1978). The rejection-intrusion pattern: A central family dynamic. *Journal of Marital and Family Counseling, 4(1),* 5–12.

Nerin, W. F. (1986). *Family reconstruction: Long day's journey into light.* New York: Norton.

Nichols, M. (1984). *Family therapy: Concepts and methods.* New York: Gardner.

Nichols, M. P. (1987). *The self in the system.* New York: Brunner/Mazel.

O'Hanlon, W. H., & Weiner-Davis, M. (1989). *In search of solutions: A new direction in psychotherapy.* New York: Norton.

Omer, H. (1981). Paradoxical treatments: A unified concept. *Psychotherapy: Theory, Research, and Practice, 12,* 320–324.

Palazzoli, M., Cecchin, M., Prata, G., & Boscolo, L. (1978). *Paradox and counterparadox.* Northvale, NJ: Jason Aronson.

Paul, N. L., & Grosser, G. H. (1981). Operational mourning and its role in conjoint family therapy. In R. J. Green & J. L. Framo (Eds.), *Family therapy* (pp. 377–392). New York: International Universities.

Pinsof, W. (1983). Integrative problem-centered therapy. *Journal of Marital and Family Therapy, 9,* 19–35.

Pinsof, W. (1992). Toward a scientific paradigm for family psychology. *Journal of Family Psychology, 5,* 432–447.

Rado, S. (1956). *Psychoanalysis of behavior. Collected papers,* 1922–1956. New York: Grune & Stratton.

Rado, S. (1962). *Psychoanalysis of behavior. Collected papers,* Volume 2, 1956–1961. New York: Grune & Stratton.

Rado, S. (1969). *Adaptional psychodynamics: Motivation and control.* New York: Science House.

Religious values in psychotherapy. (1991). Special issue of the *Journal of Psychology and Christianity, 10(2).*

Riegel, K. (1976). The dialectics of human development. *American Psychologist, 31,* 689–700.

Rohrbaugh, M., Tennen, H., Press, S., & White, L. (1981). Compliance, defiance, and therapeutic paradox. *American Journal of Orthopsychiatry*, *51*, 454–467.

Rosen, R. C., & Leiblum, S. R. (1988). *Sexual desire disorders*. New York: Guilford.

Rosen, R. C., & Leiblum, S. R. (1989). Assessment and treatment of desire disorders. In S. R. Leiblum & R. C. Rosen (Eds.), *Principles and practice of sex therapy* (Second edition, pp.19–47). New York: Guilford.

Rosen, S. (1982). *My voice will go with you: The teaching tales of Milton H. Erickson*. New York: Norton.

Rustad, L. C. (1984). Family adjustment to chronic illness and disability in mid-life. In M. G. Eisenberg, L. C.Sutkin, & M. A. Jansen (Eds.), *Chronic illness and disability through the life span* (pp. 222–242). New York: Springer.

Rychlak, J. (1968). *A philosophy of science for personality theory*. New York: Houghton & Mifflin.

Sager, C. J. (1976). *Marriage contracts and couple therapy*. New York: Brunner/Mazel.

Sager, C. J., & Hunt, B. (1979). *Intimate partners*. New York: McGraw-Hill.

Sanford, J. A. (1974). *Jesus, Paul and depth psychology*. King of Prussia, PA: Religious Publishing Company.

Sauber, R., L'Abate, L., & Weeks, G. (1985). *Family therapy: Basic concepts and terms*. Rockville, MD: Aspen.

Scarf, M. (1987). *Intimate partners*. New York: Random House.

Scharff, D. E., & Scharff, J. S. (1987). *Object relations family therapy*. Northvale, NJ: Jason Aronson.

Scharff, D. E., & Scharff, J. S. (1991). *Object relations couple therapy*. Northvale, NJ: Jason Aronson.

Seligman, M. (1991). *Learned optimism*. New York: Knopf.

Seltzer, L. (1986). *Paradoxical strategies in psychotherapy: A comprehensive overview and guidebook*. New York: Wiley.

Stanton, M. (1981). An integrative structural/strategic approach to family therapy. *Journal of Marital and Family Therapy*, 7, 427–439.

Sternberg, R. (1986). A triangular theory of love. *Psychological Review, 93*, 119–135.

Strong, S., & Claiborn, C. (1982). *Change through interaction: Social psychological processes of counseling and psychotherapy*. New York: John Wiley.

Stuart, R. B. (1980). *Helping couples change*. New York: Guilford.

Turner, N. W. (1982). Conflict-utilization in marital-dyadic therapy. *The Psychiatric Clinics of North America, 5(3)*, 503–518.

Turner, N. W. (1985). Divorce: Dynamics of decision therapy. *Journal of Psychotherapy & the Family, 1(3)*, 27–51.

Van Kaam, A. (1969). *Existential foundations of psychology*. New York:

Basic Books.

Von Franz, M. (1981). *Puer Aeturnus*. New York: Sigo Press.

Wachtel, E. F. (1982). The family psyche over three generations: The genogram revisited. *Journal of Marital and Family Therapy, 8(3)*, 335–343.

Watzlawick, P., Weakland, J., & Fisch, R. (1974). *Change: Principles of problem formation and problem resolution*. New York: Norton.

Weeks, G. (1977). Toward a dialectical approach to intervention. *Human Development, 20*, 277–292.

Weeks, G. (Ed.). (1985). *Promoting change through paradoxical therapy*. Homewood, IL: Dow Jones.

Weeks, G. (1986). Individual system dialectic. *American Journal of Family Therapy, 14*, 5–12.

Weeks, G. (1987). Systematic treatment of inhibited sexual desire. In G. R. Weeks & L. Hof (Eds.), *Integrating sex and marital therapy: A clinical guide* (pp. 183–201). New York: Brunner/Mazel.

Weeks, G. (1989). *Treating couples: The Intersystem Model of the Marriage Council of Philadelphia*. New York: Brunner/Mazel.

Weeks, G. (1990). Paradox. In J.Zeig and W. Munion (Eds.), *What is Psychotherapy?* (pp. 262–265). San Francisco: Jossey-Bass.

Weeks, G. (1991). A metatheory of paradox. In G. Weeks (Ed.), *Promoting change through paradoxical therapy* (Revised edition, pp. 302–316). New York: Brunner Mazel.

Weeks, G. (Ed.). (1991). *Promoting change through paradoxical therapy* (Revised edition). New York: Brunner/Mazel.

Weeks, G., & L'Abate, L. (1979). A compilation of paradoxical methods. *American Journal of Family Therapy, 7*, 61–76.

Weeks, G., & L'Abate, L. (1982). *Paradoxical psychotherapy: Theory and practice with individuals, couples, and families*. New York: Brunner/Mazel.

Weeks, G., & Treat, S. (1992). *Couples in Treatment*. New York: Brunner/Mazel.

Weeks, G., & Williams, J. (1984). Paradoxical interventions with children in a school setting. *American Journal of Family Therapy, 12*, 47–57.

Weeks, G., & Wright, L. (1979). Dialectics of family life cycle. *American Journal of Family Therapy, 7*, 85–91.

White, M., & Epston, D. (1990). *Narrative means to therapeutic ends*. New York: Norton.

Williamson, D. S. (1981). Personal authority via termination of the intergenerational hierarchical boundary: A "new" stage in the family life cycle. *Journal of Marital and Family Therapy, 7(4)*, 441–452.

Williamson, D. S. (1982a). Personal authority via termination of the intergenerational hierarchical boundary: Part II. The consultation process and the therapeutic method. *Journal of Marital and Family Therapy, 8(2)*, 23–27.

Williamson, D. S. (1982b). Personal authority in family experience via termination of the intergenerational hierarchical boundary: Part III. Personal authority defined, and the power of play in the change process. *Journal of Marital and Family Therapy, 8(3)*, 309–322.

Zilbergeld, B. (1978). *Male sexuality*. Boston: Little, Brown.